W9-AFK-783

CHARLES SCOTT
AND THE "SPIRIT OF '76"

Charles Scott. Drawn by Thomas Campbell from the original of Lewitt. Printed by C. R. Milne, Ghent, Ky., April 1838. (Courtesy of the Virginia State Library)

CHARLES SCOTT

and the

"Spirit of '76"

Harry M. Ward

UNIVERSITY PRESS OF VIRGINIA
Charlottesville

THE UNIVERSITY PRESS OF VIRGINIA
Copyright © 1988 by the Rector and Visitors
of the University of Virginia

First published 1988

Library of Congress Cataloging-in-Publication Data
Ward, Harry M.
    Charles Scott, and the "spirit of '76" / Harry M. Ward
        p. cm.
    Bibliography: p.
    Includes index
    ISBN 0-8139-1152-4
    1. Scott, Charles, 1739-1813. 2. Kentucky—Governors—Biography.
3. Generals—United States—Biography. 4. United States. Army—
Biography. 5. Kentucky—History—Revolution, 1775-1783.
I. Title.
F454.S43W37 1988
976.9'03'0924—dc19
[B]
                                                        87-23728
                                                             CIP

Printed in the United States of America

CONTENTS

ILLUSTRATIONS

MAPS

PREFACE

The era of the American Revolution imprinted on a national consciousness ideals for the establishment and future preservation of a Republic, governed by a free people. The war itself was a shared experience, won by sacrifice and the shedding of blood. Indeed the War for American Independence has a double legacy: the ideals to be achieved and implemented and the injunctive obligation that freedom can be maintained only through the persistent and careful vigilance of the people, who are willing to give of their blood in its defense. Historians have written of the bifurcation in American character. The heritage of the Revolution, too, calls upon Americans to cherish liberty, and, even if at times contradictory to this objective, collectively to employ arms in its defense. Charles Scott, as much as anyone of his time, represents both the making of this legacy and its application in a succeeding generation.

Charles Scott's military and public career spanned three wars, the complete cycle of Indian campaigns of the Old Northwest, and the opening and securing of the Trans-Appalachian frontier. Through merit, he rose from private to general. Whether scouting in the French and Indian War, commanding light infantry and serving as chief of intelligence in the Revolutionary War, defending Virginia against invasion, or leading the Kentucky volunteers in the West, Scott was always ready for the special assignment. Joining Washington's army after the battle of White Plains in the fall of 1776, he served with distinction throughout the remainder of the northern campaigns. In charge of raising Continental troops for the Southern Army in Virginia, he would be made a prisoner of war at the siege of Charleston, South Carolina. After the war Scott began life anew on the frontier, where he experienced the danger, hardship, and aspirations of the pioneers. As patriotic enthusiasm swept the western country on the eve of the War of 1812, emblematically and literally he was the embodiment of the "Spirit of '76"— the rallying cry for patriotic unity in Kentucky. Charles Scott participated in and helped shape the events that brought the colonies into nationhood. He shared in the exuberance of western Americans in being a new people, who were capable of determining their own destiny and influencing that of the world.

This biography considers three major areas of Scott's life: "soldier citizen and citizen soldier," pioneer, and governor. Unquestionably, though certainly far from ranking with the "demigods" and the "first string" among the founding fathers, Scott nevertheless is a significant figure of the Revolutionary War era and the period of the founding of the Republic. That he has not previously had a biography is largely owing to the paucity of his personal papers. Although many of Scott's official letters exist in the original or in copy, little of his private correspondence remains. George M. Bibb, Scott's son-in-law, a distinguished lawyer, judge, and secretary of treasury under President Tyler, had planned to prepare a biography of Scott, to be based on the family papers that had come into Bibb's custody, but the collection was destroyed. As Daniel Drake, that "Franklin of the West" in early Cincinnati, noted after making inquiries about papers of Revolutionary War officers: "It is understood, that Gov. Scott's papers came in possession of his son-in-law, the present Hon. George M. Bibb, who carefully placed them in a box with a design to the ultimate preparation of a work; but the mice found their way into the box and nibbled the papers into thousands of fragments."

My interest in Charles Scott began some twenty-eight years ago when I started my first college teaching assignment in Scott County, Kentucky (a county is also named after Scott in Indiana), and has been sustained by extensive research into the history of the Revolutionary War and of early Virginia. Curiously, I find that my residence in the Richmond area for the past twenty-two years is not far from the location of Scott's original farm. One of my delights has been to revisit an area of my youth, via this biography. Having been born in West Lafayette, Indiana, and raised in the "champagne" country—to borrow Gen. James Wilkinson's description of the Indiana-Illinois prairie—I find that Scott's Ouiatanon campaign has special meaning. For example, during summers on the farm of my Hoosier pioneer grandfather, Andrew Jackson Gilfillan Fuller, one of my favorite pastimes was fishing along the banks of Pine Creek, the site of Scott's men in routing the Kickapoo Indians.

I am especially grateful to Lowell H. Harrison, Don Higginbotham, Richard C. Knopf, and Brent Tarter, whose critical readings of the manuscript in reference to their specialties greatly added to its improvement.

Many persons of various institutions assisted in searching out materials relating to Scott. I would like to thank the staffs of the Virginia State Library (where the vast amount of the research was accomplished), the Virginia Historical Society, the Filson Club, the Kentucky Historical Society, the Kentucky Department of Library and Archives, the University of Kentucky Library, and the Library of Congress. I would like to express particular appreciation to Mary Lou Madigan of the Kentucky Historical Society, Nettie Watson and Christine Schultz (field archivist for the Kentucky Guide Project) of the Filson Club, Jeffrey M. Duff of the Kentucky Department of Library and Archives, Claire McCann and Mrs. Terry Warth of the University of Kentucky Library, Mary Plummer of the Presbyterian Historical Society, Eric Pumroy of the Indiana Historical Society, and Bruce Laverty of the Historical Society of Pennsylvania. Anne Hallerman of the Virginia State Library and Sue Ratchford of the University of Richmond Library secured most of the interlibrary loans. Moss Vance, editor of the *Woodford Sun* (Versailles), was very helpful in answering queries and providing a featured article on Scott in his newspaper. Rather unusually, I thank a hospitable citizen of Frankfort, William K. Morris, who provided transportation to the Kentucky Department for Libraries and Archives at its new "suburban" location.

I am also grateful to the University of Richmond for granting a sabbatical and a summer fellowship.

John Murray, fourth earl of Dunmore, governor of Virginia 1771–75. Copy by Charles X. Harris of Sir Joshua Reynolds's oil on canvas. (Courtesy of the Virginia Historical Society)

William Woodford. (Courtesy of the Virginia State Library)

General Charles Marquis Cornwallis. By John Singleton Copley, engraved by Benjamin Smith (London, published 1798). (Courtesy of the Virginia State Library)

Governor Charles Scott. By Paul Sawyier, after an ivory miniature by Matthew Jouett. Hangs in Old Capitol Annex Hall of Governors. (Courtesy of the Kentucky Historical Society Library)

Effingham Tavern, Cumberland County, Va., built 1775 across the road from the courthouse and burned in 1930s. (From the collections of the Valentine Museum, courtesy of the Virginia State Library)

Cumberland Gap, Lee County, Va. Steel engraving by S. V. Hunt from a sketch by Harry Fenn, published in William Cullen Bryant, ed., *Picturesque America* (New York, 1872). (Courtesy of the Virginia State Library)

"Kentucky River from High Bridge." Line etching in James Lane Allen, *The Blue-Grass Region of Kentucky and Other Kentucky Articles* (New York, 1892), p. 309. (Courtesy of the Virginia State Library)

Peyton Short. (Courtesy of the Virginia State Library)

Charles Scott's cabin near the Kentucky River, Woodford County, Ky. In William E. Railey, *History of Woodford County* (Frankfort, Ky., 1938), opp. p. 249. (Courtesy of the Kentucky Historical Society)

Charles Scott's house, Woodford County, clapboarded and with wing added since Scott's time; burned 1972. (Courtesy of the *Scott County Journal and Chronicle*, Scottsburg, Ind.)

Little Turtle, Miami Indian leader. After a portrait attributed to Gilbert Stuart. (Courtesy of the National Anthropological Archives, Smithsonian Institution)

James Wilkinson. Unidentified artist, oil on canvas. (Courtesy of the National Portrait Gallery, Smithsonian Institution)

Anthony Wayne. Copy by Arnold Levshenko of etching in Historical
Society of Pennsylvania of original (now missing) by Jean Pierre Henri
Elouis. (Courtesy of Wayne State University Libraries)

Phoenix Hotel in Lexington, Ky., including Postlethwait's Tavern.
(Courtesy of the Kentucky Historical Society Library)

Jesse Bledsoe. (Courtesy of
the Transylvania University
Photographic Archives)

First permanent State House, Frankfort, Ky., built 1793–94 and destroyed by fire, Nov. 25, 1813. In Richard H. Collins, *History of Kentucky,* 2 (Frankfort, 1874), opp. p. 246. (Courtesy of the Kentucky Historical Society Library)

Kentucky Lt. Governor's Mansion (Old Governor's Mansion). (Courtesy of the Kentucky Historical Library)

William Henry Harrison. By Albert Gallatin Hoit, oil on canvas.
(Courtesy of the National Portrait Gallery, Smithsonian Institution)

CHARLES SCOTT
AND THE "SPIRIT OF '76"

"Duty to My Country and the Glorious Cause"

Charles Scott, at age sixteen, was an orphan when he enlisted in George Washington's Virginia Regiment. Patriotic zeal swept Virginia in the wake of Braddock's defeat on July 9, 1755. The Virginia legislature voted to put into the field a new force to halt Indian depredations and to join with British regulars and other provincials to drive the French from the colony's northern frontier. Like many young men eager to answer the call to arms—chiefly the sons of the farmers and gentry and immigrant drifters—Scott saw adventure beckoning. His decision would determine a lifetime—in war and on the frontier.

In spite of being on his own, Scott could take pride in his family heritage. His forebears had been in Virginia since the mid-seventeenth century. His great-grandfather and grandfather managed a thriving plantation in New Kent County. Col. John Scott, the grandfather, was prominent in the life of the county and the parish: vestryman for St. Peter's Parish, churchwarden, justice of the peace, sheriff, and coroner. Two sons, John, Jr., and Edward, along with Stephen Hughes, acquired a 4,000-acre estate in Goochland County (lying in that part which later became Cumberland and then Powhatan County); this was later divided into tracts of 1,333⅓ acres held individually by each of the two brothers and Hughes. When John, Jr., died in 1729, unmarried, he left his Goochland estate to his brother Samuel and his sister Jean, to be equally divided between them and their heirs. Samuel Scott, Charles's father, therefore inherited 666⅔ acres bordering the south bank of the James River and the lower side of Muddy Creek.[1]

Samuel farmed the land that John, Jr., had left him and added acreage, only in time to sell most of the surplus lands because of hard times. Contrary to the provision in John, Jr.'s will that the Muddy Creek tract should be held for Samuel's heirs, Samuel Scott sold 310 acres of these lands to Gideon Patteson.[2] Samuel Scott served as a vestryman, justice of the peace, and, from 1752 until his death three years later, as burgess from Cumberland County (separated from Goochland in 1744).[3] He died intestate. An inventory and appraisement of his estate shows that he was of modest means; holdings included, for example, a few cattle, eighteen hogs, three horses, and four black slaves. Numerous court actions were brought against the estate. The administrator, Alexander McCaul, a Richmond merchant, had to sell off much of the personal property.[4]

Charles Scott was born about April 1739. His mother, whose name is unknown, probably died about 1745. Charles's older brother, John mentioned as "son and Heir at Law of Samuel Scott decd." in the court record of June 1765, died before 1762, after which time Charles Scott was regarded as eldest son and heir. Two younger brothers, like Charles, were minors at the time of their father's death. Edward Scott chose Gideon Patteson as his guardian, and Joseph (b. 1743) chose his elder brother, John. Charles Scott also had a sister, Martha.[5]

The area where Scott grew up had religious diversity. Among the first settlers were French Huguenots who established Manakintown across and down the James River about twenty miles from the Scott farm and had dispersed throughout the region. Their close kinship and thrift led them to prosper. Other residents included a few Quakers, Presbyterians, and Baptists. Scott's own religious preference is not known; most likely he was never affiliated with any religious group.

Scott had very little, if any, formal schooling. His spelling, constantly changing, reflected phonetic renderings of the local dialect. But he soon learned the rudiments of business transactions and record keeping. Tobacco was the leading staple and its receipts were the currency. Hogsheads of tobacco were rolled by land or sent by canoes or barges downstream to the warehouses in Richmond, at the Falls of the James. Scottish and English groups dominated the entrepôt trade, and Scott later, as his father before him, would have many dealings with them. The community included the very rich, such as Carter Henry Harrison, and the very poor—indigent transients, new immigrants, servants, and slaves. Travelers, from gentry to foreign visitors, passed through, following the course of the James and spending convivial evenings at a plantation or tavern.

Several months after Scott's father's death, the Cumberland Court, on July 29, 1755, ordered the churchwardens of Southam Parish to "Bind out Charles Scott orphan of Samuel Scott according to Law." But before a scheduled court hearing could be held to determine his guardian, Scott joined the Virginia Regiment, which was his right whether or not an orphan. In addition, the Virginia government would soon even condone the recruitment of servants. At the time of his entry into the service Scott was listed as a carpenter, and probably an apprenticeship-guardianship was being arranged with someone, possibly with Gideon Patteson, as his younger brother had already done. If the guardian was Patteson, this fact might have affected Scott's decision, for the court records show that Patteson was tried on a charge of assault and battery and also on a count of illegally detaining a servant (acquitted).[6]

William Mosby, whose family were neighbors to Scott in Cumberland County, who grew up with Scott's sons, and who also became a neighbors of Scott in Woodford County, Kentucky, recalled that Scott was a runaway apprentice. Mosby, whose recollections in old age were usually verifiably accurate, also asserted that Scott was part Indian—but on this point there is no corroborative evidence.[7]

Footloose and having made his decision to join the army, Scott went to nearby Albemarle County to sign up in David Bell's company. Bell's size-roll of July 1756 describes Scott as then seventeen years of age, "Dark and swarthy with blk Hair & slim made," 5'7" tall. There were a number of other adolescents in the company. Most of the enlistees, however, were in their twenties; the oldest, an English barber from Yorktown, was forty-eight. A good many of the company were immigrants—listed as Scottish, Irish, and English. Scott did not have the darkest complexion of the new recruits. Moses Johnson, age thirty-three, "a planter" of Prince William County, was described as "Black as a Mulatto with black Hair." Scott easily fitted the requirements of a soldier. The "general Instructions for the Recruiting Officers of the Virginia Regiment" prescribed that no officer should enlist any man under sixteen or over fifty years of age or under 5'4" high, "unless they are well made, strong, and active."[8]

Scott may have been among the twenty-two recruits whom Bell brought to Winchester on October 4. Washington planned to send Bell's troops, essentially a ranger company, to Fort Cumberland, on Wills Creek at the Potomac (now Cumberland, Maryland), and into the countryside as protection to the inhabitants amid renewed Indian hostilities. Some of the company's recruits were still straggling into Winchester in late October. Washington blamed its captain for this dilatoriness and threatened him indirectly with a court-martial if the lack of discipline in the company continued.[9]

By November detachments of Bell's company were employed as rangers and as relief forces to outlying posts—a dangerous assignment. Some 150 Indians, divided into small parties, were located about Fort Cumberland alone, committing "outrages" and murders "heightened with all Barbarous Circumstances." Scott learned quickly the ways of the Indians and did his share of scouting. A skirmish between a party under Capt. Richard Pearis and that of French and Indians led to a victory of sorts, with Pearis returning with the French officer's scalp; this was enough to frighten the enemy away during early 1756.[10]

During the spring and summer of 1756 Scott alternated between scouting and garrison duty. He quickly rose to the rank of corporal, and by June received pay as a sergeant.[11] So many of the troops were of such poor quality that it was easy for a serious, spirited young man to stand out. From Fort Maidstone, a stockade on the Potomac at the mouth of Great Cacapon River below Fort Cumberland, Scott logged many hours in the "constant Scouting parties of the Light Horse, &c" that Washington required of Bell's troops. He probably also assisted in escorting supply trains. For the remainder of 1756 and early 1757 Scott did duty mainly at Fort Cumberland and Fort Washington on Patterson Creek.[12]

As ordered by Governor Dinwiddie in April 1757, Washington reduced the Virginia Regiment to ten companies, with only seven captains retaining their commands. Bell was one of those superseded, and most of his men, including Scott, were put into Capt. Robert McKenzie's company, stationed at Fort Pearsall (Fort McKenzie), on the South Branch of the Potomac, directly below Fort Cumberland. Scott undoubtedly participated in the numerous "ranging Parties" sent out to find the "enemy in their Lurking Places" and to protect settlers.[13] Every morning, as soon it was light enough to see, the scouting parties set out to look for Indians, ten to fifteen miles between forts. In addition to the duty of searching for and pursuing Indians, scouting was considered necessary training for service on the frontier—to make the men good woodsmen.

Another offensive against Fort Duquesne was planned for 1758. The Virginia Assembly created the Second Virginia Regiment (under Col. William Byrd), in addition to Washington's First Regiment. Both regiments came close to meeting their authorized strength of 1,000 each. By July 1758 the new British commander for the whole expedition, Brig. Gen. John Forbes, could count on 6,000 men—in addition to the Virginians, 1,600 royal troops, 650 Indian auxiliaries, and the rest provincials from North Carolina, Delaware, and Pennsylvania.[14] Much of the early campaign would be taken up in cutting a new road from Raystown (Bedford) to Fort Duquesne.

Fort Cumberland, which had been briefly garrisoned by Maryland troops, once again became the main base for the Virginia troops. Scott, for a while, was on scouting missions out of Fort Pearsall and Fort Pleasant, also on the South Branch. On McKenzie's size-roll at the time he was listed as twenty years old (an error by one year), of "thin visage," and, in contrast to Bell's description of 1756, of "Fair Complexion" and with "brown Hair," height the same, at 5′7½″.[15]

Washington had a dangerous mission for Scott. On August 13 he sent McKenzie's company to waylay the road at the Great

Crossing (Fort Necessity); Sergeant Scott and four privates, who were "active Woodsmen," were to go on reconnaissance up to Fort Duquesne. Although McKenzie's men returned to Fort Cumberland on August 19—sooner than expected because their food had spoiled—Scott and his patrol proceeded toward the French fort. On August 24 Scott returned to Fort Cumberland, and as Washington reported to the British colonel Henry Bouquet, Scott, "when within two Miles of Fort Duquesne, unfortunately came upon a few fresh Tracks making Inwards, which he follow'd, apprehending they were just at hand, till his Provisions were expended, and was thereby oblig'd to Return without making any discoveries worth mentioning." Several days later Washington sent Scott with five men "once more to try their Success at Fort Duquesne." Again it seems that Scott happened upon little intelligence. In writing to Bouquet, Washington offered an evaluation of Scott's mission, although the particular incident alluded to is obscure: "I can answer for his good endeavours, but is it not more tedious than dangerous bringing a Prisoner such a Distance." Probably Scott's prisoner was Thomas Glen, a British dragoon who had been sent to the French as a messenger and who was accused of desertion.[16]

By early November, Scott (as one of four sergeants in McKenzie's company) had joined the combined British and American troops at an advanced base nine miles west of Loyalhanna. From here final preparations were made for an assault on Fort Duquesne. The French, because of the defection of Indian allies and the fall of Fort Frontenac (Ontario), whence they had expected supplies and reinforcements, burned and evacuated Fort Duquesne. On November 15 Forbes's army, divided into three brigades, under colonels Bouquet, Montgomery, and Washington, began the march. Opening the road as they went, the army moved a few miles each day. On November 25 the troops entered the smoldering ruins of the fort.[17] Scott, for the first time, witnessed victory in war.

Scott accompanied Washington and most of the Virginians to Fort Loudoun (Winchester). Spending the winter at the fort, he received a promotion to ensign. Washington had written the Virginia governor for a dozen blank commissions, so that he could fill up vacancies in the officer ranks by promotion of his best sergeants.[18]

During most of 1759 Scott spent his time in charge of work details (road and fort building), escort duty, and patrolling. Colonel Byrd now replaced Washington as commander of the Virginia force, and some troops were engaged in construction work at forts Pitt, Ligonier, Venango, and Presque Isle; most, however, were stationed at Fort Loudoun and at posts on the South Branch of the Potomac. In July 1759 Byrd and 500 troops were camped at Fort Bedford, where they assisted in opening the road from that place to Redstone Creek and served as escorts for supply trains. The Virginians would continue on duty in Pennsylvania and the Winchester area until the summer of 1760.[19]

Virginia's frontier war then shifted southward. The Cherokees laid siege to British posts (Fort Loudoun on the Little Tennessee and Fort Prince George in South Carolina). Gen. Jeffery Amherst dispatched Col. James Grant with 2,500 men toward the Lower and Middle Towns of the Cherokees. William Byrd received orders on June 23 to lead Virginia troops against the Overhill Towns. Scott volunteered for the expedition, and in July 1760 he was named the fifth captain. Scott's assignments are not known, and he may have participated only in the initial phase of the Cherokee campaign. The Virginia troops proceeded very slowly, cutting roads and building forts along the way, toward their ultimate objective, the Great Island (at present Kingsport, Tennessee) in the Holston River. Eventually 540 Virginians were garrisoned at the Great Island, and the remainder of the 740-man regiment was stationed at forts Attakullakula, Chiswell, Fauquier, and Lewis. Lt. Col. Adam Stephen, who succeeded Byrd as commander of the regiment, made peace with the Indians on December 18, 1761. The Virginia troops—those who had not already left because their enlistments had expired—then marched back over the road that they had built, and dispersed for home. One significance of the expedition was that the road-building provided an avenue for migration into far southwestern Virginia and also, at a later time, Kentucky. Though the assembly had extended the life of the regiment until May 1762, Governor Fauquier had Stephen disband it in February 1762, but not before an extra year's pay over and above time of service had been voted for the officers.[20]

It is not known when Scott left the army and settled on the Muddy Creek farm. The first mention of him in the county records after he entered the army was when he did not show up in court on September 28, 1761, to prosecute his suit against Tarlton Fleming; the suit was dismissed.[21] The Muddy Creek farm now belonged to Scott because of the death of his brother John.

On February 22, 1762, Scott married Frances Sweeney (on the face of the marriage bond spelled Swiny and signed Sweny). Frances's immediate family remains a mystery, but it seems that on her mother's or grandmother's side were the Howards of Gloucester County. There were Howards also nearby Scott's residence; Allen Howard at mid-century was one of the great landowners along the James, with one of his six plantations, at Deep Creek, located in Cumberland (later Powhatan) County.[22] Frances was likely the daughter or granddaughter of Merritt Sweeney (d. 1751) of Elizabeth City County[23]—this conjecture, however, is based only on the facts that Scott's son was named Merritt and his grandson Merritt Sweeney Scott. There were Sweeneys in neighboring Albemarle County, and Scott enlisted with Aaron Sweeney, but there was apparently no direct relation of Frances to that branch. Part of the marriage arrangement was the signing of an indenture between bride and groom, whereby Frances retained sole right to her property in slaves.[24]

In 1762 Charles Scott was listed with six tithables; in 1768, four. If one uses the method at the time for arriving at a slave population census—that is, multiply by two the number of slave tithables—it would seem that Scott had the use of about ten slaves.[25] He built a water gristmill on his land at Muddy Creek.[26] Eventually he recovered the half of his landed inheritance that had been sold by his father to Gideon Patteson, but not until the county court reversed a jury verdict favorable to Patteson on a point of law. Scott's repossession of the land was effective December 1764.[27] Thus he was confirmed in possession of the full 666⅔ acres.

Flour and tobacco provided Scott with a modest income. With enough slaves, he did not have to bother with menial labor and could give his attention to business affairs and marketing, probably at the wharfs and warehouses at the small village of Richmond, about thirty-five miles down the river. Scott occasionally lounged at Benjamin Mosby's tavern, eight miles away, which doubled as the courthouse and was the hub for social and public discourse. Perhaps encounters with the fledging lawyer from Hanover County, Patrick Henry, who had one-third of his clients in Cumberland County, led to insights politically and rhetorically. Scott also took an active role in the local militia, and in July 1766 he was appointed one of the two captains.[28]

A happy domesticity prevailed. Frances was an enterprising housewife and excellent cook. According to one family tradition, "Mrs. Scott was a famous housekeeper, and her admirers said that she could get up a good dinner with buckeye chips" (a reference to the later years in the Ohio Valley).[29] She kept an eye open for her property rights and in at least two cases for this period appeared as a plantiff along with her husband. Although almost nothing is known about Frances as a person, comments upon her death in 1804 indicate that she was well liked. Scott never mentioned her by name in his few extant private letters (other than the single surviving letter to her). Frances ("Frankey") formed her own circle of women friends, as evidenced by the fact that the four witnesses to her will were women. Her sons, when adults, referred to her as "the old lady"; "old" was a common frontier term indicating great respect and affection— Scott referred to both of his wives as "the old lady."

The family was growing. Elizabeth ("Eliza," also "Betsy") was born about 1763. Then came four sons during the next decade, probably in this order: Merritt, Samuel, Daniel, and Charles.

As gentleman farmer Scott had a good life. Yet, for one who had attained manhood in the frontier wilderness, there was a void—lack of excitement, adventure, risk. But events again intervened that shaped the man. Scott, at age thirty-six, answered the call to defend Virginia's independence.

As the Revolutionary movement quickened in early 1775, Scott raised a volunteer company in Cumberland County.

Startling news aided his effort. On the night of April 20–21 Governor Dunmore's marines seized the powder from the Williamsburg magazine and hauled it aboard the HMS *Fowey.* On May 2 Patrick Henry gathered militia in Hanover County and marched toward Williamsburg. Approaching the capital, however, Henry and his troops went home when the receiver general gave him a bill of exchange in payment for the confiscated powder. Militia from other counties were prepared to join the fray if one ensued. On Wednesday, May 3, Scott collected his volunteer company at the courthouse—in case Patrick Henry needed further aid. The Cumberland Committee of Safety showed its appreciation for this effort by voting Scott and his troops "the most cordial Thanks" for "their spirited Offers of their Service in defending this Colony against Wicked Invaders" and their "readiness to march forward on a late Alarm."[30]

On June 8 Governor Dunmore fled Williamsburg to the safety of the *Fowey* at Yorktown, whence he asked for support for the royal standard from the inhabitants of the lower Tidewater. Dunmore was ready to use what little force he had to subdue the rebels, expecting that he would soon receive reinforcements from England. The Virginia county committees decided to send troops to Williamsburg to ward off an anticipated "invasion" by the governor, and on June 30 the Cumberland committee asked Scott to detach twenty-five men of his volunteer company to the capital. The Albemarle County committee also called upon Scott, in the absence of Charles Lewis, to command its military contingent at Williamsburg. By mid-July 250 men from the various counties encamped at Waller's Grove on the southeast edge of the town.[31]

Shortly after Scott arrived at Williamsburg, he was selected, presumably by the other officers, to be the commander in chief. The Virginia Convention, without making an official appointment, recognized Scott as commander of the volunteers at Williamsburg. The *Virginia Gazette* reported on July 14 that "Capt. Charles Scott, of Cumberland is chosen commander of the troops now in this city. He served last war in the Virginia regiment with great reputation, and is an excellent woodsman."[32] Scott thus became the first commander of Virginia forces during the Revolution, even though this was a temporary command of short-term volunteers.

Most of Scott's citizen soldiers were men of means and not accustomed to stringent military discipline. A picnic atmosphere prevailed. Indeed, the whole band would be somewhat derisively referred to as the "orchard" men, and George Gilmer complained to Thomas Jefferson that the troops who "have been some time placed in the grove" were "totally inactive" and that there was no order. "Capt. Scott, our Commander-in-Chief, who's goodness and merit is great, fear[s] to offend, and by that every member are rather disorderly. We appear rather invited to feast than fight."[33]

The volunteer officers assumed authority that more properly belonged to the civilian members of the Virginia Convention. Scott and other officers wrote the Norfolk committee that if the rumors they heard of "some of you desserting the Glorious Cause" were true, they would "assist the proper side" with all the force that they had, upon approval of the Convention. Furthermore, they took it upon themselves to compel officials of the royal government to recognize the new regime. The receiver general was told to deliver all the king's revenue to two captains, who would wait upon him, or to enter into a "solemn compact" with them, pledging not to do anything with the monies unless directed by the Convention "on penalty of Confiscation of your whole Estate, and being treated as a traitor to the American Cause." John Blair, clerk of the governor's council, on behalf of the receiver general duly replied that, except for some £41 on hand, he had no funds in his keeping. Naval oficers and customs collectors were also ordered to deliver all monies in their charge to the officers at camp.[34]

Scott and the officers informed the Convention of their actions on July 26, 1775. The delegates, meeting in Richmond, were not especially pleased with this military policy-making that affected civilians. Although acknowledging the officers' "best Motives," the Convention, intending to maintain the traditional constitutional principle of civilian over military authority, directed Scott and his colleagues "to desist from carrying their Resolutions into Execution."[35]

The Convention's rebuke did not dampen the zeal of the gentleman volunteers. Dunmore was now actively soliciting slaves to abscond to his ships, a fact which infuriated the officers, themselves slaveholders. The governor's cutter had actually taken slaves. Also Josiah Phillips, at the head of a band of outlaws ostensibly allied with Dunmore, was marauding throughout Princess Anne County with impunity. The officers addressed another letter to the Convention, stating that they should crush Phillips's ruffian band and also retaliate against Governor Dunmore by kidnapping him, if possible, and seizing his property. "We think it high time, to establish the doctrine of Reprisal," the officers declared. They would, however, submit to the direction of the Convention. Again Charles Scott headed the list of signatures. The Convention, on August 3, had this letter read and referred it to the committee on the state of the colony. Not wishing to discourage the officers' initiative in the field too much, the Convention simply resolved that it approved the enthusiasm of the officers and the volunteers and that they should continue to be on guard against any attack.[36]

While the Virginia Convention met—July 17 to August 26—a state of war actually existed; the battle of Bunker Hill had been fought, and bankcountry Virginia riflemen were on their way to join Washington's army. With additional British reinforcements in the north, there might at any time be a full invasion of Virginia. The Convention created two regiments, with Patrick Henry elected the colonel for the first and William Woodford for the second. On August 17 balloting was held for the other field officers, and Scott was elected lieutenant colonel of the Second Regiment. He was allowed 12s. 16d. per day for his service as "commander in chief" of the volunteers at Williamsburg.[37]

The new little army bivouacked at College Camp, behind the college outside the town limits. Scott's younger brother Joseph served in the Second Regiment as a lieutenant. Patrick Henry, who had been designated commander in chief, arrived at the camp on October 7, and his first orders "Continued the Command in Colo. Scott Till further Orders." Henry had no real military experience, while other field officers were veterans of the last war. The next day Henry assumed full command. Countless details had to be attended to, from latrine making to teaching the men the military exercises, according to *The Manual of Exercises* (London, 1764), which had been adopted for all military units by the Virginia Convention. Scott must have had some say about the "Woods Exorcise," which was required one day a week. Scouting parties were sent out along the James and York rivers.[38]

Dunmore began his offensive on October 12, seizing military stores and cannon in the Norfolk and Portsmouth areas. Reinforced with sixty crack troops under Capt. Charles Fordyce from St. Augustine, he dispatched a force, including loyalists and his "Ethiopians," to Great Bridge on the south branch of the Elizabeth River, twelve miles below Norfolk, and on November 14 at nearby Kemp's Landing he routed about 300 militia.[39]

To hinder Virginia troops from descending the James, the Virginia governor sent several vessels up the river. Fortunately Scott, with 215 men, crossed the James before the sloop *Kingsfisher* prevented other crossings. He encamped a few miles downriver opposite Jamestown, where he awaited Col. William Woodford and the rest of the Second Regiment. Scott put out several small craft to intercept an oyster boat headed for the British ships and forced it ashore. That night his men had an oyster feast "and skimmed the shells in contempt at the Kingfisher and her tenders."[40]

Several days later, informed that Dunmore was heading for Suffolk with 200 of his best troops, Scott quickly marched to that town, where he hoped he could contain the British detachment until he was reinforced by Woodford. Actually Dunmore's move to Suffolk proved a false alarm. Woodford finally reached Suffolk, where he found a message from Scott that he was now at Deep Creek, seven miles west of Great Bridge, which was guarded only by "Tories & Blacks." Scott asked permission to attack by a flanking maneuver across the south branch of the Elizabeth River a few miles below. Woodford refused, but let Scott advance up to the bridge, and sent him two companies under Maj. Alexander Spotswood. Scott captured a group of loyalists on their way to Great Bridge and disarmed others who had taken the oath of allegiance to the king.[41]

When Scott arrived at Great Bridge about November 25, he saw a stockade, named Fort Murray after the governor, John Murray, earl of Dunmore, located on the northernmost of two islands, each of which anchored the bridge. The stockade, dubbed the "hog pen," guarded the bridge and its approaches and could hold three or four companies. The forty-yard bridge had plank causeways leading up to it. The one on the south side of the stream where Scott's troops were was about 160 yards long; from there a road for 400 yards ran past a dozen houses. Scott pitched his camp near a church where the road forked.[42]

For a week, before Woodford arrived on December 2, Scott had his hands full, with his men constantly encountering enemy patrols. The first day at Great Bridge some of his troops confronted a British ranging party and killed sixteen blacks and five whites. The next day Scott's boat guard a few miles away was attacked; fifty men sent to their relief, though "obliged to pass through a very heavy fire from the enemy," made it back, suffering only two fatalities to seven for the enemy. Writing to a friend in Williamsburg (probably John Page) on December 4, Scott noted: "Last night was the first of my pulling off my clothes for twelve nights successively. Believe me, my good friend, I never was so fatigued with duty in my whole life; but I set little value upon my health when put in competition with my duty to my country and the glorious cause we are engaged in." In a second letter of the same date, Scott said he had sent Lt. Col. Edward Stevens and one hundred men across the south branch, and about midnight they encountered a British guard of about thirty men, consisting mostly of blacks. "Our people being too eager, began the fire immediately, without orders and kept it up very hot for near 15 minutes"; two of the enemy were killed and two captured.[43]

During the night of December 6 Woodford sent Scott and 150 soldiers over the south branch to attack an enemy party of 70 men. Scott "unluckily fell in with" a four-man guard escorting a wagon hauling supplies from Norfolk. The British guardsmen fired on Scott's men, thereby alerting the British detachment. In the ensuing action Scott's troops killed one white man and four blacks and took two black prisoners. The only American casualty was a soldier "grazed by a Ball in the Thumb."[44]

For the time being, while waiting for reinforcements of Virginians and Carolinians, Woodford was content to keep on the defensive. Scott had thrown up a breastwork immediately below the south causeway. Little help could be expected from the inhabitants of the area. Scott noted that the American camp was surrounded by "enemies; I do verily believe that nine tenths of the people are tories, who are the poorest, miserable wretches, I ever saw. . . . there is as much provision within 10 miles round as would serve us one day."[45]

For Dunmore, if he was going to strike, now was the time, before the American force could receive more men and artillery. He, however, miscalculated the number and quality of the American troops. Catching the Americans by surprise, before daylight on Saturday, December 9, 120 regulars and grenadiers of the Fourteenth Regiment under Captain Fordyce rushed across the bridge six abreast and up the south causeway toward the American breastwork. The causeway went through a swamp bottom, on the west side (the American left) of which was a thicket.

Fordyce had supposed that the American redoubt would be unmanned, but it was occupied by Lt. Edward Travis and two dozen troops. Holding fire until the enemy was within fifty yards, Travis and his men gave a deadly volley. The British soldiers recoiled slightly and then proceeded forward slowly. Scott's troops and other American soldiers came forward quickly, and Edward Stevens's Culpeper riflemen took to the thicket, with the British now caught in a crossfire. Capt. Samuel Leslie with about 230 blacks and loyalist volunteers was ready on the north island to bring up rear support for Fordyce. But when Fordyce, hit by fourteen bullets, fell dead within twenty yards of the American breastwork, his men then hastily retreated across the bridge. In all, the battle lasted no more than twenty-five minutes. The British left thirteen dead on the field and seventeen captured; since they had carried back some of

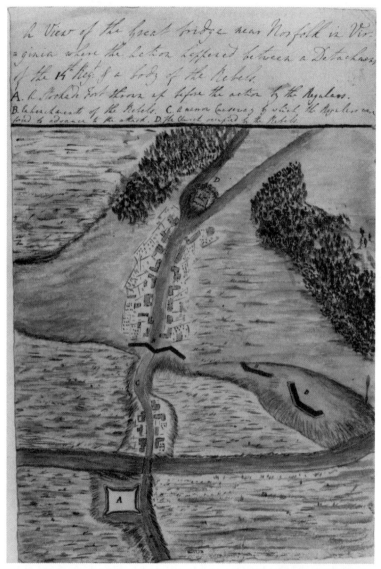

"A View of the Great bridge. . . ." Undated but presumably drawn shortly after the battle of Great Bridge, Dec. 9, 1775. (Courtesy of the William L. Clements Library, Henry Clinton Papers, Ann Arbor, Mich.)

their own dead and wounded, their casualties probably numbered about sixty. The Americans had not a single man killed; only one was wounded, slightly in the hand. Dunmore, who had remained in Norfolk, realizing that his position there was now untenable, quitted the breastwork at the town and embarked his troops and local tories aboard his ships in the harbor.[46]

On the day after the battle, Woodford's force mustered at 897 men, 400 of whom were sent to secure Kemp's Landing, which, Scott said, "they did without interruption." On December 12 Col. Robert Howe, with 340 North Carolina regulars, three companies of Patrick Henry's First Regiment, and a few scattered minutemen of companies ordered down by the Committee of Safety, arrived in camp—boosting the army in the field to 1,275. The next day Woodford collected all the American force at Kemp's Landing. In the evening of December 14, the American troops occupied Norfolk. Howe, having been commissioned a colonel in the Continental line by Congress, assumed general command the next day, with Woodford continuing in charge of the Virginia troops in the field. To Scott, Norfolk was "the most horrid place I ever beheld. Flags are continually passing, asking water, provisions, or to exchange prisoners. Duty is harder than ever I saw before."[47]

Not much excitement prevailed at Norfolk for the rest of December—only occasional firing between HM sloop *Otter* and the troops on shore. Dunmore sent our parties to obtain provisions for the crowd of soldiers and refugees aboard his ships but was largely unsuccessful because American troops blocked the roads and the populace was uncooperative. With the arrival of HM frigate *Liverpool*, Dunmore sent a flag to Howe to demand provisions and that the Americans cease firing on his ships; if they did not comply, he would bombard the town. Dunmore notified Howe on December 31 that women, children, and remaining loyalists should leave Norfolk. Between 3 and 4 P.M. on January 1, 1776, the *Dunmore*, *Kingsfisher*, *Otter*, and *Liverpool* began cannonading the waterfront buildings. The Americans returned the fire, but the British artillery was too much for them, and they had to pull back. British marines and sailors landed and set aflame the buildings at the wharf. A wind fanned the fire through the wooden warehouses, where pitch and turpentine were stored. The Americans used the occasion to burn residences and commercial properties belonging to loyalists. After a conflagration of fifty hours, nine-tenths of the town was in ashes.[48]

It now made sense to evacuate Norfolk, and the Convention, acting on a request of a council of war which included Scott, on January 15, 1776, ordered the American troops to leave the town and take post at Kemp's Landing, Great Bridge and other places that the commander and a council should deem fit. The Convention also called for destroying the remaining houses in the town that belonged to loyalists. Not until several weeks later, however, did the army leave Norfolk. Dunmore's ships meanwhile still hovered in the port. On January 21 a landing party engaged the Americans; three on each side were killed, and several wounded. On January 25 Woodford went home to Caroline County on a leave of absence, and Scott temporarily took charge of all the Virginia troops in the field—Robert Howe still having the overall command.[49] Patrick Henry, who was still the nominal commander in chief of the Virginia troops, had been snubbed by the Committee of Safety when it had ordered the First Regiment to assist Woodford at Great Bridge. Henry had remained at Williamsburg and, for all practical purposes having been superseded in the chief command by Woodford, resigned his commission in February 1776.

Scott tried his own hand at prisoner exchange, making several offers to Dunmore, but the governor refused to pursue negotiations. Scott commented that "we have taken up some of the worst of the tories, and coupled them to a negro with handcuffs. The most stupid kind we discharge." After burning most of what was left of Norfolk on February 6, the American force took post at Kemp's Landing, Great Bridge, and Suffolk. Dunmore's troops encamped for the winter at Tucker's Mill Point (today Hospital Point), near Portsmouth, under cover of the warships. For additional protection the British dug an eight-foot-deep entrenchment for a quarter mile between coves.[50]

Scott had hoped to go home on furlough in February, but the colony's Committee of Safety asked him to stay in the field. Robert Howe planned to return to North Carolina, in view of a tory uprising there, but, with Woodford still absent, he stayed on until May. Edmund Pendleton, head of the Virginia Committee of Safety and president of the Convention, anticipating Howe's departure, wrote him that "anything you may think of further service, you'l please to communicate to Lieut. Col. Scott, upon whom the command will devolve."[51]

For Scott, there was tangible recognition of his service. On February 13 Congress, in accepting the Second Regiment into the Continental line, elected him lieutenant colonel. Andrew Lewis (a brigadier general in the Continental line, as of March 1) arrived in Williamsburg on March 18, 1776, to assume full command of the American force. Scott, however, continued in charge of the Virginia troops in the lower Tidewater. Gen. Charles Lee came to Williamsburg on March 29 to take charge of the American troops in Virginia for a while, as part of his mission to assist the southern colonies in defense preparations. During the lull in hostilities, discipline was all the more a problem. Among Scott's troops at Suffolk the spread of venereal disease caused concern. So did drunkenness: all tippling houses were ordered not "to sell spiritious liquors to the Soldiers under pain of Confinement." On April 16 Col. John Peter Muhlenberg of the Eighth "German" Regiment arrived and took over from Scott the command at Suffolk. Other American troops were distributed at various positions around Portsmouth and Norfolk—to keep a check on Dunmore's base at Tucker's Mill Point. In May, Muhlenberg led a detachment to join Woodford at Kemp's Landing, with Scott and most of the Second Regiment staying at Suffolk.[52]

On May 22 Dunmore took leave of Tucker's Mill Point, and five days later his ships anchored at Gwynn's Island in the Chesapeake at the mouth of the Piankatank River. Here he hoped to have an effective base of operations for the whole lower Chesapeake and to be relatively safe from attack. Gen. Andrew Lewis, who resumed the American command when General Lee left in mid-May, deployed his force at Hampton, Yorktown, Jamestown, Burwell's Ferry, and Williamsburg. Most of the troops, however, were posted at the capital. Dunmore, who had a variety of options of where to attack, expected that he might have aid from Sir Henry Clinton's fleet on its return from the unsuccessful siege of Charleston.[53]

Scott, meanwhile, was elected by Congress on May 7 colonel in the Fifth Regiment, replacing Col. William Peachy, who had resigned. Although it was several months before he received his commission, Scott took over the duties as acting colonel of his new regiment.[54] He was not unhappy with the change in assignment, for the Second Regiment had experienced a great amount of fractiousness. Rev. David Griffith, chaplain and surgeon to the Third Regiment (one of the new Virginia regiments), commented that the Second Regiment was "the Worst disciplined Regt. in the whole line (Though they boast of being Veterans) & the Officers & Men are, in general, the most profane & disorderly of any I ever met with."[55]

On July 9, with selected companies from four regiments, General Lewis led a successful onshore cannonading of Dunmore's ships, which were anchored off Gwynn's Island. During this action Scott remained at Williamsburg. Dunmore sailed up St. Mary's River in Maryland, causing some havoc along the banks. After pausing briefly at St. George Island, the Virginia governor's fleet sailed out of the bay on August 7, his lordship leaving Virginia forever; half of the vessels headed for New York and the others southward.

Until the end of September, Scott and the Fifth Regiment were stationed at Hampton and Portsmouth, where they were joined by militia. He was now "Charley Scott" to his troops.[56] Meanwhile, Congress ordered six Virginia Continental regiments to join Washington's army. The first, second, and third regiments, leaving Virginia in late August, made it just in time for the battle of Harlem Heights. On September 10 General Lewis informed Congress that he was sending on, as ordered, a brigade under Adam Stephen, consisting of the fourth (Thomas Elliot), fifth (Scott), and sixth (Mordecai Buckner) regiments. The march was delayed because half of the men were sick, but in October the three regiments were on their way.[57] On reaching Chester they found orders from Congress, of October 24, 1776, to repair to Trenton, and there await further orders from Washington.[58]

For nearly a year Scott had been constantly in the field. He had almost no time to snatch from his duties to visit his family. Possibly he went home for several weeks in late spring and in August or September. Frances had her hands full with the young children, but there were ample slaves to tend the farm and the mill.

The war for Virginia independence had succeeded. The royal governor had been driven out. For Scott, service had been exceedingly wearisome, and now, without much respite, he would be fighting in a larger war in the North. Yet he had come a long way from his first military experience as a woodsman and scout. The War for Independence afforded him, like many other veterans, an opportunity for both upward mobility and distinction as a professional military officer.

"Leg Them Dam 'Em I Say
Leg Them"

Serving as a Continental officer in the theater of war gave Charles Scott an immense sense of honor and pride. Like others of the officer corps, he too considered himself the most dedicated and virtuous of patriots, performing the most effective contribution to American independence. Scott expected plenty of action in joining up with Washington's army, but instead of pitched warfare over the next several months, there would be constant duty in prodding the enemy and skirmishing. In spite of the lack of clear victory, even with the American failures in the two large battles at the end of the year, the British would discover that the war was far tougher than they had anticipated, and they would gain respect for American arms.

Ordered to join Gen. Nathanael Greene's force at Fort Lee on the Hudson, Scott's and the other two regiments of Adam Stephen's brigade left Trenton on November 8. Unfortunately, 324 sick men in the brigade had to be left behind. On the way the Virginians expected an opportunity to concert an attack with Hugh Mercer's "Flying Camp," then at Amboy, against Staten Island. On November 16 Stephen's brigade arrived at Amboy, only to find that Mercer was gone. A "parcel of Tories" and British sailors in the area were made captives. Scott was disillusioned, as was his brigade commander, over confronting so many people disaffected with the American cause. Wrote Stephen, at Amboy, on the twenty-second: "The men are greatly irritated at finding a Number of disaffected & mischevous persons, daily supplying the Enemy; and Cannot with Chearfulness Submit to rough the Rigours of War, & forgo Domestic Felicity; to fight the Battles of a People, who are not willing to distinguish their Friends from their Foes." Since Fort Lee surrendered to the British on November 18 and Washington's army was now in full retreat in New Jersey, Stephen's brigade simply waited to hook up with the main army at Brunswick.[1] It was a doubly discouraging experience for Scott, not only to find so many tories but also to enter Washington's army as it ignobly fled from the British.

Disassembling part of the bridge over the Raritan River at Brunswick temporarily delayed the British advance. On December 1, after exchanging artillery fire with the British across the river, the American army headed for Princeton, and then to Trenton. Scott's regiment was one of several units that served as a covering party for the army when it left Princeton and also for the Delaware River crossing on December 8–9. On the eighth this detachment skirmished with Cornwallis's advanced troops.[2]

Over the Delaware, in Pennsylvania, for the next two weeks Scott's regiment helped patrol the river from Coryell's Ferry to Yardley's Ferry and constructed earthworks at places where the enemy might cross. Stephen's little brigade (still only fit for duty, Scott's regiment, 121 men; Elliot's, 200; Buckner's, 199) encamped just above the elbow of the river, at McKonkey's Ferry.[3]

Cornwallis halted the pursuit and posted troops at several garrisons in New Jersey, including nearly 1,600 Hessians at Trenton. At the American encampment the news of Gen. Charles Lee's capture at Basking Ridge on December 13 caused dismay. Perhaps it was a portent for Scott's own rising career, as Benjamin Rush reported: "Since the captivity of Gen Lee a distrust has crept in among the troops of the abilities of some of our general officers high in command. They expect nothing now from heaven taught & book taught Generals." Having in mind Stephen and Mercer, Rush recommended that "the next promotions" take into consideration "genius" and the ability to gain "the confidence of the troops."[4]

There was much talk at the American camp that there should be at least one major stroke against the dispersed enemy before settling down for the winter. A victory of any kind would spur reenlistments in an army that was scheduled to all but disappear on January 1. A council of war, therefore, decided on a three-pronged attack on Trenton in the early morning after Christmas. In the main column, to be led by Washington, Stephen's brigade and a group of artillerists were to be in the advance, to attack any enemy pickets and to seize "such posts" that might prevent American troops "from forming in the streets" of Trenton.[5]

The Delaware crossing began at nightfall. At 6 P.M. Scott's regiment and the rest of Stephen's force debarked from the Durham boats at the New Jersey side of McKonkey's Ferry, and from the brigade, a "chain of sentries" protected the landing of the rest of Washington's troops. Instead of the expected six hours, the entire crossing was not completed until 3 A.M. Of the two other divisions, James Ewing's, which was to block the escape route south of Trenton, was unable to cross the river, and John Cadwalader's, which was to attack the garrison at Bordentown as a diversion, arrived too late to be of assistance. At 4 A.M. Washington's force began the nine-mile march to Trenton.

Four miles from the town, Washington divided his troops into two columns. The right wing under John Sullivan took the River Road that led into the lower end of Trenton, and Nathanael Greene with Stephen's and Stirling's brigades headed down the Pennington Road, leading into Trenton from the north. Both columns were to attack simultaneously. Snow and sleet thickened as the men protected their weapons by tucking the firing pans into their armpits or into their blankets and clothing.

At the head of the American force, Scott and the other men of Stephen's brigade soon had some action. At 8 A.M. they arrived at a Hessian outpost above the town, and the firing commenced. Shortly, bugles and drums sounded the alarm in Trenton. Sullivan began the attack from the River Road. In the town only Col. Johann Rall's regiment was on duty, the other two being allowed the festivity of Christmas. But Rall's troops were sleeping at the alarm posts at the lower end of the town. With American artillery firing down the two main streets, Capt. William Washington and Lt. James Monroe of Weedon's Third

Virginia Regiment led a charge that captured the enemy's cannon on King Street. Although the Hessians turned out quickly, the Americans, who "entered the town in a trot," soon were pouring out a deadly fire from cover of houses, trees, and hedges. The snowstorm beating in the face of the enemy made their ammunition too wet to fire. In less than an hour it was all over. Of the 1,586 men at the garrison, 918 surrendered—the rest being able to escape across Assunpink Creek because of the failure of Ewing's support in that quarter.[6]

With the German prisoners and captured stores, the American army retraced the route back across the Delaware. Facing the bleak prospect of a dimished army at New Year's, Washington yet had another chance of success in the field, which would further encourage soldiers to stay beyond their original enlistments. Eighteen hundred Pennsylvania and New Jersey militiamen were expected to join the American army. On December 30 Washington's force again crossed the Delaware and encamped on the south side of Assunpink Creek (South Trenton). Cornwallis at Princeton, however, still had a major British force with him, and General Howe, upon hearing of Washington's action, immediately sent Cornwallis toward Trenton.

Scott, commanding a detachment of the Virginia fourth, fifth, and sixth regiments, joined other units under Brigadier General Roche de Fermoy, on January 1, to contest, as much as possible, an enemy advance on the Princeton road. The American troops took position at Five Mile Run (halfway between Trenton and Princeton), just south of Maidenhead (Lawrenceville). Around noon on January 2 British light infantry and Count von Donop's jaegers passed through Maidenhead. An American picket shot a mounted jaeger from his horse, and a party of American riflemen, concealed on each side of the road, gave point-blank volleys that threw the Hessians into confusion. At this moment de Fermoy inexplicably rode off for Trenton, and Col. Edward Hand, the senior regimental commander, decided to make a stand on the south side of Shabbakonk Creek. The Americans pulled down the wooden bridge over the creek. The British, expecting a major encounter, formed a battleline and brought up artillery, which scoured the wooded American position on the other side of the creek. After a half an hour of artillery fire, the British forded the swollen creek. One group of the American troops contested the enemy on the road after they had crossed and kept up a fire at intervals while plodding slowly backward along the muddy road. Scott and his men kept between the road and Assunpink Creek, thus preventing a flanking movement. From high ground overlooking Stockton's Hollow, south of a ravine intersecting the road at right angles, a deadly fire from Capt. Thomas Forrest's artillery forced a British advance party to deflect toward Scott's Virginians. Steadily retreating, all the American troops passed through upper Trenton, again taking advantage of cover from the buildings and gardens in firing on the enemy, until they reached the bridge where Queen Street crossed the Assunpink. There Col. Daniel Hitchock's New Englanders were waiting and provided cover for the weary detachment as they crowded across the narrow stone bridge.

It was nightfall as Scott and his men got across the bridge, with the British detachment of 1,500 now on the opposite bank. Cornwallis, with the rest of the army, would not come up until several hours later. Firing continued after the Americans passed over the bridge, and American batteries opened up on the British troops below. The enemy had to withdraw to a safe distance, thus ending the running battle along Assunpink Creek, known as the second battle of Trenton. Between 20 and 30 Americans were killed and more than 10 wounded; one estimate of British casualties was 200. Major George Johnston of the Fifth Regiment commented that, from the engagement, Scott "acquired immortal honor."[7]

Washington formed a three-mile battleline on the south side of the creek, extending from his left on the Delaware River eastward to Mill Pond (adjacent to the creek); earthworks were thrown up along the ridge and below at the bridge. Arthur St. Clair's brigade held the ground just east of the bridge; about a mile up the creek John Cadwalader's troops were in an open field; and a mile farther, at the extreme right, Hugh Mercer's brigade guarded Phillips Ford.[8]

Scott had the perilous duty of guarding the Queen Street

bridge. Tradition has it that the commander in chief rode down to inspect Scott's post. According to one version, after addressing Scott's men, Washington rode off as if to rejoin the army, but went only a few paces and sat silently on his horse. Scott, who hitherto had not said anything, when he thought Washington was gone, told his men: "Well, boys, you know the *old boss* has put us here to defend this bridge; and by G—d it must be done, let what will come. Now I want to tell you one thing. You're all in the habit of shooting too high. You waste your powder and lead; and I have cursed you about it a hundred times. Now, I tell you what it is, nothing must be wasted, every crack must count. For that reason, boys, whenever you see them fellows first begin to put their feet upon this bridge do you shin 'em." Supposedly Washington gave out a hearty laugh, and Scott turned around astonished.[9] Another non-contemporary version has Scott, unmindful of Washington's presence, uttering "tremendous oaths" in exhorting his men to defend the bridge to the last extremity.[10]

But Scott did not have to make a stand at the bridge. Washington soon had another plan. Fortunately the American army had been reinforced by the Pennsylvania and New Jersey militia in larger numbers than expected, bringing the total force to around 5,000; many, however, were raw troops. Washington had not counted on a full thrust by the British army. Yet he needed a face-saving alternative to immediate retreat back across the Delaware. Perhaps, in maneuvering, Washington might hold the advantage. In the evening of January 2, Cornwallis arrayed his army for battle on the opposite bank of the Assunpink; with the arrival of reinforcements from Maidenhead and Princeton the next morning (intelligence of which Washington was apprised), the attack would begin. By not crossing at the several fords, however, Cornwallis missed the opportunity to trap the American army; he also neglected to send out effective scouting parties. At midnight, leaving behind 400 men at intervals and campfires burning on the higher ground, Washington marched his whole army around the British left and headed toward Princeton to intercept the British reinforcements and also to strike at the Princeton and Brunswick garrisons.

Cornwallis, discovering Washington's ruse in the early morning, headed toward Princeton. Two of the three British regiments at Princeton, beginning their march to join Cornwallis, met Hugh Mercer's brigade just outside the town. In the ensuing bloody affair Mercer's men were routed, and he was mortally wounded. With the arrival of the main American army at the site of the battle, Col. Charles Mawhood, the British commander, had no choice but surrender or attempt a breakthrough with a bayonet charge against a large number of Americans on the road. Mawhood succeeded, and, with cover from his dragoons at his rear, hastily retreated down the road toward Trenton. Scott's regiment in Stephen's brigade had the assignment to provide cover to the army baggage and supplies. What action Scott saw during the battle of Princeton, if any, was in the harassment of Mawhood's fleeing troops.[11]

After the battle, Washington's army went into winter cantonment at Morristown, on a plateau surrounded by rugged hills. This position enabled a close watch of British troops at Brunswick and Amboy; it would also be at the flank of the British army should it move to Philadelphia or the Hudson River. The Virginians, however, were stationed at various encampments below Morristown. Scott's and the other two regiments of Stephen's brigade went immediately to Chatham, seven miles southeast of Morristown, from whence they operated as light infantry, chiefly on the lookout for enemy foraging parties. About January 10, Scott's regiment captured some seventy Highlanders and a large number of baggage wagons. As an indication of the mobility of the Virginia troops, they were at Mount Bethel Meeting House (near Quibbletown Gap) on the fourteenth, northwest about fifteen miles to Springfield on the twenty-third, Westfield and nearby Scotch Plains on the twenty-seventh, and then along the Old York Road to Quibbletown, the twenty-eighth.[12]

Scott, early on February 1, led 500 Virginia and Connecticut infantry from Quibbletown toward Metuchen. About the same time, Gen. Sir William Erskine and 180 men set out from Brunswick. Heading northeast toward Metuchen (equidistant about six miles from Brunswick and Quibbletown), Erskine's men joined another foraging party from Brunswick of 850 men under Lt. Col. William Harcourt. The British troops then moved to the uncut fields and haystacks at Drake's Farm, outside Metuchen.

Scott came upon a picket of five British dragoons. He had his men open fire and pursue them; all got away except the officer in command. Early in the afternoon, Scott, leading an advance party of ninety men, encountered part of the British foraging troops. He ordered an attack on the Black Watch, which was serving as a guard for the foraging party. Erskine then directed Hessian grenadiers who had been gathering hay to take position to the right of the Black Watch—making the number of men opposing Scott 230. For fifteen minutes "bullets flew like hail." Scott's men drove the grenadiers back to their cannon. Col. Andrew Ward of Connecticut and the other 400 Americans did not initially come to Scott's assistance. The grenadiers returned with 300 fresh men and a fieldpiece, which forced Scott to give way. Ward and the other men now came up in three columns.

One soldier of Ward's Connecticut troops remembered the exact moment: "The logical advice of Col. Scott where we were going into the action Mentioned I always remember & the glib manner in which he Spoke it fearing they would fire too high which is said is apt to be the case in the beginning of an Action he Said 'Take care now and fire low bring down your pieces fire at their legs, one man Wounded in the leg is better [than] a dead one for it takes two more to carry him off and there is three gone leg them dam 'em I say leg them.'" Erskine brought up the rest of his troops to outflank the Americans. Before the superior fire and man power, Scott had to call a retreat. His men lined up at the edge of the woods, and Ward's men ducked behind the fences of a hayfield—now about a quarter of a mile from the enemy. According to an American view, Scott's and Ward's men "formed again, and looked the enemy in the face until they retreated"; to the British, the Americans "very soon dispersed and run except poping from behind Rails. At last the whole went off." Seven Americans—two of them officers—lay wounded on the original ground that Scott had held. Several British soldiers "dashed out their brains with their muskets and ran them through with their bayonets, made them like sieves." Lt. William

Kelly, adjutant to Scott's Fifth Regiment, was one of the officers murdered. Wounded in the thigh, he surrendered and was immediately clubbed to death with his own musket. Scott's losses overall were nine killed and fifteen wounded.[13]

The brutal killing of Kelly and the other officer led to a bitter correspondence between Stephen and Erskine which was widely publicized in the newspapers. "If the British officers do not restrain their soldiers from glutting their cruelties, with the wanton destruction of the wounded," threatened Stephen, the United States, "contrary to their natural disposition, will be compelled to employ a body of furious Savages [Indians], who can, with an unrelenting heart, eat the flesh, and drink the blood, of their enemies."[14]

The battle of Drake's Farm could have been more decisive for the Americans. Andrew Ward faced a court of inquiry for his delay in coming to Scott's aid. "Difference of training," writes the only historian of the battle, was a factor, but "not the whole story, though it probably explains why the Americans came up piecemeal, and could not take advantage of their superior position, and explains the rapidity with which Erskine and Harcourt converted the situation to their advantage after they were surprised." Artillery also had given the British an edge.[15]

Scott, nevertheless, emerged somewhat a hero. Washington gave implied praise. Virginians back home, from two letters published in the *Virginia Gazette,* learned of the "heroic" actions of Scott and the other Virginians. Robert Forsyth, General Stephen's brigade major, wrote: "Our hickory hearts, as usual behaved like heroes. Ninety of them, under the command of the brave Col. Scott, beat, at fair cutting, 230 of their best troops." Stephen boasted that most of his officers behaved like heroes and that his brigade "in a campaign or two will surpass any troops in the world."[16]

Relentlessly the Americans kept up the pressure on the British foraging. Hardly could a party leave Brunswick or Amboy without being attacked. The constant harassment drastically reduced provisions and fodder and caused great suffering at the Brunswick and Amboy garrisons. General Stephen in mid-March commented (and he had a reputation for exaggerating) that "fighting is now become so familiar that unless it is a very great affair we do not think it worth mentioning." Stephen considered his "Division" an "excellent school for a young soldier. We only fight eight or ten times a week—in short I have got my men in such spirits—that they only ask when the enemy come out and where they are—without enquiring into their numbers and so fall on."[17] At thirty-eight, Scott was not "a young soldier." Even for such a durable outdoorsman the constant mobility and skirmishing in the dead of winter was an extreme hardship.

The annoying tactics of Scott's men and other light infantry did create a healthy respect by the British for the American soldier. William Harcourt, an adversary of Scott in the New Jersey fighting, noted that although American troops "seem to be ignorant of the precision and order, and even of the principles, by which large bodies are moved," they "possess some of the requisites for making good Troops, such as extreme cunning, great industry in moving ground and felling of wood, activity and a spirit of enterprise upon any advantage . . . they are now become a formidable enemy."[18]

In early March, Scott took a much-delayed furlough. So many field and general officers did the same and extended their leave that Washington sternly requested them to return. On April 7 he ordered all the officers of the first, third, fourth, fifth, and ninth Virginia regiments—and two weeks later those of the second and eleventh—to proceed immediately to camp. Back on the farm in Powhatan County, Scott received the welcome news that Congress had elected him brigadier general on April 1, dating his commission the next day.[19]

Scott returned to the army about May 9. A week earlier, Washington had written Capt. Caleb Gibbs to tell Scott, if he was in Philadelphia, to "proceed on to hd. Quarters. add that I hope the useless punctilios, which have but too much Influence on Officers, to the great detriment of the Service, and which serves to distress me (as I can never compleat any arrangement) will have no effect upon him." All of Scott's field officers except one were on furlough. Scott evidently was at Morristown on May 10 when Washington rearranged the army and directed Scott and Woodford to bring their brigades "into compact order." Scott's new command consisted of the fourth, eighth, twelfth, and six-teenth Virginia regiments in Stephen's division (Stephen had been promoted to major general on February 19). From May 19 to about May 24, with Generals Stephen and Maxwell both ill, Scott assumed acting command "upon the lines."[20]

With summer approaching, the army prepared for a new campaign. On May 28 Washington moved the army south to Middlebrook, in the foothills of the Watchung Mountains, about seven miles up the Raritan River from Brunswick. Howe, on June 13–14, took his whole army to Brunswick, from whence he sent out two columns, one toward Somerset and another toward Middlebush—thus indicating to Washington's council of war, which included Scott, that the British intended to head for Phil-adelphia. Howe expected to lure Washington down from the hills into battle. The British set up redoubts along an eight-mile line from Middlebush to the Millstone River. Their conduct was very perplexing, noted artillery general Henry Knox: "It was unaccountable that people who the day before gave in very gas-conading terms that they would be in Philadelphia in six days should stop short when they had gone only 9 miles." In case the British continued toward Philadelphia, Scott's brigade and those of Sullivan and Muhlenberg and Daniel Morgan's riflemen would form the front of the American army.

On the morning of the nineteenth, "without Beat or Drum or Sound of Life," Howe took his army back to Brunswick. Wash-ington, on the twenty-fifth, came down out of the hills to Quib-bletown and put Stirling's division off his left flank to secure the passes. Howe, a day later, suddenly moved in two columns to-ward Woodbridge and Bohampton, where he hoped to sur-round Stirling's troops and gain the passes to Middlebrook. After heavy skirmishing, the British troops withdrew.[21] On the twenty-eighth an enemy detachment of 2,000 came within two miles of the American lines. Scott, as a young Virginia captain observed, was "sent out to feel their pulse but they did not seem 'fightish.'" Howe's army entered Amboy the next day and on the thirtieth embarked for Staten Island. Scott with "a Body of Light Troops," including Morgan's riflemen and Thomas Con-way's brigade, served as a "corps of Observation," keeping close to the retreating enemy. Slightly delayed by rain, Scott entered Amboy at dusk, just after the last British soldiers had embarked. Leaving guards to protect any stores the British might have left behind, Scott then withdrew to about four miles out of the town. This "was expedient to do," Washington commented, since staying in the town overnight "might have induced the Enemy, whose Boats were ready, to throw over a Superior force in the Rear." Scott returned the next morning to carry off any abandoned supplies he could find.[22]

It was a guessing game as to what Howe would do next. When word came that the British army had set out to sea, Washington, expecting that Howe would ascend the Hudson River to aid Burgoyne's invasion, marched the American army as far as Smith's Clove, a pass in the Palisades near West Point. But Howe's army did not appear, and Washington surmised that the British army, still shipboard, was heading for Philadelphia by sea; hence he made another long trek back through New Jersey to the Delaware. Scott and his men who made the full march were as weary as the rest of the troops.[23] In Washington's view, however, all this activity was the best discipline—although surely the common soldier did not see it that way, and it was not easy either on the middle-aged generals. But Scott and the other generals had only themselves to blame for the futile marching, for the decisions were made in councils of war. Although the British were sighted off the Delaware Capes at the end of July, they left the bay, hovering off the Jersey coast. Thoroughly frustrated, Washington rested his army at Germantown, five miles from Philadelphia.

During the brief inactivity, Scott had time to ponder his status in the army. Never caring much for his portly Virginia colleague and former tavernkeeper, Gen. George Weedon, Scott concluded that Congress had wrongly ranked Weedon above himself. Although Scott had been appointed lieutenant colonel and colonel after Weedon's appointments, apparently his claim was based on his assuming the colonelship of the Fifth Regiment before the date of Weedon's commission. The order of rank that Congress adopted was determined by the previous regimental ranking. Scott later would have the sense to be discreet on the subject, while Weedon would not. Yet, perhaps feeling the effects of exhaustion and of the summer's heat, Scott could not resist the temptation to apply to Congress through a Virginia delegate, Benjamin Harrison, for "justice" in the matter. "I am Sensibly hurt," he informed Harrison. Patriotism was paramount, but an officer had to defend his honor. "I wish to serve my Country but I cannot submit to indignity and make myself unhappy," Scott said. "I will sooner quit the Service altogether which would indeed make me exceedingly unhappy." Scott requested Harrison to apply to Congress to place him in his "proper Rank" next to General Muhlenberg "and not mark me out the Disgraced exception from the Genl. rule of promotion by Seniority." Scott contended that Congress had been misinformed as to the seniority of the Virginia officers. He would welcome "the Strictest Scrutiny" into his character and conduct. Congress considered Scott's complaint.[24] Thus Scott initiated among the Virginia generals the controversy about rank that was kept before Congress for the next eight months. Ultimately the ruling would be decided in Scott's favor, with Woodford ranked first, then Muhlenberg, Scott, and Weedon, in that order.[25]

On August 7 Washington, upon consulting his generals, concluded that the British were again heading for the Hudson, and therefore the army started in that direction. Three days later it was learned that the British were off the Maryland coast, south of the Capes of Delaware. Could Howe be aiming for the Carolinas? Or the Hudson? Washington held his army at the Crossroads, along Neshaminy Creek, twenty miles north of Philadelphia. A decision on August 22 once again to go to the Hudson was countermanded soon afterward when news arrived that the British Fleet had entered upper Chesapeake Bay—leaving no doubt that Howe would advance toward Philadelphia from the south. On the twenty-third, the American army encamped at Germantown.[26]

It had been a long, hot summer. Both armies in full battle strength were now to confront each other in the open. In spite of their ragtag condition, the American troops were in high spirits. To them and their countrymen, a victory might end the war. For Scott and the other officers, this might also be the hour of glory.

Crossing the Schuylkill River, the American troops on August 26 reached Brandywine Creek, a mile north of Wilmington. There it was learned the British had landed at the Head of Elk. Eventually the American army took position on the north side of Red Clay Creek, near Newport, on the main road to Philadelphia. Greene's and Stephen's divisions—chiefly Virginia Continentals under Woodford, Muhlenberg, Scott, and Weedon—advanced to White Clay Creek. On September 3 Scott's and Woodford's brigades went out to assist William Maxwell's light infantry, posted at Cooch's Bridge on Christiana Creek. But before Scott's troops got there, although it seems that his Twelfth Regiment arrived in time to be of some assistance, Maxwell's troops had been put to flight by a strong force of British advanced units. Scott's and Woodford's men now made camp with the main army.[27]

In order to check the British advance on Philadelphia, Washington put most of his army on the east side of Brandywine Creek at Chad's Ford. The creek was deep enough so that the British would have to cross at one of the numerous fords—and Washington thought that Chad's Ford, if not the actual place of crossing, would serve as a point of maneuverability up and down the creek. The hilly and wooded banks of the Brandywine, flowing southeast to below Wilmington, offered the last natural barrier before the Schuylkill.

At daybreak of the eleventh, the British marched in two columns: the right, commanded by Baron von Knyphausen, went directly toward Chad's Ford, and the other column, under Cornwallis, outflanking Washington's right, moved to just above the forks of the Brandywine (six miles from Chad's Ford) and about 2 P.M. made the crossing. Throughout the day heavy artillery fire was exchanged by both Knyphausen's men and the Americans at Chad's Ford. Washington had suspected that the British might try to outflank him and had pulled most of Sullivan's division up the Brandywine—but not far enough. When Washington startlingly learned that Cornwallis had crossed beyond his right—threatening to catch the American army, with

Knyphausen on the American left, in a pincers movement—he rushed troops at Chad's Ford, including Scott's brigade, to support Sullivan.

It was late afternoon when Scott found himself on wooded Birmingham Meetinghouse Hill, exhausted after leading his men hurriedly over the rolling countryside and fences four miles from Chad's Ford. Cornwallis, with the main part of his force, reached the hill, and a steady small-arms fire ensued from both sides. Most of the troops from three divisions—Sullivan's, Stirling's, and Stephen's—defended the hill. Sullivan's men were the first thrown into confusion. Then, as the British light infantry pushed up the hill, Scott's brigade also gave way. Scott's men had been fighting three companies up the hill and had not been aware of other British light infantry ascending the hill from the other side. All the American troops were forced off the hill, except Woodford's brigade, which fought valiantly in an attempt to delay the British advance so that the American force could regroup. Scott's brigade, at the bottom of the hill, kept in reasonably good order and did what it could to protect Woodford's rear. But, with the enemy bringing into action heavy artillery, Woodford's men also had to take to the woods down the back of the hill. As the retreat became general, Scott, according to one of his officers, "came riding by and asked [Col. Josiah] Parker [of the Fifth Virginia Regiment] what he intended to do. He said. 'Fight Them.' Scott told him the whole army was in confusion, he had better cover the retreat. He did so, not without several hot fires from the British."

To resist further the British advance, Stirling's division took position at two hills to the rear, on each side of Forks Road. Woodford's and Scott's brigades came up, expecting to pass along the road under cover of Stirling's troops. However, they were suddenly attacked by Cornwallis's left wing, which had not been engaged in the assault of Birmingham Meetinghouse Hill. This force, because of the swamp and the rugged ground, had moved farther to the left than intended—and hence encountered Woodford's and Scott's brigades. Because of the suddenness of the attack and the weariness of already battle-worn soldiers, whose ammunition was running low, the two Virginia brigades scattered. The British then attacked Stirling's troops at the two hills, both of which were carried by the British in fierce hand-to-hand combat. Scott and other officers collected some of their retreating men and formed about four hundred yards to the rear of the hills, but they too were again quickly overrun. Meanwhile the other British force from Birmingham Meetinghouse Hill was stalled in the nearby swamps and woods.

Washington, learning of the failure to hold a position on the right flank, ordered up Greene's division and part of Francis Nash's brigade from Chad's Ford. Greene's division—Muhlenberg's and Weedon's Virginians—created a wedge between the enemy and the retreating Americans. Weedon's men, in a "ploughed field" in a pass between hills, gave the enemy such a "terrible firing," killing "nearly all" the officers of two regiments, that the British advance was halted. Since it was now nightfall and his troops were somewhat in confusion, Cornwallis did not press his attack. Darkness also brought a cease-fire on the American left, where Knyphausen had succeeded in crossing the Brandywine and gaining the Chester Road. While the British occupied the battlefields, Washington's army retreated to Chester; then, crossing the Schuylkill, the army encamped at the Falls and at Germantown.[28]

The battle of Brandywine had demonstrated both the tactical ability of General Howe and the capability of the British army for swift mobility. To prevent another disadvantageous situation, Washington, on September 14–15, recrossed the Schuylkill and formed a three-mile front between the enemy and Swede's Ford. This location in the Chester Valley would block Howe's route to Philadelphia by way of the upper fords of the river. On the sixteenth, the British, in three columns, marched toward the American army. Washington drew up a line of battle slightly beyond the crest of the south hills of the Chester Valley. Brief skirmishing by advance units was halted by a heavy rain in the afternoon which lasted until the next morning, drenching both men and weapons and making a quagmire underfoot. A dense fog greatly limited visibility. Scott's brigade was ordered to attack an advance party from Cornwallis's column but was unable to do so because of the adverse weather conditions. During the

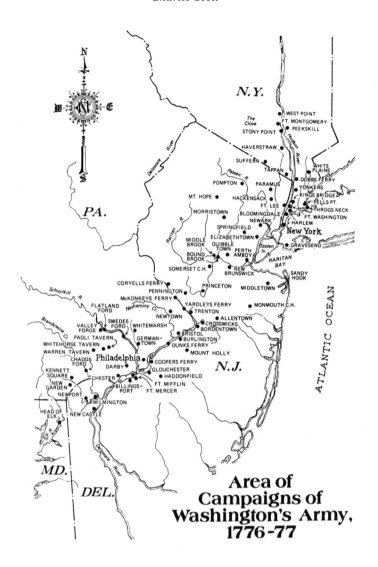

Area of campaigns of Washington's army, 1776–77. (Reprinted with the permission of the publisher from Harry M. Ward, *Duty, Honor, or Country: General George Weedon and the American Revolution* [Philadelphia: American Philosophical Society, 1979])

night Washington's troops climbed down from the muddy hills and withdrew to Yellow Springs. Thus ended before it had barely begun the "battle of the Clouds."[29]

Washington, on the nineteenth, brought the army across the Schuylkill, still intending to guard the upper fords. A detachment under Wayne, left behind near Paoli, south of the river, was surprised by a large British force and suffered heavy casualties. On September 22 Howe crossed the Schuylkill, twelve miles below the American position; thus the way was open to Philadelphia. Howe, however, refrained from immediately entering the city and instead encamped near Germantown, sending part of his army under Cornwallis on the twenty-sixth to occupy Philadelphia. After some mobility, Washington brought his army to the hills at Skippack Creek. While a majority of the generals at first voted against an attack (Scott and four other generals persistently favored an offensive), on October 3 the decision was to attack the British force at Germantown.

At 7 P.M. four columns started on the fifteen-mile march to Germantown: Sullivan, Wayne, and Conway to enter the town at the center by way of Chestnut Hill; John Armstrong and the Pennsylvania militia to the enemy's left and rear, along Manatawney Road; Greene's and Stephen's divisions and McDougall's brigade, by a circuitous route along Skippack and Lime Kiln roads, to attack the enemy's right; David Forman's New Jersey militia, along the Old York Road, to the rear of the enemy's right; Washington, Stirling, and Nash would hold troops in reserve. The attack was planned to begin simultaneously at 5 A.M.

On schedule Sullivan's troops started the attack, penetrating into the center of the town and driving "the enemy before them, who fled with the greatest confusion and precipitation." Greene's column, with the major part of the army (including Scott's brigade), which had the greatest distance to cover, did not reach the town until 5:45 A.M. They, however, attacked "with spirit." A dense fog, arising from the intense musketry and from a fire that the British had set to a dry buckwheat field, greatly limited visibility.[30]

Stephen's two brigades (Scott's and Woodford's) soon stumbled around helplessly in the haze-covered woods and underbrush at the edge of town. General Stephen, allegedly intoxicated, heard the firing at the Chew house, where Maxwell had cornered a British regiment, and, breaking the battle plan, ordered his Virginia troops toward this scene of action. The Virginians came across Wayne's troops, who had come down to assist Maxwell. Here "the left wing supposed the cannon-balls fired by the right at the house came from the enemy." As a result, Wayne's and Stephen's troops engaged in such a brisk fire that both retreated. Sullivan's troops, to the right of Wayne, also panicked when a light horseman rode up and shouted that they were surrounded. Because Germantown "abounded with small enclosures strongly fenced with rails," the mounted officers lost touch with their men. Scott's and Woodford's brigades became separated. Washington was horrified to see the swarm of troops running out of the fog toward the rear. As General Greene later put it, the Americans "fled from Victory." These and other mistakes allowed the British to regroup and counterattack, aided by a reinforcement under Cornwallis from Philadelphia. Gen. Charles Grey's troops pursued some of the fleeing Americans as far as Swede's Ford. On the night of the battle Washington headed the army to a previous place of encampment, twenty-three miles from Germantown, at Pennypackers Mill.[31]

Germantown was as disappointing as Brandywine. While Brandywine was a defensive operation on the part of the Americans, Germantown was an attack that seemed to have every advantage and opportunity for success. With victory within grasp, retreat was the more humiliating. Washington, nevertheless, praised the bravery of the troops. One good result of the battle—which the commander in chief noted, and Scott could agree—was that the soldiers could now "see that the enemy are not proof against a vigorous attack."[32] This the British now well knew themselves.

In mid-November, with the army now posted on the hills at Whitemarsh, fourteen miles above Philadelphia, Scott and his brigade had the task of intercepting enemy supplies between Chester and Philadelphia. Before entering the assignment, Scott sat down at the Whitemarsh Church and wrote his wife—the only one of his letters to her still in existence.

Dear Frankey,

I take this favourable oppertunity by Majr Meane to inform You that we are in High spirits and full of hope of Bringing This most Horrid War to a Conclusion by Defeating Genl. How in a fiew days

I am to march tomorrow morning with my Brigade to Cut off the Enemys Supplies of provisions from the Shiping. Colo. Morgan with his lite Coar and Genl. Woodfords Brigd. marches at the same time. I make no doubt of Success and indeed doing something very Cleaver   Mr Lawson who I do not long since wrote by will leave you some money Which please dispose of in Supplying Your Wants in the Best manner You Can if any of my Frends has been kind enough to Credit You Pray let it be Your first Care to discharge these Debts. I dont know what Sum Mr Lawson may have left You as I do not know Your Necessaty, but directed Him to leave with You what ever You might stand in need off, pray take notice of the Sum that I may Account with him for it. pray dont wish to see me sooner than my Duty to my Country will allow me to Leave the Service with Credit, no time Shall be lost when thats the Case I am

Dear Frankey &c
Chs. Scott[33]

Scott's "High spirits," however, might have been tempered somewhat by the news of the loss of the Delaware forts: Fort Mifflin on the sixteenth and Fort Mercer on the twenty-first.

At a council of war on November 24 ten officers opposed an attack on Philadelphia, while Scott and four others (Stirling, Wayne, Woodford, and De Kalb) favored an attempt. Scott advised in his brief written opinion that an advance party to enter the city should be taken from General Greene's division, since Greene's troops were "the flower of the Army, and . . . it will require the best Men we can pick to effect the landing if opposed." However, Scott soon changed his mind. On November 30 he was one of six generals favoring cantonment of the army at Wilmington, Delaware; the other generals preferred other locations, with only Pulaski holding out for a winter campaign. Somewhat apologetic a few days later, in answer to a circular letter from Washington, Scott said he had thought there would have been "a probability of success" in attacking the British in Philadelphia; "but after your Excellency returned from reconnoitring the Enemy's lines and hearing your opinion with regard to their strength, I lost every idea of a Winters Campaign."[34]

On December 4 the British army, in full force, "by a sudden and rapid march," took post at Chestnut Hill, within one and a half miles of the American position. Washington arranged an order of battle, with Greene and Sullivan in the front line and Stirling and Lafayette (with General Stephen being cashiered, Lafayette was given Stephen's division, including Scott's brigade) in the second. On the morning of the fifth "the two Armies lay like Saul & the Philistines with only a small Valley between, and a General Action every moment expected." For the next several days there were numerous encounters between advanced troops of both armies. Unable to use a flanking maneuver to advantage and to draw the main American army into battle, Howe withdrew to Philadelphia on the eighth. The successive minor actions of December 4–8, of what is called the battle of Edge Hill, nevertheless was costly to both sides: 350 British casualties and 100 American.[35]

On December 18 the army took up winter cantonment at Valley Forge, on the west bank of the Schuylkill, twenty-five miles northwest of Philadelphia. For several weeks Scott's men were busy building huts. His brigade—along with those of Woodford, Wayne, and Enoch Poor—held the western flank of the front line. Scott himself stayed at Samuel Jones's spacious Georgian house, overlooking a fifty-acre farm (now Valley Brook Farm), three miles from Washington's headquarters.[36]

It was a white Christmas at Valley Forge; four inches of snow fell during the day and evening. Scott undoubtedly was a guest of Washington for dinner on the twenty-sixth, for he was brigadier officer of the day, and it was Washington's custom to invite the officers on such assignment to dinner (later changed to the day after the special duty). Scott was brigadier of the day ten times from December 26 to March 3 (on the eve of going home on furlough). Dinners with the officers of the day were plain:

usually meat, hard bread, potatoes, a little toddy or Madeira wine, and perhaps hickory nuts for dessert.[37]

Scott lived in style at the Jones house, where Sir William Howe had headquartered briefly after the battle of Brandywine. His Welsh host had a plentiful supply of hard cider. The daily horseback rides through the snow and ice to inspect the men or to meet with Washington might have been a stiff endurance test for some of the stout, overweight general officers, but for Scott they were a means of breaking the boredom and keeping in physical shape.[38]

One effect of the Philadelphia campaign was the deepened rancor between Scott and Adam Stephen, which apparently had been growing since the Virginians had joined Washington's army in New Jersey. It is understandable why the two men did not get along. Washington himself had a dislike for Stephen for his insubordination, recklessness with the truth, and opportunism, a reputation going back to the French and Indian War; Stephen also had had the audacity to try to unseat Washington as a burgess from Frederick County in 1761. The Scottish physician-farmer, in his mid-fifties, had been high-handed in public and private affairs. What Scott probably disliked most about Stephen was his taking patriotism lightly. On one occasion Stephen even boasted how easy it was to make the rank of major general. Scott also was probably offended by Stephen's improprieties; once the old bachelor (who kept a mistress at home) was observed taking snuff with some of the camp follower prostitutes. Benjamin Rush, who had originally backed Stephen for promotion, now called him a "sordid, boasting cowardly sot." At his court-martial, Stephen was charged with "Acting unlike an Officer" and with "Drunkenness or drinking so much, as to act frequently in a manner, unworthy the character of an officer." Actually an able officer, Stephen was undone mainly by his cockiness and outspokenness.

Facing the charges of misconduct, Stephen reported to Washington on October 9 that "General Scot has been an incumbrance to me for Some time." Stephen blamed Scott for the precipitous loss of Birmingham Meetinghouse Hill during the battle of Brandywine: "To my great Surprise I found Genl Scot marching off his Brigade from that Advantageous position without my Orders or Knowledge. . . . It took a long time to form them in tolerable order, as the Enemy were firing upon them; & I am Confident by this unseasonable Manoeuver the Enemy escaped Considerable Loss, & it Shortened our Stand." Moreover, "on the 16th of September when drawn up in order of Battle, waiting your Exellencys Orders—Genl Scot Movd off with his Brigade without my Knowledge." Concluding his complaint against Scott, Stephen said: "I had great inclination to let all these things pass hoping that the least Reflexion would have brought him to alter his Conduct; but besides Aspersing me to your Excellency, he goes through the Division alienating the affection of the officers, & breeding bad blood."[39] It was no problem for Washington, though, whose side to take—Scott's or Stephen's.

Meanwhile, the thoughts of the officers and men turned toward home. The arduous campaign and now the prospect of a long, cold winter disheartened many of the soldiers. Many officers, largely because of the hardships of their families, resigned their commissions.[40] Surely Scott also had such qualms. But, at least, with the New Year he could be grateful that he was alive and well. Like other Virginians, he had expected that a victorious campaign in 1777 might well have ended the war, and indeed, coupled with the surrender of the British at Saratoga, it probably would have. But, for the present, Scott would have to forgo the idea of returning to "Domestic Felicity," as he prepared for further difficult service in the field.

III

"A Corps of Light Infantry Composed of the Best"

Wintertime Valley Forge was an ordeal. Restlessness among the men pervaded the camp; because of boredom there was no end to disciplinary infractions, assaults, near mutiny, and desertions. Sickness was rife. In January, Scott's brigade, with its largest complement of men thus far, including several hundred Virginia militia, at 1,287 had only 473 effectives—the rest comprised 104 sick present, 253 sick absent, 154 on command and extra service, 50 on furlough, and 253 wanting shoes and clothes. Not only did the controversy over the ranking of the four Virginia generals come to a head, with a congressional committee and a board of general officers making the final determination, but Scott and other brigadier generals protested Congress's promotion of Thomas Conway, an Irish-Frenchman, to major general, a decision which disregarded seniority, proven merit, and experience.[1]

Light infantry was still Scott's chief interest. Much of his experience with the army thus far had been commanding such troops. As distinguished from actual cavalry (dragoons), which several states had supplied for Continental service, the light infantry of the main army usually consisted of regular regiments or detachments of personnel selected from various units—both mounted and dismounted infantrymen—operating at the front of the army to harass enemy outposts and advance parties, particularly those foraging. Light infantry served as patrols in order to secure areas between the two armies and to collect

45

intelligence. In maneuvering toward battle, the light infantry was the first to engage the enemy. Scott felt that the light infantry should be put on a more established basis. He recommended to Washington that there should be specifically a "light corps" of 1,000 men, half riflemen and half "Musqueteers," all of whom would be "chosen men," commanded by officers "of known bravery," without reference to seniority or state quotas. "One hundred Horsemen of the same Stamp should be annexed to, and do duty with the Corps. As much is to be expected of these Troops the greatest care should be taken in the choice of officers."[2]

At Valley Forge the officer ranks in the Virginia brigades were practically depleted. In February, Washington noted that all the Virginia field officers were "in a manner absent." Muhlenberg was the first Virginia brigadier general to take furlough, and by mid-March the other three—Woodford, Weedon, and Scott— also had left the army. Washington reluctantly consented to the leaves of absence, providing that the generals first decide which officers to retain in their brigades. Scott left Valley Forge for home about March 14. He stopped off at York, Pennsylvania, the temporary capital, to visit with members of Congress. He returned to Valley Forge about May 20. Scott's brigade, considered essentially as light infantry, along with Woodford's and the North Carolina brigades, formed a division commanded by Lafayette.[3]

While the British pulled out of Philadelphia on June 16 to 18, Washington asked his generals what course the American army should take. Scott had become more conservative in his views on confronting the enemy, and in his answer, brief as usual, he thought that "by no means" should the army "risk a general Action," nor should it leave the strong ground of Valley Forge "untill the route of the Enemy is certainly ascertained. I have not the most distant Idea of having it in our power to annoy the Enemy on their march to Amboy, if that should be their route." Thus Scott was one of the ten officers who supported Charles Lee, who, however, did not want to attack the enemy at all. Only Wayne would fight immediately.[4]

While the British army slowly pushed on across New Jersey

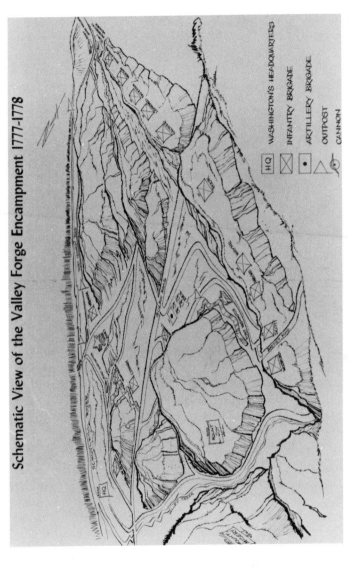

Schematic View of the Valley Forge Encampment 1777-1778

Schematic view of the Valley Forge encampment. (Reprinted with the permission of the publisher from John B. B. Trussell, *Epic on the Schuylkill: The Valley Forge Encampment, 1777–78* [Harrisburg: Pennsylvania Historical and Museum Commission, 1974]) toward New York, Washington in the night and early morning of June 18–19 abandoned Valley Forge. Crossing the Delaware, the Americans encamped at Hopewell township in New Jersey. Washington committed part of his force as light infantry to sound out and harass the enemy and, in the event of a battle, indicated that he would bring up the rest of the army. Scott, with 1,500 "Picked men," was "to gall the enemys left flank and rear." Daniel Morgan and 600 riflemen and 50 Continental dragoons under Lt. Col. Anthony White were to probe the enemy's right, while cooperating with the brigades of Dickinson and Maxwell and Cadwalader's Pennsylvania militia already in the advance.[5]

Scott's elite detachment set out on its mission on the evening of the twenty-fourth. The remnant of his brigade was left under the command of Col. William Grayson, who had charge of the "Additional Regiment" in the brigade. Scott's force remained separate from the others, and on June 26 was three miles from the British encampment at Monmouth Courthouse. Meanwhile, Washington ordered Lafayette to form a junction "as expeditiously as possible with that under the command of Genl. Scott" and "to use the most effectual means of gaining the enemy's left flank and rear, and giving them every degree of annoyance." By nightfall, Lafayette joined Scott with 1,000 additional troops under Wayne. All the American advance detachments—4,000 select troops and 1,200 militia—were to take orders from Lafayette. The Frenchman held a quick meeting with Scott, Maxwell, Wayne, and Dickinson at Robin's Tavern, and largely upon the insistence of these generals it was decided to press closer to the enemy and attack their rear guard the next day. On June 27, after coming up to a mile of the British lines, Lafayette and Scott, however, upon orders from Washington, countermarched and the next day were in Englishtown, a safe seven miles from Monmouth Courthouse. A delay in forwarding provisions and inadequate communications had been the basis for Washington's decision.[6]

Maj. Gen. Charles Lee had deferred to Lafayette in command of the advance troops, thinking they would be kept as a minimum force. Discovering, however, that the forward units amounted to half the army, he asserted his right to command by the fact that he was the senior major general. At Englishtown, on the twenty-seventh, Lafayette placed his army under Lee, who had arrived with Varnum's brigade and that part of Scott's (Grayson's) troops that had been left behind. Washington, meanwhile, came up with the rest of the army to Cranbury, three miles distant, and rode into the advance camp in the afternoon, where he met briefly with Lee, Lafayette, Maxwell, Wayne, and Scott. It was decided that Lee would lead an attack on the British rear the next morning. Lee was instructed by Washington to work out the details with his generals. At a meeting at Lee's quarters at 5 P.M., however, no plan of attack was presented. Lee would later insist that because he had insufficient intelligence of the terrain and the enemy's exact location, he could not form a precise battle plan. Lee, nevertheless, as Washington ordered, readied his troops for an advance at dawn.[7]

At 5 A.M. Sunday, June 28, the American van—Scott's detachment, the rest of his brigade, Varnum's, Wayne's, and Maxwell's brigades, and other troops under colonels Richard Butler and Henry Jackson—set out and an hour later arrived at Monmouth Courthouse on the rear and left flank of the enemy, who had begun to march. Lee with the rest of his force came to about a half mile of the courthouse on the right. British troops charged Colonel Butler and were repulsed; Scott's detachment crossed the morass on the left of this action. Lee, expecting an enemy attack by a left flank movement, halted the advance, and sent orders by Capt. Evan Edwards and Maj. John Francis Mercer to tell Scott to stay in the woods at the American left. The orders were never delivered because by the time Edwards and Mercer arrived, Scott had retreated. Fleeing artillerymen at the center, who had run out of ammunition, gave Scott the impression of an overall collapse of the American attack. Scott persuaded Maxwell, adjacent to him, also to retreat, and Wayne, at the center, not having received orders, did the same. Lee was counting on an encirclement of the enemy, but this could not be carried out with the troops at the left and center retreating. The British brought up heavy reinforcements, and Lee had no choice but to withdraw the rest of his troops. Lee's next plan was to form his troops at an elevation back of the morass. Scott, however, kept on going and fell all the way back to Tennent Meetinghouse, where he met troops under Lord Stirling.

Lee, in his defense later, would argue that it was Scott's hasty retreat that caused the collapse of the American offensive. Scott cited two factors for his withdrawal: the confusion of the artillerymen—"they were running and the horses trotting with the field pieces"—and the British mounting a strong attack that threatened to outflank him. He insisted, too, that he had no orders from Lee and did not know what was intended. There had also been a misunderstanding between Scott's detachment and Maxwell's brigade as to which position each should take.[8] Certainly Scott was as responsible as anyone for the general retreat.

Washington, bringing up the main army, was amazed to find the advance units falling back pell-mell. Eventually, among the retreating troops, Washington spotted Lee. According to Lee's aide, Maj. John Francis Mercer, Washington inquired of Lee the reason for all the disorder. Lee replied, "I see no confusion but what has arose from my orders not being properly obeyed." Lee also pointed out the superior strength of the British attacking force and stated that he did not want to take a risk. For the time being Washington told Lee to continue in command until he could make "a disposition of the army."[9]

Tradition has it that the commander in chief, at this meeting with Lee, was so chagrined that he used intemperate language toward Lee. Supposedly Scott was present and witnessed the exchange of words. Actually there is no real evidence that he was there, and one authority demonstrates that he could hardly have been present at this time. Possibly Scott was a witness to the second meeting between Washington and Lee, when Washington took over sole command. Two unsubstantiated stories printed in the nineteenth century, nevertheless, have given currency to Scott's being present at Washington's denunciation of Lee. According to George Washington Parke Custis's *Recollections and Private Memoirs of Washington* (1860): "Scott, it is said, was very profane; and a friend after the war, anxious to reform him of his evil habit, asked him if it was possible that the admired Washington ever swore. Scott reflected for a moment, and then exclaimed, 'yes, once; it was at Monmouth, and on a day that would make any man swear; Yes, sir, he swore on that day, till the leaves shook on the trees, charming, delightfully. Never have I heard such swearing before, or since. Sir, on that ever memorable day he swore like an angel from Heaven.' The reformer abandoned the General in despair." Franklin Ellis's history of Monmouth County (1885) has another version. Scott "or another of the Virginia officers present in the battle," heard Washington, who was "enraged by Lee's excuse that he had thought it safest to retire before the enemy, who greatly outnumbered him, wrathfully burst out, 'D—n your multiplying eyes, General Lee! Go to the front, or go to hell, I care little which!'"[10]

For the remainder of the battle, Washington drew up the troops that he had initially held in reserve on a ridge—the one that Lee had selected on which to make a stand. Greene's division held the right, at Comb's Hill, and Stirling was on the high ground at the left. Of the light infantry that had participated during the early action, only Wayne's troops were committed. Scott's detachment remained at the rear. Under orders from Washington to hold the center, Wayne held off a column of advancing British infantry and horse. For a second line, Lafayette was given command of the light troops, including Scott's, and other reserves. Although Clinton mounted a full-scale attack, the battle soon became largely an artillery duel. With Gen. Henry Knox's guns from the higher ground exacting a deadly fire, the British withdrew. The intense heat of nearly 100° in late afternoon was a determining factor for both sides in quitting the battle.[11]

The British retreat at nightfall gave renewed spirit to Washington's troops, but darkness (a new moon) and the unevenness of the country, with its woods and marshes, discouraged pursuit. Two days after the battle Clinton reached Sandy Hook, from whence the British army ferried to New York, Long Island, and Staten Island. Washington's army marched northward, crossed the Hudson on July 15–18, and encamped at White Plains, awaiting Clinton's next move.[12]

From July 3 to August 12 a court-martial met to try General Lee on three counts: disobeying orders by not attacking the enemy at Monmouth, misbehavior before the enemy by making a shameful retreat, and disrespect to Washington expressed in two letters. Scott, Wayne, and Maxwell gave testimony damaging to Lee. Lee was found guilty on all three charges, though the second was reduced to "making an unnecessary, and in some instances, a disorderly retreat." He was sentenced to a year's suspension from any command in the army, a verdict narrowly upheld by Congress; an insulting letter to Congress later led to his dismissal.[13] For Lee to be made a scapegoat was a face-saving measure for Scott, whose own distant retreat was inexplicable and a major cause for the failure of the attack during the first phase of the battle. Lee's conviction, of course, also absolved Washington from responsibility for the improvised and loose tactics, the wide disposition of the advanced troops, and the broken command system.

At White Plains, Washington rearranged the army. Scott's brigade, now consisting of David Hall's Delaware regiment and four Virginia regiments—John Gibson's sixth, John Green's tenth, James Wood's twelfth, and William Grayson's Additional Regiment—formed the right wing, along with Woodford's and Muhlenberg's Virginia brigades and Smallwood's Second Maryland Brigade. At a council of war on July 25, Scott voted with nineteen other officers unanimously against taking post closer to the enemy; later he would also oppose a siege of New York City.[14]

With the army to be stationary and with the presence of the large British army in the city and surrounding area, it was urgent to have light infantry patrolling the zones between the two armies, to keep watch on the enemy and to interfere with enemy foraging parties and the like. To Scott's surprise and as if to remove any doubt in his ability that might have resulted from the battle of Monmouth, Washington appointed him to the command of a new light infantry corps. In the after orders of August 8, Washington directed that "a Corps of Light Infantry composed of the best, most hardy and active Marksmen and commanded by good Partizan Officers be draughted from the several Brigades to be commanded by Brigadier General Scott," until such time as the "Committee of Arrangement," a congressional committee at camp (appointed June 4, 1778), "shall have established the Light Infantry of the Army agreeable to a late Resolve of Congress." In addition to the men to be drawn from regular Continental army units, a New York militia regiment under Col. Morris Graham was added to the light infantry corps. Continental dragoons when acting in conjunction with the light infantry would also be under the general supervision of Scott.[15]

Although different special forces had been previously so designated (such as Scott's brigade and detachments led by him), the light infantry now was to be of a more fixed entity and would be regarded as the principal combat arm of Washington's army. Since the American and British armies in the North would avoid battle, the light infantry corps played a major role in the war of outposts—one major accomplishment occurring the following year, when Scott's successor, Anthony Wayne, with many of Scott's original light infantry troops, stormed and captured Stony Point.

On August 14 Scott received instructions for his new command. He was to take post in front of Washington's army, to secure the roads leading to the enemy's lines, and to send out a "constant succession of scouting parties," which were "to penetrate as near the Enemy's lines as possible, and to continue within observing distance at all times," always being careful to avoid surprise. Scott was to forward to Washington immediately all intelligence "worthy of notice."[16]

Scott's new command was the most important of his Revolutionary career. For three months he was in charge of the forward-probing operations of the American army about New York and was Washington's chief of intelligence. Actually Scott's authority was more on paper than real. The individual units of the light infantry corps and also the Continental dragoons attached to it from time to time were pretty much on their own in the field, and although it was Scott's responsibility to direct an espionage system, his main duty was to act as liaison between his agents and Washington.

While most of the army held post farther up the Hudson, Scott's troops secured a line from Phillip's Creek to New Rochelle (from the Hudson to Long Island Sound). From his head-quarters on the Greenburg Hills in lower Westchester County, near New Rochelle, Scott's first action in his new command was to send various patrols to Frog's Point, Long Island, and the Neutral Ground (in Westchester County between the two armies) to scout and secure intelligence. These efforts succeeded in collecting news of British troop and ship movements toward Rhode Island, information which led Washington to send Continentals to reinforce militia at Newport. Eli Leavenworth of the Connecticut Continentals and Col. Morris Graham of the New York militia served as Scott's operatives on Long Island; their principal task was to interview persons coming from the British lines and to establish contact with patriot spies in New York City. On the Jersey side of the Hudson, Scott had Maj. Alexander Clough, of the Third Continental Dragoons, employ "some intelligent person," who would pose as an illicit trader and go into New York City, carefully memorizing information so as to avoid carrying incriminating papers.[17]

With the British establishing an outpost at King's Bridge, Scott dispatched Col. Mordecai Gist and 300 men to take position on the Eastchester Road, where it crossed the Sawmill River (in Yonkers). Gist sent out an advance guard of 40 men under Capt. John Stewart and 60 Wappinger Indians (from Stockbridge, Massachusetts) led by Capt. (Chief) Daniel Nimham. On August 20 the Indians ran into a patrol of the Queen's Rangers and forced the enemy to retreat. Lt. Col. John Graves Simcoe of the Rangers, one of the most enterprising figures of the Revolution, not to be outdone, with 500 troops, including Banastre Tarleton's dragoons, marched on the thirty-first toward present Woodlawn Heights, where Stewart's and Nimham's men were posted. The Indians were at the bottom of the hill, separate from Stewart's men. As Scott put it in his report, the Indians came across "an ambuscade sirounded by a large body of Horse and foot." The Indians were herded into a field by Tarleton's troops and slaughtered—even those who had laid down their arms; this was the first instance of "Tarleton's quarter." Among the dead were Captain Nimham and his son. Scott immediately ordered out 300 troops under Richard Parker to reinforce Stewart, and as a result the British did not press an attack further.[18]

The battle of Indian Bridge, or Indian Hill, was reported in Virginia. Commented Edmund Pendleton; "What is the next Object to engage Our Attention, or is the remaining part of the Campaign to be a quiet one, except the Skirmishing of General Scott's Corps. The poor Indians I fear had been taking some grog, or they would not have been surprised *in an Old Field.*"[19]

The enemy became more aggressive after the Indian Bridge affair. To keep abreast of enemy patrols, Scott retained Gist's detachment at its previous location. He also coordinated the activities of Continental dragoon units; for example, he instructed Col. Benjamin Tallmadge to patrol between the Bronx and Hudson rivers, Maj. Henry Lee to cover the east side of the Bronx River, and Capt. Allen McLane to range freely with "an Advance party of the main body of light Infantry." Scott's instructions to McLane were typical of those he issued to officers leading parties in the field. "Your Corps being intended for an Advance party of the main body of light Infantry, You will conduct it in such a manner as to be able to give me the earliest intelligence of any Movements of the enemy & effectually prevent the incursions of small parties into the Country." McLane was also to acquaint himself "perfectly" with the roads and terrain. To avoid fatiguing his men "with excess of duty," McLane was to "move every evening into the rear of a party which will be constantly ready to cover you and allow your men to refresh without danger of a surprise." All intelligence or "discoveries of the enemys motions must be conveyed to me in the fullest & the most perspicuous manner." Whenever provisions ran low, McLane was to repair within a few miles from the encampment of the main army, where he would be supplied. Finally, to prevent surprise, Scott ordered: "Above all you will take care by possessing the Avenues leading to your Posts."[20]

Washington ordered Scott to keep a lookout for any forward movement of the enemy. Scott was to make his main camp at North Castle or Bedford. In case of the unlikely possibility of a "total evacuation" of New York City, Scott was to dispatch 100 men into the city to secure any stores and to notify the governor of New York immediately so that civil authority could be quickly established.[21]

Col. Mordecai Gist, on September 15, reported that nearly 5,000 British troops were marching out of New York City, heading along the Albany Road, in Yonkers. Scott ordered Benjamin Tallmadge and Henry Lee "to keep out Strong Patrolling parties on the Right and left of our incampment also in front." Although the enemy was not in as large numbers as assumed, British rangers and dragoons confronted Gist and his troops at dawn on the sixteenth. Gist soon found that he was outnumbered and surrounded on three sides; fortunately he was able to retreat westward over Philipse's Bridge, which the British had failed to seize, and into woods, from which he gained the Albany Road. Hearing the retort of arms, American pickets and guards in the area came up, and most were captured.[22]

Washington, unaware that General Henry Clinton in New York was under orders to send a large number of troops to St. Lucia and Florida, broke up camp at White Plains and disposed his army in anticipation of a full-scale British attack. McDougall's division was to join Gates's troops, already at Danbury, to form the left wing; De Kalb, on the Fishkill Plains, to form the right. Stirling would establish a second line around Fredericksburg (near the Connecticut line), where Washington made his headquarters. Scott's light infantry, to be joined by Col. Elisha Sheldon's Connecticut dragoons (making a total of Scott's force 1,300 foot and 400 horse), would maintain post in front of the center to "cover this army from surprise." Scott, however, had already responded to the threat of a British advance. Word of the attack on Gist's troops had brought him and the main body of the light infantry down from the camp near North Castle to White Plains. "The whole of the Infantry Lay on their arms all night," a distraught Scott wrote his commander in chief, "in the Rain without the smallest cover immaginable." Because his men were in "Such a Horred Condition," Scott bought enough rum to serve each man one gill. "I was obliged to pay the economic price of Twelve dollars a gallon for it," said Scott, "which I thought better Than letting the men Suffer." Scott himself was so weary that he was "hardly able to set up an hour togather."[23]

With the threat of a British offensive a false alarm, Scott returned to the North Castle camp. "The enemy have been very still since the Army left White Plains, untill this morning," Scott reported to Washington on September 20, when there was a clash of patrols. Scott complained that at the camp the flour had all spoiled, his men had not been paid, "owing to the inattention of the Regimental Paymasters," and he had not received badly needed shoes and clothing."[24]

The high rate of desertion in the light infantry added to Scott's troubles. In most instances, however, the men simply wanted to get back to their regularly assigned regiments. When thirty men left at one time, Scott sent forty troops to bring them back. Becoming exasperated, Scott told Washington that "I shall be proud," whenever the deserters were caught, "that they may be tryed and punished hear as it will be a good example" to the rest of his corps. When some of the deserters were taken, Scott asked permission to execute one of them—Elisha Smith, a dragoon. Washington consented, but the warrant for Smith's execution arrived at Scott's camp a day after it had expired; Scott then was unwilling to carry out the sentence, fearful that he might "commit a Blunder." Scott had other deserters tried by a court-martial, which sentenced them to one hundred lashes each; but because they were basically "good men" and had been "misled by Some officer," he again sought Washington's advice and was told to use his own judgment—and the outcome is unknown. Apparently Scott solved the problem of desertion for a while. But in early November, within four days, fifty-six New England soldiers absconded. Scott sent out troops after one group of deserters, with orders to fire on them. A fight ensued; no one was killed, but two were captured, while eighteen escaped. Scott hoped "an Example may be made at least of one," he informed Washington, "as I am well assurd that nothing Else will put a Stop to it."[25]

With Scott's camp about thirty miles directly south of the main army at Fredericksburg, Washington proposed that Scott set up a relay system of communication—a sort of "pony express," with two dragoons stationed every twelve or fifteen miles for the purpose of carrying dispatches. Washington also advised that Scott have his patrols "communicate with each other, so that if the Centre or either wing is struck, the whole chain may have notice."[26]

Receiving a report that a British force of about 3,000 was marching north from New York City, Scott went to the Hudson to get information firsthand and, if necessary, to dispose his troops to resist the advance. Washington advised Scott that he should particularly attend to guarding the pass into the Highlands near Peekskill. Only several British regiments, however, came out of the enemy lines. A party under Simcoe pursued Major Lee's cavalry to White Plains and beyond to near Scott's camp at North Castle, and, as Scott reported, there was some "Scattering fur on Wards Road and also on the North [Hudson] river." In case of any further British advance, Scott planned to position his corps between the enemy and Croton Bridge "and Dispute every Strong ground with them until I Reach peaks Kills." Meanwhile, he placed Lee's troops "on every road Leading this way and so Disposed of the other hors that they will be able To Support him in case he should be Run by them. Gists Corps will skirmish with their Flanking Parties."[27]

The British, merely extending their outposts to the area essentially evacuated by the Americans, took possession of Valentine's Hill, Sneading Hill, and Philipse's Hill. One of Scott's units, some 300 dragoons (Frenchmen and Hessian defectors) commanded by Col. Charles Armand (marquis de La Rouerie Tuffin), stayed in the neighborhood of Sneading Hill and alarmed the British post several times. But, as a Hessian captain at the British post commented, "since these enemy patrols ran into my sneak parties," Armand's men then kept at a safe distance.[28]

The enemy only persisted in sending out strong foraging parties. Nevertheless, Scott requested that Washington secure the pass at the Continental Village for good measure in case his patrols in that area had to retreat. Scott wished that he could be more active himself in the field. "I am Still so onwell," he wrote Washington, "that I am not able to Reconnoiter the Country myself, but I Trust that my faithful officers (for so I may with Propriety say) will not mislead me."[29]

George Baylor's Third Dragoons from Virginia (also styled "Mrs. Washington's Guards") joined Scott's corps in September and were stationed at Old Tappan (Harrington) on the west bank of the Hudson. Generals Cornwallis and Knyphausen each led British troops across the Hudson: Cornwallis to attack Baylor's dragoons, and Knyphausen, the miltia, who, however, were alerted in time and escaped. Late at night, September 27–28, Maj. Gen. Charles ("No Flint") Grey and a detachment from Cornwallis's force stealthily approached Baylor's position. Baylor's men were asleep in three barns, the officers in the several houses. Grey's men surprised and butchered a dragoon guard of about a dozen men at the Hackensack Bridge. Living up to his reputation, Grey had his men remove the flints and charges from their muskets and attach bayonets. Undiscovered, the British raiders rushed the sleeping Americans. Of Baylor's 104 troops, 67 were killed, captured, or wounded. Baylor was severely wounded by being bayoneted through the lungs. Maj. Alexander Clough was killed; all but one officer were captured. The British buried the American dead in the local tanning vats; reinterment years later revealed excessive multiple wounds, substantiating charges of British atrocity. After this affair, Cornwallis, as did Knyphausen, recrossed the Hudson back to New York. Two days later, Col. Richard Butler with 300 men and Henry Lee with some of his cavalrymen, who had been assigned by Scott to check British foraging along the east bank of the Hudson, surprised a Hessian party of 150, and killed 10 of them and captured 19, without any American loss. Scott commented that "this in Some Measure Compliments For poor Baylor."[30]

On October 1 Scott moved his camp northward three miles to near Bedford. He had convinced Washington this was a better defensive position. Gen. James Clinton was assigned to cover the pass into the Highlands at the Continental Village. Thus Washington had strong protection on both his right and left flanks, and, as a Hessian officer noted, Washington's "cordon, under General Scott, had been extended from the Hudson River behind Sing Sing to Bedford." Scott's and the British patrols still occasionally collided. Washington thought some of Scott's officers were not vigilant enough in guarding against surprise attacks and wanted Scott to reprimand the officers. Scott defended his officers, and Washington then merely insisted that the officers be warned against the dangers of not fully reconnoitering an area.[31]

About October 10 the British withdrew from their stations in lower Yonkers, and King's Bridge once again became the forward enemy post. Scott had Colonel Armand's "Foreign Legion" operate between Tarrytown and the heights across from King's Bridge. On October 12 Armand captured a Hessian picket of twelve men near King's Bridge, but he had to let all but two go because an enemy party gave chase. Scott later increased the range of Armand's patrol duty to include cooperating with other American scouting parties around White Plains.[32]

In addition to directing the field activity of the light infantry, Scott continued to give attention to intelligence gathering, a duty which he found both worrisome and demanding. Not only did Washington need information but so also did Admiral D'Estaing, whose fleet remained in American waters (first at New York and then at Providence and Boston) until early November. Scott barraged Washington with reports on the coming and going of British ships and embarkation and debarkation of troops. Too frequently, all that he had was speculation. At one time, Scott's agents reported the imminent departure of all British troops in New York City for the West Indies, which, of course, would not be the case. Thus Scott's main problem was to establish the credibility of his intelligence reports. General Greene complained that "our intelligence from N York is altogether equivocal and uncertain," and General McDougall also had his doubts. "General Scotts character for combining particulars and balancing evidence I am a stranger to," commented McDougall.[33]

Washington insisted on corroborating evidence, usually from Scott's light infantrymen, who picked up information from deserters and the like. The commander in chief was often impatient with the delays in getting intelligence from Scott—delays that were unavoidable because of the necessity of protecting the

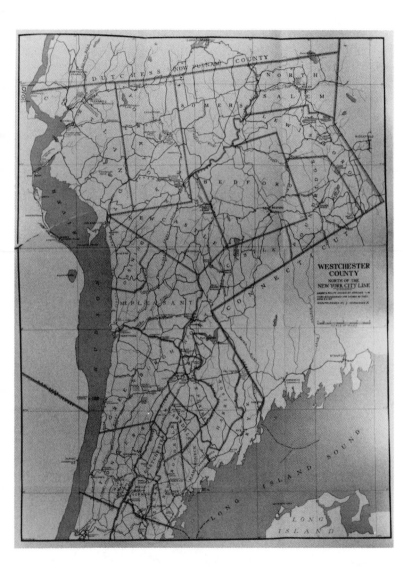

Westchester County north of the New York City line. (Reprinted with the permission of the publisher from Otto Hufeland, *Westchester County during the American Revolution* [White Plains, N.Y.: Westchester County Historical Society, 1925])

agents at all costs and also because in most instances the intelligence had to be carried from Manhattan to Long Island, and then by boat across Long Island Sound through the "Devil's Belt" to the Connecticut shore, and then by land to Scott's headquarters.

Extreme precaution had to be taken to conceal the identity of Scott's spies. Instead of having an agent pass through British lines—as, for example, the unfortunate Nathan Hale had done earlier—it was deemed best to employ a solid, respected resident, preferably a merchant, who in the normal run of business would be allowed to make outside contacts. So secret were some of Scott's sources that neither he nor Washington could identify them. The real identities of two super-spies, known only at the time as Samuel Culper, Sr., and Samuel Culper, Jr., were not established until one hundred fifty years later. Culper, Sr., was Abraham Woodhull of Setauket, Long Island, and Culper, Jr., was Robert Townshend, a merchant from Oyster Bay who moved to New York City at the start of the war. The two men began their secret correspondence under Scott and continued in the secret service until the end of the war. Townshend mingled among British officers at taverns and social functions, collecting information for James Rivington's tory newspaper. As a society reporter Townshend thus had the perfect guise for obtaining information.

The spy system followed a basic pattern. Townshend, as a merchant in New York, made purchases for friends in Oyster Bay and Setauket and slipped messages to Austin Roe of Setauket, who transported the goods. At Setauket, a British outpost, Roe learned from signals via Woodhull's clothesline when and where American messengers could be contacted. Usually Roe would meet with Lt. Caleb Brewster, whose whaleboat would deliver the message to Col. Benjamin Tallmadge on the Connecticut shore. Tallmadge, who used the code name John Bolton, forwarded the message to Scott, who then relayed it to Washington.[34]

Scott did not do much to develop a cipher system—this was left for his successor, Tallmadge, to accomplish. Though Scott, who was very concerned about the authenticity of the reports he received, preferred to have the full identity of the person submitting intelligence, he went along with Washington's view that names could be withheld or false signatures used on the letters as long as the handwriting was known.[35]

The British of course had their espionage system as well. Scott once got hoodwinked at his own game. Mrs. Ann Bates, formerly a Philadelphia schoolteacher, married to a British soldier, posed as a peddler and gained full access to Washington's encampments in the summer and fall of 1778. On her last trip she was recognized by a British deserter and had to get back to New York by the most direct means possible. Some of Scott's light infantrymen took her into custody, though not knowing her mission, and brought her to Scott. She explained that she was a soldier's wife "in the Centre Division & had forgot something about five or six Miles below the Plains." Scott wrote out a pass for her, thus unwittingly abetting one of the most dangerous British spies.[36]

A big headache for Scott was Capt. Eli Leavenworth, who commanded a small party on Long Island. Leavenworth's chief duty, so it seems, was to roam in the British unoccupied areas to gather intelligence at random and when possible to deal with secret agents. Leavenworth admitted that he got most of his information from strangers. Scott would go for long periods without hearing from him, and though some of his intelligence was correct and useful, often it was suspect. Eventually Scott lost confidence in Leavenworth, "being fearfull he had turn'd his thoughts more to his own interest than the public good." Leavenworth seems to have used his position as a military officer to extort goods from the local populace, particularly from suspected tories, and then sold them in different places. Washington directed Scott to make a full inquiry and, with sufficient evidence, to have Leavenworth arrested, along with anyone else involved, and sent to headquarters. Scott informed Washington on October 17 that "I have wrote Capt. Leavenworth in Premtory Terms to confine himself to his duty and not Risk the Displeasure of his Country for the paltry consideration of a horse thief with a fiew hard dollars in his Pockit." Scott, who originally had hesitated to recall Leavenworth, "fearfull it cause an alarm," finally ordered Leavenworth back to camp and appointed another officer in his place; he also "had several persons employed" in an attempt "to fix a Charge" against Leavenworth for plundering.[37]

Other officers in Scott's command offended the local citizenry. In Norwalk, Connecticut, Capt. Josiah Stoddard of the Second Continental Dragoons rescued one of his men, Gershom Dorman, who had been jailed for assault on a local citizen. Washington intervened to order Dorman back to the custody of the civilian authorities. Scott protested to Washington that the soldier was on assigned duty when arrested and insisted upon upholding military jurisdiction over any misdeeds of his men. Too many "of these select Men are enemys to this army," Scott pointed out, and "if they are Suffer'd to Stop and arrest the officers and Soldiers of this Detachment when they think themselves abused, and without first acquainting me, I shall never be able to know when I am in Safety, and of course Cannot be accountable for the Safety of the troops under my Command."[38]

On another jurisdictional matter, Scott arrested Elijah Wadsworth, a deputy commissary of issues assigned to his light infantry, for neglect of duty. Washington advised Scott that by a resolve of Congress only the commander in chief or a general officer in charge of a post had the authority to do this. Besides, it was very difficult "to get people of common honesty to undertake the lower duties of the Staff," and unless there was a criminal act it was "better to report them to their superiors and have them removed, than to enter a quarrel with them."[39]

With many enlistments about to expire, Scott's corps faced dissolution. Scott suggested that the problem could be solved by giving furloughs for the winter. He talked to his men and reported that most of the troops of Armand's regiment, whose time would expire December 1, "would Chearfully inguage for the war" if they could get home by December 1 and stay until spring. Scott believed that by adopting this policy two-thirds of the light infantry and dragoons would return. Washington, though he feared "a pernicious precedent to the Army," reluctantly consented, provided "the men cannot be induced to continue in the service by the common means. The Corps is too valuable to be lost to the Army."[40]

Although Scott had complained of being ill, apparently personal and economic problems back home bothered him more. He was ready to resign from the army. On October 21 he wrote to Washington: "My long indisposition and other Obvious reasons I am afraid will make it indispensable necessary for me to Retier from this Honor and most Desirable Command, however I'll hold out as long as I possably Can and when Necesaty Compells the Measure I hope for your Excellencys Indulgence." Scott reiterated his request a week later. Washington understood, though he would dislike losing "so valuable an Officer"; if Scott could not "reconcile the Situation of your private affairs with your continuance in the service," he would not "be expected to make an absolute sacrifice of the former for the latter." Washington reminded Scott that only Congress could accept the resignation of a general officer. Scott, however, did not care to apply to Congress at this time and asked for a furlough instead. Washington agreed and stated that Scott's next in command could temporarily take charge of the light infantry.[41]

Scott was very grateful, but he did not like the idea of Col. Mordecai Gist's succeeding him. He felt Gist "was no way equal" to the task. Scott had "kept him always Detached from the Corps where he had don no other duty than that of keeping Constant Scouting partys." Scott advised Washington to give Gist a separate command, and Gist would then "take no offence at being deprived of the Command of the whole Corps." Washington agreed with Scott and told him that he never had any intention of handing Scott's command over to Gist. "If Gist will not be satisfied where he is at present, I must recall him," said Washington. Rather, Col. David Henley would take over as acting commander of the corps.[42]

The army would soon move across the Hudson for winter cantonment at Middlebrook, New Jersey, and the light infantry would be dissolved temporarily, with the men going back to their original units. The corps would be revived in the spring. Col. Benjamin Tallmadge, already well experienced in clandestine operations, would take over supervision of Scott's intelligence network. In several weeks the three depleted Virginia brigades (Woodford's, Muhlenberg's, and Scott's) and a Delaware regiment would be arranged into a division under Stirling, with Col. William Russell becoming acting commander of Scott's brigade.[43]

Scott left for home about November 16–18. On his way his "indisposition" again bothered him, and he had to rest a few days in Delaware. One cannot speculate what Scott's infirmity was—perhaps the gout, which plagued so many of the other generals, but, given Scott's activity in the field nearly twenty years later, it would seem this was not the case. During his stop, Scott inspected a quartermaster depot and was shocked at "the Idolness in the Waggoners and the Willful Wast of Forage." In reporting to the quartermaster general, Nathanael Greene, he said that "however unhappy" he was "at the loss of time on the Road," he could "rejoice at the Misfortune when I Reflect that it has put in my power to make this early Discovery of abuse which perhaps might not have happend untill Too late for Remedy." Scott recommended that a new superintendent for the depot be appointed, namely Dr. William McMechen, a surgeon in the Fourth Virginia Regiment, who was "on the Spot, a Man of property and a *Gentleman*." McMechen "has done as much as any person could Possably do in his way for the Country without any thoughts of a reward." Scott also mentioned to Greene that "I have In a great Measure Declind all thoughts of Resigning as I find it very Disagreable to my Frends."[44] Interestingly Scott omitted reference to his ardent patriotism, which he had so often cited in the past as the compelling reason for continuing in service. The war had been drawn out, and in Scott's mind there was no doubt of the inevitability of winning independence. His inclinations now were perhaps more that of the professional soldier: to stick out the war so as not to forfeit either material rewards or honor and glory. Scott did not know that he was bidding farewell to Washington's army. As he headed southward, so did the war.

"To Stop the Progress of the Enemy"

"It being a matter of importance that the inclosed should reach Genl. Scott as speedily as possible," wrote Washington on March 6, 1779, to General Weedon, who was enjoying a tranquil retirement in Fredericksburg, Virginia, "I have taken the liberty to put in under cover to you and to request you to direct the Deputy Quarter Mr. at Fredericksburg to forward it immediately to him by a special Messenger. As I do not know to what particular place to direct it, I must beg of you to send it where Genl. Scott will most probably be found."[1]

Scott was not hard to reach. He probably was sipping a toddy at his farm or enjoying the camaraderie of friends and furloughed officers at the Effingham Tavern, near the new Cumberland courthouse (about five miles west of the old county seat). The letter from the commander in chief said that in compliance with Governor Patrick Henry's request for a general officer to be sent to Virginia, Scott was to superintend recruiting in the state. Washington enclosed a list of officers furloughed and on command in Virginia, who would assist Scott and lead the troops northward as they were collected. The officers were to be notified in the newspapers. Scott was to go to Williamsburg, where he would receive further orders from Governor Henry. Washington hoped most of the recruits would reach camp by May 1, and Scott was also to return by that time.[2]

Specifically, Scott would be in charge of collecting 2,216 soldiers, rank and file, which the Virginia assembly, in the October session, had voted to be raised by volunteers or by draft. When Scott returned to headquarters, he would reassume command of his brigade (as of March, the fourth, sixth, eighth, and additional Virginia regiments and a Delaware regiment). Aiding Scott's task was Washington's proclamation to pardon all deserters who returned to the army by May 1.[3]

On March 31 Scott attended a special meeting of the Virginia Council of State called by Governor Henry to work out details for collecting the troops. The council ordered the state's commissary of stores to send clothing for 1,000 men to Fredericksburg. Such material, however, was in short supply. Scott wrote Washington that nothing was really being done in the state to provide clothing, without which, according to law, the troops could not be marched out of the state. Washington assured him that he could count on a large supply of clothing from Philadelphia.[4]

Scott found that recruiting as well as military procurement under state auspices could be inefficient and even obstructionist. The rendezvous were set for April 20 at Alexandria (for those coming from north of the Rappahannock) and April 25 at Fredericksburg (for those from south of the river). Scott placed advertisements in the newspapers and sent out express letters to local authorities. Arriving at Alexandria on the twenty-first, he found "not one rag of Clothes nor a Single man." He immediately notified Governor Henry, pointing out the "inattention" of the county lieutenants and requested that "the Cloths may be Hurryed up." Receiving no reply from the governor by April 24, Scott informed Washington frankly that the clothing would not be ready in time "to render the men of any use this Campaign." But Washington was to rest assured that "However Ruinous this Business may be to me what ever respects my own duty has and Shall be don with all possible Expedition."[5]

Since the new troops had not arrived at Alexandria, as he had ordered, Scott next went to Fredericksburg, where he found about 400 recruits and 200 of the reenlisted men; 400 of these he was able to send on to the army with minimal clothing, but there were no garments left for the other troops. Scott ordered several officers into active service to assist him, since most of the officers on Washington's list to be called back to duty had returned to camp. This Washington approved, but he advised Scott not to "reclaim" any of those from several western counties who were to be stationed at Fort Pitt. With the spring planting done, there would be more troops—but there was still the lack of clothing. A notice in the *Virginia Gazette* of May 1 exaggeratedly asserted that at Fredericksburg "General Scott has already collected 1400 men to fill up the Virginia regiments to the northwards and more daily coming in."[6]

Although Scott had not been able to meet Washington's deadline, he was determined to finish the job and hoped he would soon lead the rest of the Virginia Continentals to Middlebrook. Events, however, intervened. All Continental troops from states south of Pennsylvania were to be committed to the southern theater. The British were sending large reinforcements to Georgia, which could be a prelude of an invasion to sweep through Georgia and the Carolinas.[7] Gen. Benjamin Lincoln commanded a force in that state, chiefly militia, that could not alone resist a strong effort by the enemy. Washington's letter to Scott of May 5 urgently had new orders.

> I am now to inform you, that the Original Intention of bringing those levies to reinforce the Army here is changed and that they are destined, as a reinforcement to the Southern Army. Our Affair in Georgia grow daily more alarming, and unless a Force of more permanent Troops than Militia can be collected sufficient to Stop the Progress of the Enemy in that Quarter we shall have a great Deal to apprehend. South Carolina considers herself in imminent Danger. . . . you will exert yourself to collect them with the utmost expedition, at such Places as you Judge most convenient and to have them equipped and Marched to join the Southern Army. . . . There is not a Moment's Time to be lost.

The men who had been destined for the Northern Army—those remaining levies that had been voted for by the Virginia legislature—were now to constitute a brigade of three regiments under Scott. Officers would be sent from Middlebrook, from whom Scott would select to fill the commissioned ranks of the brigade.[8] Washington notified Governor Rutledge of South Carolina to expect the brigade under Scott, whom "I can venture to recommend as a good man, and a brave and intelligent Officer. I hope his health will permit him to join you."[9]

There was yet another surprise for Scott. As British strategy concentrated on the conquest of the Deep South, it became essential that the British disrupt the sources of supply, finance, and manpower in Virginia that would sustain an American defense. To damage Virginia commerce—seize or destroy tobacco and ships—was a primary objective. For this purpose, a British expeditionary force left Sandy Hook, New Jersey, under the command of Commodore George Collier and Maj. Gen. Edward Mathew. It was a formidable fleet: four men-of-war and lesser ships, accompanied by twenty-eight transports. Aboard was a land force of 1,800 men.

The British fleet passed the Capes of Virginia on May 8. Sailing up the Elizabeth River, on May 11 the enemy took possession of Portsmouth, which they spared except for the destruction of several public buildings. The British also occupied Norfolk. Over the next several days raiding parties plundered Smithfield and burned Suffolk and some plantation houses (which, however, Collier blamed on privateers). The British burned the Gosport naval yard, seizing or destroying 137 vessels (some of which were under construction). Large quantities of tobacco and naval stores were destroyed or carried off, including, at Suffolk alone, 9,000 barrels of salted pork, stored for Washington's army, 8,000 barrels of pitch, tar, and turpentine, and other stores.[10]

The House of Delegates on Monday, May 10, directed Scott to march the Continental levies immediately to Williamsburg and to call up any Continental officers in Virginia whose services he might need. Lt. Col. Benjamin Temple's First Continental Dragoons, then at Winchester, were requested to serve under Scott's command.[11]

Scott stationed the Continentals at Williamsburg. Expecting the enemy to advance on the capital, he began constructing earthworks. Of 5,000 militia called up, only a few were able to get to Williamsburg; some militia in the lower counties, however, were of service. Scott sent militia under Robert Lawson to Suffolk, where they saved some of the stores from the enemy. Elsewhere, Scott posted troops on the south side of the James, across the York, and at Hampton.[12]

It soon became evident that the enemy expedition was a limited search-and-destroy mission. Washington, upon receiving an account of the invasion, held fast that Scott should give primary attention to readying his brigade to march southward. The commander in chief considered the Virginia militia sufficient to contain the Collier-Mathew expedition. The Virginia House of Delegates was of the same opinion, stating on May 20 that the militia and the regulars in the state not going with Scott could provide for "the immediate defense of Virginia."[13]

The British ships, loaded with tobacco and other plunder, including some slaves, crossed over toward Hampton on May 25, but Collier and Mathew, "finding that they should meet a warm reception" from Scott's troops there, took the fleet out into the bay. On the morning of the twenty-sixth, with the exception of several ships left behind to raid in the upper Chesapeake in Maryland, the fleet set out to sea. In only four days the Collier-Mathew fleet sailed into the Hudson, ready to assist in attacks on Verplanck's Point and Stony Point. The booty brought back to New York, by one estimate, was worth £80,000 to £100,000 sterling.[14]

The Virginia assembly expressed its gratitude to Scott for his promptness and effort in taking charge of the defense of Virginia during the crisis by directing the governor to present him with "the finest gelding that can be procured, and caparisoned in the best manner," as "a small testimony of their sense of his activity and zeal in the late invasion of this Commonwealth." The assembly also voted Scott £500. Thomas Jefferson, the new governor, about a month later informed Scott that he was glad that Scott had selected a horse but warned that he might not be pleased with the caparison. Pistols were difficult to obtain, and although "the caparison is preparing," noted Jefferson, "I fear (when I take a view of our workmen) it will hardly be worthy the givers or receiver."[15]

At the end of May, Scott brought his Continentals from Williamsburg to Petersburg, where he promised Washington he would have them regimented and marched to South Carolina as soon as possible. Scott reported on June 10 from his home (about forty-five miles from Petersburg), where he had gone for a few days, that he had collected about 1,300 men. There was still a shortage of clothing—principally shirts, shoes, and stockings—and more arms had to be obtained. Another problem was securing the services of subaltern officers. Fear of the torrid climate and of disease during the summer season in South Carolina hindered recruitment in all ranks.[16]

Pressed by Washington to get the Virginia Continentals to the Southern Army, Scott at least had two detachments marching southward by the end of June: 400 men under Col. Richard Parker and the First Virginia Dragoons commanded by John Jameson. But Scott was unable to send the rest of the troops to Lincoln's army. He needed surgeons; two were detached from the northern medical department to be assigned to him, only one of whom showed up much later. Although the Virginia government decided to give the soldiers money to purchase their own clothes—a decision which helped Scott to get Parker's and Jameson's detachments on the way—clothing was still in short supply. While Scott was to receive one out of every twenty-five eligible men in each county (with the counties organized into twelve districts with eight places of rendezvous), many localities were deficient in sending their quotas. The draft was put into effect, but, although there were penalties for county lieutenants and officers not doing their duty, there were no legal liabilities for not delivering the required number of men to the army. From thirteen counties, for example, by May only 174 of the required 370 troops had been sent to Scott.[17]

Scott had Col. George Baylor's troop of horse, which had come down from Washington's camp, employed in the pursuit of deserters. Scott felt that he needed more authority to deal with deserters as well as fractious officers. Facing a desertion problem similar to that he had experienced while commanding the light infantry the year before, he asked Washington to empower him "to Execute Some proper Objects, or I am fearfull we Shall Loose the Greater part" of the troops. Scott also wanted permission to accept the resignations of officers, although he had already allowed the resignation "of a Lt Carny a Rascal who ought not to Have Born the rank of a Corporal." Other concerns also troubled Scott, particularly the reluctance of Virginians to accept any certificates for goods, since they "have by some means or other Been so used By our Auditors & others," and the refusal of civil authorities to grant warrants for the impressment of wagons.[18]

Virginia Continentals were needed more than ever for Lincoln's army. In midsummer most of the active duty terms of the South Carolina militia in Lincoln's army expired. Congress, by resolution (July 27) and a letter from its president, John Jay, ordered Scott to march the rest of his troops immediately to South Carolina.[19] But summer passed into fall, and Scott did not send on any more men.

At last, in late October, shortly after the failure of the siege of Savannah by Lincoln's little army and a French fleet—whereupon Lincoln moved to Charleston—Scott sent Col. William Heth with 300 men and Col. George Baylor's Third Regiment of Continental Dragoons to Charleston (arriving December 2). Those remaining at Petersburg were chiefly troops of Abraham Buford's regiment.[20] Thus Scott had nearly completed his mission. Washington was pleased to learn that Scott was sending the detachments from Petersburg. With the "sickly season" over, Washington expected the enemy to launch an offensive. He also told Scott: "I hope the approaching Season will also help to repair your Health." Writing on November 16, Washington said that he had no objection to Scott's going southward himself, but Scott should "give the most pointed order to the Officer who shall be left, to bring on the rear, not to lose a moments time in getting them under march." Congress, not having word that the two detachments of Scott's troops were on their way to Charleston, on November 11 directed General Lincoln to hold a court of inquiry on Scott "for disobedience of the orders of Congress" in its resolution of July 27.[21]

A full-scale British invasion in the South commenced in late January 1780, when Gen. Henry Clinton and about 8,000 troops in a fleet of 10 warships and 90 transports under Adm. Marriott Arbuthnot arrived at the mouth of the Savannah River. On February 11 the fleet entered North Edisto Inlet, about forty miles south of Charleston. Landing at Simmons (now Seabrook) Island, Clinton took his troops across John's Island and the Stono River to James Island, where Fort Johnson was captured on March 6. For over a month Clinton consolidated his position in the harbor, making preparations for a siege. Except for Fort Moultrie (which the British ships passed at will) the harbor was abandoned by the Americans. On March 29 the British land force crossed the Ashley River and entrenched itself about twelve miles above Charleston on Charleston Neck, and the siege began.[22]

Washington, when he heard that the British fleet had cleared from New York, immediately sent the last of the Virginia troops remaining at his camp at Morristown—Woodford's brigade—south to join Lincoln at Charleston. By mid-February Woodford's brigade of some 750 men made camp with Scott's remnant troops at Petersburg. The Virginia governor and council, fearing that Clinton on his way to South Carolina might invade Virginia, ordered Scott to hold his troops in Virginia. The suspension of Scott's march was not lifted by the Virginia executive until about February 15, by which time the British entry into the Savannah River had been confirmed.[23]

Woodford's brigade and Col. Charles Harrison's artillery regiment left Petersburg on March 11 for the 500-mile journey to Charleston. While Scott had no troops to lead to Charleston (the 400 men, chiefly Buford's regiment, at Petersburg were still not clothed), he could not sit by while Woodford would be the only Virginia general at Charleston and perhaps become a hero. Professional jealousy was involved, and also "Beau" Woodford, the "Damndest Partial Rascal on this earth without exception," according to one of his disgruntled orderly sergeants, was not exactly a favorite with the men or the other Virginia generals. Scott had been ordered to South Carolina, and he would now go. Accompanied by Maj. William Croghan, Scott headed for Charleston without any troops! Leaving Petersburg on the same day as Woodford, Scott and Croghan, riding down through the interior country by way of Salisbury and Camden, arrived at

Charleston on March 30, eight days ahead of Woodford. That same morning Lincoln's army discovered the British entrenching themselves only 3,000 yards from the American lines at Charleston. Lincoln immediately took Scott and Croghan on a tour of the American batteries and earthworks. Scott "appeared upon the grand parade" the next day, when he took over the command of Col. Richard Parker's Virginia troops. On April 2 Lincoln ordered Col. Archibald Lytle's North Carolina volunteers to be brigaded with Scott's Virginians.[24]

On April 8 Clinton summoned Lincoln to surrender, but the American commander, expecting further reinforcements, refused. At this time the American force numbered 5,150 (about 2,500 of which were militia); the British, being reinforced, had three times this number, in addition to naval control and superior firepower. Clinton's army completed the first parallel and opened up batteries on Charleston on April 13. Although there was still an escape route across the Cooper River, Lincoln, under pressure from the Charleston authorities neither to evacuate nor surrender, vetoed a resolution of his officers in a council of war for the army to leave the city.[25] A major factor also was the refusal of the local militia to accompany the rest of the army out of Charleston.

The enemy now began to close the last exit for escape. On April 14 Lt. Col. James Webster, assisted by Tarleton's dragoons and Patrick Ferguson's light infantry, attacked an American force of about 700 militia and Continental cavalry, commanded by Isaac Huger, at Monck's Corner, a supply depot across the Cooper River on which Lincoln depended for provisions. The rout was complete: the British captured 120 officers and men and 400 horses. Scott, on April 18, with 100 men crossed to Lemprieres (Hobcaw) Point, across the Cooper, and took charge of the American troops at the post. The next day, however, he was recalled to Charleston to attend a council of war. On April 25 Haddrell's Point, on the north bank of the harbor, and on April 26, Lemprieres Point fell to the British. Fort Moultrie, on Sullivan's Island at the entrance of the harbor, the last American outpost, surrendered on May 7. The vise tightened. On Charleston Neck the enemy completed the second zigzag parallel, 600–800 yards from the American lines, and on April 21 began a third parallel.[26]

On April 20 Lincoln called a council of war and pointed out the futility of continuing resistance; even if the American troops could get across the three-mile-river, notwithstanding the lack of boats, they were "waisted and worn down by action, fatigue, & famine" and would be "closely pursued as we must by the enemys horse & infantry." The council voted unanimously to propose surrender. The terms that Lincoln submitted did not quite suit Clinton and were rejected. Evacuation, still possible for another few days, was voted down by a council of war the next day—again, a decision influenced by the Charleston officials. Some heated action took place on April 24, with the Continentals attacking two British work parties; one of Scott's regimental commanders, Richard Parker, was killed.[27]

By May 7 the British had completed the third parallel, and batteries were in place. Not only could a more telling fire be aimed into the American lines and the city itself, but the British were now in a position to carry the American works by storm. On May 8 Clinton sent his "last summons," calling upon Lincoln to avoid needless bloodshed and destruction. Lincoln and his council of war again replied unsatisfactorily. On the ninth, wrote one British officer, "the Rebels began with huzzaing and a violent Cannonade from every Gun they could fire seemingly at Random as if in a drunken Frensy, and without doing us any harm. We fired very little but from our Mortars." The British pushed several more saps toward the American works.[28]

Charlestonians had a change of mind, and on May 10 two petitions, totaling 407 names, were presented to General Lincoln requesting immediate surrender. Lincoln and his officers met and agreed to accept Clinton's terms. On the morning of the eleventh, as British troops crossed a drained canal twenty-five yards in front of the American lines and waited for a signal to storm the works, a flag was sent by Lincoln offering surrender. All hostilities ceased.[29] At that moment, Scott must have cursed himself for his sudden eagerness to join the Southern

Army. In effect, he had arrived just in time to become a prisoner of war.

At the surrender ceremony, just past noon on May 12, 1780, Scott delivered 448 men fit for duty of the two Virginia regiments (William Heth's and Samuel Hopkins's) of his brigade. In all, 5,684 Continentals and militia were made captive. Scott was one of the six prisoner brigadier generals: the others, William Woodford, William Moultrie, Lachlan McIntosh, James Hogun (militia), and Louis Le Bègue de Presle Duportail (Continental army chief of engineers). According to the terms of the capitulation, all Continental officers were to be confined to Haddrell's Point (present-day Mount Pleasant), five miles east of Charleston across the harbor, where, although prohibited from going beyond any river, creek, or "Arm of the Sea," they would have freedom of mobility within a six-mile radius. The enlisted Continentals were to be placed on board prison ships in the harbor. The militia were allowed to return to their homes as prisoners on parole. Contrary to the articles of capitulation, on the fourteenth the 274 prisoner officers were brought together and ordered to surrender their swords. Some officers resisted, shouting "Long Live Congress!" The British guards subdued the troublemakers, with several killed and wounded on both sides, and the swords were collected. The generals were confined to quarters. Several of the officers were wearing a cloth bound around the left leg, a symbol of defiance and also a tribute to General Lincoln, whose lame leg was always wrapped with gauze.[30]

Scott and the other officers reached Haddrell's Point on May 18. Since the barracks at the post could not hold all of them, some went to neighboring houses, and others built huts in the woods. Scott was probably quartered in one of the houses. William Moultrie, as the senior brigadier general, had charge of arrangements. Moultrie and Charles Cotesworth Pinckney, a colonel of a South Carolina regiment, stayed at the plantation house on Snee-farm, belonging to Pinckney's cousin, Charles Pinckney. General Lincoln and his aides were permitted parole and took passage to Philadelphia.[31]

Scott initially found his captivity intolerable. He had left Virginia with his financial situation in chaos—and now it was all the more difficult to attend to his affairs. The inadequacy of provisions added to his and the other officers' misery. The British held up full rations on the erroneous grounds that the Americans were inflating the number of officers. For a while, the officers subsisted mostly on fish and crabs. Yellow fever broke out among many officers, and there was a lack of medicine. Without hard money, they found it almost impossible to make purchases.[32]

Haddrell's Point and the surrounding area seemed a land of desolation—a "flat country," wrote Duportail, where the water was not fit to drink and "the soil is nothing but sand which burns the flat of the foot and blinds one when the wind blows." The pine trees gave no shade "and interrupts the little air one might enjoy." One could see a few blacks "covered with a few miserable rags" and "wretched peasants only a little less dark than their negroes—who go about barefooted and without education or politeness."[33]

Scott had some of his own personal items put up for auction in Charleston, and he asked the commandant for permission "to sell some Negroes"—whether they had accompanied him or whether the reference was to his slaves in Virginia is not known. Nevertheless, he did obtain some cash and credit. A list of items sent to him, for £78.8.2, in August 1780 indicates Scott's needs at the time: candles, bread, brown sugar, a cask of port wine, three tablecloths, coffee, four pans, a coffeepot, four tumblers, six glasses, six cups and saucers, six knives and forks, thirteen fowls, two quire paper, a grog can, butter, pepper, plates, chocolate, and blue cloth.[34]

By November (General Woodford had been sent to New York, where he died November 13) Scott was assuming responsibility for the welfare of the Virginia line in captivity. He had great difficulty in getting the Virginia government to send supplies. In January, however, some relief from Virginia arrived, and Scott was able to exchange tobacco, flour, and leather for clothing, sugar, butter, and other commodities. For thirty-one officers he obtained portmanteaus, chests, trunks, boxes, barrels, kegs, cases, saddlebags, clothing (coats, waistcoats, jackets with sleeves, hunting shirts, breeches, and 732 pairs of "overalls"), combs, shoes, shoe brushes, and "a number of half Soals & Heel Lifts."[35]

The tobacco sold for 5*s*. sterling per hundredweight and the flour 30*s*. After pressing the British authorities, including Cornwallis, Scott obtained permission to receive tobacco in unlimited quantities from Virginia. Unfortunately he sent to Virginia only a copy of the permission from the Charleston commandant, which his brigade major had secured, and Gen. William Phillips, commanding a British invading army in Virginia, at first refused to consider this a sufficient licence. Another problem was that Charleston merchants discounted tobacco by 10 percent since the vouchers were not in triplicate. Scott, as did other officers, acquired personal debts in anticipation of getting tobacco and other supplies from Virginia. He wrote Jefferson, "I made it my business to procure credit on my own Account and distribute to those in need, what Articles their situation or health demanded."[36]

Not until early 1781 did Virginia establish a regular transport of tobacco to Charleston for the relief of the prisoners. David Ross, the state's able commercial agent, took charge of the shipment. The quantities were so large—with officers securing private supply from friends in addition to that of the state's—that special boats were needed. Cornwallis's invasion of Virginia in the spring of 1781 threatened to disrupt the Virginia tobacco shipments. Lafayette, then commanding the American army in Virginia, arranged with Cornwallis that under certain conditions the supply would continue (for example, that the vessel carrying the tobacco would stay clear of the British army).[37]

Later, in December 1782, after Scott and the other officers had been paroled or exchanged, Col. Maurice Simonds, who represented Ross in Charleston, without waiting for Scott to submit all the necessary vouchers, which would have taken some time, successfully got the Virginia government to liquidate his accounts with Scott and with other officers. Simond's estate in Charleston had been attached, and it was also costing the state to keep the accounts open.[38] Thus Scott got reimbursement where he had used his own credit in securing supplies under the state's authority.

More troublesome was Scott's attempt to collect from the federal government £450 of £550 for medical supplies for his fellow captive officers—mainly for bark, vinegar, sugar, and wine (Scott deducted £100 for his own use and that of his staff). He had his aide-de-camp, William Kelley, who resided with him at Haddrell's Point and did all his paperwork, public and private, keep an account of the purchases. Unfortunately Kelley deserted from Haddrell's Point taking all of Scott's financial records with him. Later when Scott was called upon to justify his claim for reimbursement he had no exact proofs of the transactions. He conducted a long struggle to get reimbursement, even later visiting the federal capital for this purpose. With affidavits from many of his officers and the senior surgeon of the Virginia line at Haddrell's, Cornelius Baldwin, Scott eventually convinced Congress that he had purchased 160 pounds of bark and was awarded $1,066^{60}/90 in 1786. His claim for reimbursement for the other medical supplies was unsuccessful—largely because his case rested on the hearsay testimony of Dr. David Oliphant, who had been the director of hospitals for the Southern Army.[39]

Scott had hoped for an immediate exchange of prisoners. The most likely quid pro quo would be to trade the American Continentals held at Charleston for the Convention prisoners (captured at Saratoga in 1777): desertions from the Convention army had now reduced it to about the size of the captive Continental force at Charleston. But Congress dragged its feet, determined not to honor, so it seemed, any commitment that had been made (in the articles of capitulation signed by General Gates) for release of the Convention troops. Lord George Germain, of the British war ministry, advised the British commander in chief in the South, Cornwallis, not to expect Congress to agree to a cartel for exchange, especially since Congress was now using the "pretence" that the service time of most of the captive American troops would soon expire, whereupon, being no longer soldiers, they could not be considered prisoners of war. Although the British ministry had considered sending the American prisoners captured at Charleston to the West Indies as a protest to Congress's violation of the Saratoga Convention, it decided ultimately on a gradual and limited policy of parole.[40]

For Scott to be exchanged, the Americans would have to have an available British brigadier general or his equivalent. There would be negotiations, and, of course, there were other American generals also waiting for exchange. In the meantime, Scott could apply for a parole, which would allow him to return home. On January 30, 1781, he made such a request to Cornwallis, stating that "the very derang'd situation" of his "domestick affairs" demanded immediate attention in person.[41]

Cornwallis granted Scott's request. Around the end of March 1781 Scott headed for Virginia, where, in the area not far from his home, there was an invading British army. A letter to him on his journey from General Greene mentions "your continuing your route to the army under the command of Lord Cornwallis," signifying that Scott perhaps went behind Cornwallis's lines in North Carolina, probably to negotiate further matters pertaining to the supply of the American prisoners at Haddrell's Point.[42]

Scott was so "feeble as to be unable to walk," according to a report by James Taylor nearly sixty years later, which he claimed to have heard firsthand from Scott (in 1792) and also from Scott's wife. The complete account regarding Scott's trip home has inaccuracies and does not quite fit the context of Scott's journey. Otherwise, it is worth retelling. As the story goes, when Scott and his servant came up to a spring, Scott had his attendant spread his cloak under a tree so that he could rest and put bottles of brandy, "spirit and wine" into the stream to cool. Scott had his servant keep an eye open for anyone passing along the road, for he was interested in seeking directions and in learning if any American or British troops were around. Shortly, "a small dirty looking Indian" was spotted, and Scott asked his servant to summon the newcomer. As the Indian approached, Scott noticed he was wearing a coat, with a book protruding from one of the pockets. After greeting each other and shaking hands, Scott asked, "Where are you from?"

"Lower Cattaba [Catawba] Town."

"Where are you going?" again asked Scott.

"Upper Cattaba," replied the Indian. "Me going to preach."

"Oh," said Scott, "do you Preach?"

"Oh yes. Me preach sometimes."

"Well," continued Scott, "do you get any pay for preaching?"

"O yes," remarked the Indian, "each town pay me 20 shillings a year."

"That is damn'd poor pay," declared Scott.

"Damn'd poor preach, too, Sir," replied the Indian.

At this exchange, Scott

burst out in an immediate fit of laughter—which he was unable to restrain for some time: when he got composed he felt a glow over him & wiped considerable perspiration from his forehead . . . he felt much strengthened by the impulse, raised himself up, had his wine & brandy & provisions brought forward, drank & ate more he said and with better appetite than he had done for months, of which the Indian partook with him.

Scott "from that moment" would "frequently burst out in loud fits of laughter at his interview with the Cattaba Indian," and it "materially assisted in bestirring him to health. By the time he arrived at home he was perfectly restored, but yet feeble from his close confinement."[43]

Returning to the Muddy Creek farm, Scott could relax and recover from his ordeal as a prisoner. His family's bout with smallpox around this time proved not to be serious. There was a new addition to the family—Martha (b. 1781). With another infant daughter, Mary ("Polly"), his family had grown to seven children: Merritt, Samuel, Daniel, Charles, Elizabeth ("Eliza"), Mary, and Martha. Scott had just missed Eliza's wedding to a neighbor, Littlebury Mosby, Jr.[44]

On parole Scott would be free from the arduous demands of army life—even as Cornwallis's army passed down the river across from his home in June 1781. Meanwhile, there was still the matter of exchange. Congress entrusted General Greene with the responsibility of negotiating with Cornwallis the release of American prisoners in the South. By a cartel of May 3 a trade of the enlisted prisoners and some of the officers at Charleston was arranged for an equal number of captive British or loyalist soldiers. Nearly 900 American troops and officers were brought to Jamestown Island in July and marched to Richmond for discharge. By August 1781, of the brigadier generals captured at Charleston, only Duportail had been exchanged; Woodford and Hogun had died, and Scott, Moultrie, and McIntosh were on parole.[45]

Scott had to wait quite a while longer for his exchange. It was thought that the prisoners gained from the British surrender at Yorktown might facilitate matters. An arrangement to trade Scott, seven colonels, and two lieutenant colonels for Cornwallis did not succeed, and Cornwallis instead was exchanged for a former president of Congress, Henry Laurens, who had been captured at sea and confined to the Tower of London.[46]

General Moultrie, who had been originally scheduled for exchange with Lt. Col. Lord Rawdon, was traded "by composition" for General Burgoyne. With this accomplished, Washington, on February 21, 1782, wrote General Rochambeau, asking if he would give up Rawdon, who was a captive of the French, for Scott. Rochambeau complied, and Scott ended his parole status in July 1782. When Cornwallis heard of Scott's exchange, he pointed out the irregularity—but the war had halted and proper procedure now mattered little. Washington notified Scott that he was now considered back on active duty and ordered him to report to General Greene; in the meantime Scott was to assist General Muhlenberg, who headed the Continental recruiting service in Virginia.[47]

Scott expected to join Greene's army. But the commander of the Southern Army wrote that he did not have a command for Scott and the Virginia line was "too weak to offer you one." Rather, Greene requested that Scott continue to superintend recruiting in the district assigned to him by General Muhlenberg. Although the bounty for enlistment was only £12, Greene thought Scott would not have much difficulty in obtaining recruits, with the aid of other Virginia officers. The Virginia legislature had voted to raise 3,000 troops for 1782; it was hoped that many soldiers of the Southern Army whose times had expired would reenlist.[48]

During October and November 1782 Scott was acting commander of the Virginia line while Muhlenberg was sick. The rendezvous for the new troops was the tavern at Cumberland Old Courthouse, not far from Scott's farm. In addition to keeping track of the troops, Scott also signed numerous discharges, some of the soldiers going directly to his home for that purpose.[49]

While acting as commander of Continental troops in Virginia, Scott set off a controversy that proved to be immensely damaging to the reputation of Gen. Nathanael Greene. Captain Clough Shelton dropped by the courthouse, carrying a packet of army mail, and urged Scott to open two letters, both addressed to James Hunter, one from Robert Forsyth (November 7) and the other from John Banks (November 2). Hunter was a partner of John Banks and Company. The letters indicated that Robert Burnet and Forsyth, both of whom were aides to General Greene, were also members of the mercantile firm. Particularly surprising in Forsyth's letter was the intimation that possibly Greene was also a silent partner and wanted to be included in a new commercial house to be established by the company in Charleston. With the Southern Army in destitute condition, Greene had gone security for bills of exchange, drawn upon Robert Morris, the superintendent for finances of the United States, for payment for supplies to be delivered by Banks and Company, which would benefit by a 11-13 percent commission on goods obtained. Thus it appeared that the commander of the Southern Army was engaged in profiteering from the furnishing of supplies for his own army. The letters enclosed $8,000 in bills of exchange, signed by Greene. Scott, in perusing the letters, immediately concluded that "it was evident something wrong was going on, some speculation, some private business in Trade." Scott sent the letters to Governor Benjamin Harrison, who rebuked Scott for opening them. Scott replied that he had done simply his duty, and "should any letters under similar circumstances fall into my hands, I shall think it a duty I owe my Country to make what discoveries I can from them. I shall be exceeding sorry after explaining this matter if it dont meet your approbation."[50]

Governor Harrison informed Greene of what happened but assured him that he did not believe there was any collusion between Greene and Banks and Company. Greene was extremely upset by Scott's action and willingness to sully his character. Writing from Charleston on February 18, 1783, Greene addressed Scott on the propriety governing the relationship of one officer to another. "It is perfectly right, for a free people to watch over their liberties to inspect into the conduct of public officers and to examine with delicacy and with candor every public transaction," he said. But "it is inconsistent with the first principles of good government which are tranquility and public confidence to raise jealousies and create suspicions from incidents that are not only innocent but necessary," and "this becomes the more criminal and less excusable when it is leveled at characters where there has been no just grounds for suspicion." Greene, therefore, regarded Scott's conduct toward him "not only indelicate but exceeding improper." It wounded "the feelings of a man of sensibility to be obliged to appeal to the public to remove the private suspicion of individuals." If Scott had any doubt of the "propriety" of Greene's conduct, he should have kept the letters and have notified Greene immediately to seek an explanation.[51]

That Greene might have been involved in profiteering in the supply of his own army was a subject of investigation from many different sources and would pester him until his death in 1786; probing continued even many decades afterward. Greene could not forgive Scott for initiating the slander. Scott's eagerness to imply wrongdoing on Greene's part perhaps confirms a character trait of his own. It was not the first time that a superior had accused Scott of going behind his back and sowing dissension— this had also been a charge leveled by generals Stephen and Lee earlier. Furthermore, Scott had many times written to Washington of the malfeasance of other officers, particularly staff.

With so long a period of inaction in the field, Greene seems to have been losing popularity among his troops, a fact that Scott may have been well aware of in making his decision to expose Greene. In April 1783 the enlisted men of Col. George Baylor's Virginia regiment of Continental dragoons in Greene's army mutinied and set out for Richmond to demand redress of their grievances from the Virginia government—namely the lack of pay and inadequate food. General Greene wrote Scott to afford whatever aid he could toward apprehending the mutineers. The commander of the Southern Army told Scott that the sufferings of Baylor's men were only pretended, as they had plenty of provisions when they left. On their way, the mutineers sent a petition to Governor Harrison, who laid it before the Council of State, where it had a sympathetic hearing. Gen. Daniel Morgan was called out of retirement in order to meet with the mutineers as they approached Richmond and lead them to Winchester; this was done without incident.[52]

Only several hundred Virginia Continentals were collected in late 1782 and early 1783; what few men Scott enlisted were sent on to the new Continental depot at Winchester. After news arrived in March 1783 of the signing of the preliminaries of peace, recruiting stopped, and in its May session the Virginia assembly set about liquidating the accounts for the maintenance of the Continentals.[53]

On the prospect of peace, Scott recorded his feelings in a letter to General McIntosh on May 3, 1783. He was pleased with "the Glorious Event of Gaining our End in a manner at least eaquil to our most Sanquin Expectations. The Prelimanary articles of Peace wear Red in the City of Richmond on this day Last with the Greatest parade Possible." Every "Article of Merchandise fell immediately as low as ever they wear & our Tobo. Took a Rappid rise which put Joy on the Countenance of Every planter indeed Every body Seams happy but our little Pimping Traiders."[54]

The war was over. With the army dismantled by the end of 1783, except for several hundred troops under General Knox at West Point, Scott left the army with a retirement brevet rank of major general.[55] The long service given his country in winning its independence had entailed hardship and sacrifice. Soon the material rewards for his military service would lead him to the "land of the western waters" and new adventure. The "Spirit of '76" would be transformed into a frontier spirit.

"Wolves Might as Well
Have Been Pursued"

Although Charles Scott anxiously waited to claim the bounty of war, much of it would escape him, as it did most of the Continental army officers. By an act of the October 1780 Virginia General Assembly, Scott, as a brigadier general with continual service during the war, was to receive 10,000 acres. With allowance for 1,666⅔ acres for marginal land and 1,666⅔ acres for an extra year's service (1775–76, before Independence), Scott was entitled, in all, to 13,333⅓ acres in western lands to be distributed by the state. The commutation certificates voted by Congress in March 1783 for a bonus of five years' full pay, in lieu of a life pension, could also be exchanged for lands. Uncollected bounty lands for service in the French and Indian War could now also be claimed in the western country. Little is known about Scott's transactions in western lands. A good deal of land was traded back and forth, claims overlapped, and officers often joined forces with each other or acted in another's stead. A warrant holder had to "locate" the land or have someone else do it for him; he was also responsible for the surveys. Various fees had to be paid, and it could also be expected that there would be the costs of court litigation. If the different steps to gain title to the land were not completed within time limits, the land reverted back to the state, as "waste and unappropriated" property. In all, the system was expensive and complex, and thus many of the military grants were forfeited.[1]

Scott undoubtedly sold his federal bonus certificates, which depreciated rapidly to about twelve cents on the dollar and were picked up quickly by speculators gambling on a later return to their par value. If Scott had kept the federal certificates, he could have exchanged them later at full value for land in the U.S. Military District, north of the Ohio, but he would have had to settle in the area to redeem the land warrants. What happened in the military district may be indicative of the situation pertaining to military land bounties overall: about two-thirds of the 9,900 warrants issued before 1800 were sold at an average of $10 per 100 acres. Most of the warrants were acquired by speculators. The same was true for the Virginia Military District, also north of the Ohio, left to the state as a condition for its cession of the Northwest Territory; even though the state permitted exchange of Kentucky military lands for those in the Virginia Military District, speculators soon had full sway in the Ohio lands. As the historian of these bounty lands has aptly stated: "The voice of the speculator in Virginia warrants, relayed through the generations from heir to heir, is a far cry from the voice of the recruiting agent calling for men to help win independence. Land was thus won by the 'common blood and treasure' and gravitated into the hands of those few who had a surplus treasure with which to buy up the paper evidences of contributions to the 'common blood.'"[2]

Scott, however, did briefly exhibit extensive landholdings on paper. For example, from December 1785 to January 1786 he had his name on eight grants in Fayette County (then embracing about a third of Kentucky) for 60,639½ acres—all later withdrawn, except for 1,637 acres. He would claim, along with Nicholas Mosby, 9,759 acres in Bourbon County in 1787 and 1792.[3] Hard-pressed by debts and on the verge of insolvency, Scott opted for what meager return he could get by ridding himself of most of his land claims, and he would give attention solely to the several hundred acres where he would settle along the Kentucky River, in what would become Woodford County.

It was a leisurely existence for Scott during 1783 and 1784. His wife's slaves now numbered twenty, more than enough to run the farm and the mill. Scott visited with old friends and transacted business at the courthouse taverns in Cumberland

County and Powhatan County (created in 1777 from Cumberland County—Scott's farm was now in the northwest corner of Powhatan County). More often than not, he could be found at the tavern at Cumberland Old Courthouse. Scott wrote James McDowell in October 1783, "I recd Your letter in a public Race field Near Cumb old Courthouse where there was all Your Acquaintance[s] in that part of the World." Twins were born August 1, 1783, only one of whom, Nancy, survived beyond early childhood.[4]

Scott began to think of Kentucky—a land of opportunity. Many Virginians—especially the war veterans—were picking up and moving westward. Already pioneers plied the Wilderness Road and the Ohio River to Kentucky. Almost any crop could be grown on the virgin soil of the western bluegrass country, and wild game was plentiful. Towns were sprouting. Three counties had been formed in 1780–Jefferson, Fayette, and Lincoln—and four more in 1784–85. Judicial districts were established.[5] Overnight, it seemed, the wilderness assumed a semblance of civilization.

James Wilkinson, army officer turned storekeeper and speculator, who envisioned a grand avenue for trade from the Kentucky River to New Orleans, arrived in Kentucky in 1784 and began sending Scott glowing reports, encouraging him to settle in central Kentucky. Scott acquired land along the Kentucky River and arranged to have a cabin built. In June 1785 Wilkinson mentioned to Scott that although "not one Stake is yet Struck on your House," a Mr. Ellis had received £50 for building the structure. It seems that Ellis had already set up the foundation—a cornerstone bore the inscription "CS N6 1784." This may indicate that Scott visited Kentucky in November 1784; but there is no other evidence that he did, and the tone of Wilkinson's letters strongly suggests that Scott was not in Kentucky before 1785. Ellis had hired hands working with him, presumably also for the purpose of clearing some of Scott's land. Wilkinson advised Scott as to what he would need to take on a trip to Kentucky: "be sure you bring out a double stock of great variety and we will try to make out more with Turnips and Potatoes—get a snug little assortment of medicine; don't forget Blistering

Plaister, a plenty of Salts, Tart-Bark, Laudinum." When Scott reached the Kanawha River he should send "an active fellow" on ahead by canoe, in order to "advise us of your Approach, with the number of Pack Horses, Waggons &c that you may want."[6]

In early summer 1785 Scott journeyed to Kentucky, accompanied by Wilkinson's business partner, Peyton Short. They went by way of Redstone Old Fort (now Brownsville, Pennsylvania), down the Monongahela River and then the Ohio River to Limestone (now Maysville, Kentucky), covering the sixty miles or so from Limestone to the Kentucky River by land, a trip of more than 900 miles from Scott's farm in Virginia. Scott found it heartening to see so many persons traveling down the Ohio. If others could move their families, so could he. Scott stayed in Kentucky only a short time and by September 1785 was back in Virginia. A severe drought in Kentucky that summer and more frequent Indian depredations (albeit mostly horse thievery) lessened the edenic expectations.[7]

The frontier was always good for tall tales, and Scott had several for his Virginia neighbors, at least according to traditional lore. Out in Kentucky the corn "was so plenty, they took it in bushel baskets. If an ear fell out, it took 2 negroes to put it back." Deer were everywhere, "hundreds in a drove, with horns that would measure seven feet from tip to tip, running with the swiftness of lightning over the plain, and from hill to hill." When someone asked how these magnificent animals could move with such agility through the dense cane and undergrowth, which even a rabbit found difficulty in passing through, Scott replied, "Ah, my good sir, that's their look out: it is no concern of mine."[8]

Before he could settle in Kentucky, Scott had to exact some order from his tangled finances and to find a buyer for the Powhatan farm. Edward Carrington, former quartermaster general of the Southern Army and a neighbor at Boston Hill in Cumberland County, obliged Scott by taking over the management of his financial affairs. Carrington wrote his brother, Joseph, a business partner, in February 1786 that "new faces almost every day appear with claims against the General." Carrington provided a loan on the consolidation of most of Scott's debts—

£2,294.15.½, which Scott agreed to repay Carrington in annual installments, from December 1786 to December 1790. Carrington purchased Scott's 666⅔-acre farm and mill in September 1785 for £2,500, allowing the family to stay on the farm until the move to Kentucky. In addition to household goods, furniture, and farm equipment, Scott also sold Carrington nine colts, thirty-six cattle, eight sheep, two workhorses, and seventy hogs—with the total sale, including the farm and mill, amounting to £2,836.3. Carrington asked his brother to purchase or hire out the old slave woman that tended Scott's mill in return for supplies that Scott and his family would need to take with them to Kentucky.[9]

In late August 1786 Scott went to New York City to pursue his claim for reimbursement from Congress for medical articles that he had furnished the prisoners at Haddrell's Point in 1780–81 and finally managed to secure compensation for the bark that he had supplied but not for the other hospital stores.[10] By the end of 1786, he was ready for the Kentucky move. Leaving some of the slaves in the care or hire of Littlebury Mosby, Jr. (husband of daughter Eliza), the Scotts—probably including four sons and three daughters, although one or several of the children may have stayed behind in Virginia for a while with the Mosbys)—set out for Kentucky in early January 1787.

The Scott family traveled down the Ohio in a Kentucky boat which was more fragilely built than other flat-bottomed craft that went on to New Orleans. The rectangular Kentucky boat ranged in span from 40 to 100 feet and had a 12- to 15-foot width and an 8-foot depth (boarded 2 or 3 feet in height on both sides). In addition to a reliance chiefly on the current of the river for propulsion, various oars were used, and sometimes a sail. Among the supplies carried on the boat there would usually be a cow, a coop of chickens, and a flitch of bacon. Going down the Ohio in the dead of winter, the Scotts probably roofed their boat completely, except for the hatchway, and put in a chimney and windows, in addition to the portholes for the oars. The boat averaged considerably less than the eighty miles per day that could be attained in the spring when the water was at high level and the current the strongest. At Fort Harmar, where the Muskingum flows into the Ohio, the American commander noted in his diary, on January 19, 1787, "genl Scott passed in a Kentucky boat with his family on board with a design to settle below."[11]

Fortunately, by water and by land, the Scotts traveled during a time when there was no hostile Indian activity along the river. In wintertime the Indians customarily did not stir much, at least not in war parties, and the military campaigns of George Rogers Clark against the Wabash tribes and Benjamin Logan against the Shawnee three months earlier had a telling effect, if temporary, in keeping the Indians out of the way.

The Scotts debarked at Limestone and traversed by land to the Kentucky River. As others often did, they may have dismantled the boat and taken the lumber with them, perhaps using some of the boards for constructing wagons. The new farm (256 to 270 acres) was located on the Kentucky River at the mouth of Craig Creek. About a half mile from the junction of the stream with the Kentucky was a crossing point for travelers going from Harrod's Station (Harrodsburg) to Lexington; this location would be known by various names—Scott's Ferry, then Wilson's Landing, and last, but no longer in use, Soard's Ferry.[12] Scott's Ferry Road is still in existence. Nine miles southwest of present-day Versailles and west of Lexington, on the river in Woodford County (at this time still Fayette County), the new homestead was an ideal location for commercial enterprise—at the crossroads of central Kentucky and on the navigable part of the Kentucky River.

The Scotts' house (30 by 18 feet) was made of heavy oak logs and was one-and-a-half stories high. Downstairs there were two rooms and a hall. Floorboards were cut from ash trees; a fireplace, with large stone chimneys, was situated at each end of the house. The windows were small, and portholes were put under the eaves in the upstairs rooms. The oak doors were secured on the inside by bars. The house, expanded and clapboarded by subsequent owners, existed until 1972, when it was destroyed by fire.[13] Around the house Scott built a stockade of oak pickets, with square portholes cut at intervals. The only entrance was through a large gate. Several other small log cabins were within the stockade. Scott's overseer, one Valentine, Wil-

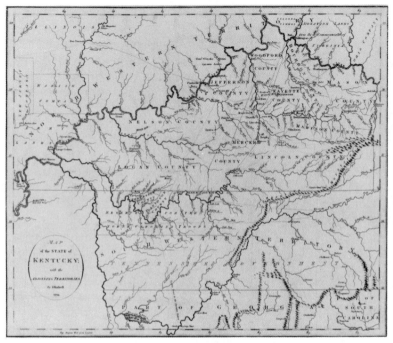

"Map of Kentucky, with the Adjoining Territories." By J. Russell, London, Dec. 27, 1794. (Courtesy of the Filson Club, Louisville, Ky.)

liam McCoy, who had served with Scott during the war, Barrett Gaines, David Williams, and an old Indian, Buffalo Fish, took their turn as guards. Scott kept "a great many dogs—some bull dogs." Every morning, the dogs were let out, and several of the men went out of the fort checking for moccasin tracks.

When the Mosby family came out from Virginia, they lived temporarily at Scott's fort. William Mosby recalled that fishing was a favorite pastime. Once he and Scott's son Daniel, age about sixteen, went fishing when they were not supposed to. They set their lines and in the evening went back down to the bank to see what they had caught. "Owl hallooed very pert. 2d time the same, and then hallooed again." This meant one thing to the boys, the Indians "were endeavouring to get around them. . . . The Indians they had been taught could halloo like owls, and these owls were on the ground." The boys ran back to the fort and told Buffalo Fish. "Big-footed chief knew it was policy to be getting out of the way in time."

At Scott's fort reading was by the light of the burning of "scale-bark hickory," considered almost as good as an oil lamp. Hunting supplied much of the food. Several times a week deer were hunted by firelight from canoes, with a torch made of green bark covered with sand to entrance the deer as they came down to the river's bank at night to drink and to eat the moss in the shoals. On one occasion Scott and Mosby, Sr., killed two fat bucks at a distance of 220 yards. Wild turkeys and even bear also were hunted. Mosby said that one bear shot by one Lillard (probably Thomas Lillard, who lived just across the river), a "great bear hunter," weighed 400 pounds. Bear hunting was another reason that Scott kept so many dogs.[14]

Not long after Scott got settled in, he was visited by a religious zealot (in one version of the story, Rev. Reuben Cave), who said he represented the Baptists in the neighborhood. He told Scott that the church members did not want "so profane & wicked a man living so near them," corrupting the morals of youth. Scott was caught by surprise. Regaining his composure, he replied, "My friend I had supposed your settlement & most others between this & Lexington would have been much pleased to have some such barrier as mine, between you & the Savages & I had flattered myself I had gained some little reputation during the late revolution, & at any rate would be some protection to the frontier settlements." The stranger said this was true but proceeded to tell Scott that his Baptist group was an orderly and peaceful society and from what they knew of Scott he should not be permitted to settle in the same community.

Scott tried a little reason and then declared that he had been fighting his country's battles in vain if he could be driven from his own land by religious fanatics. His ire grew. All of a sudden he called out to his hands and servants. "Surround this d——d rascal!" he exclaimed. "Catch him. I'll punch this scoundrel, who had insulted me & wants to drive me from my own home." Scott's dogs were snarling. The visitor ran as fast he could to his horse and made his escape.[15]

In June 1787 tragedy struck. Since April the Ohio Indians—principally Shawnee—were getting bolder, and hunting parties crossed the Ohio and penetrated the scattered settlements in upper Kentucky. A number of settlers were killed, and several communities in Jefferson and Mercer counties had to be evacuated.[16]

Young Samuel Scott and Valentine went in a canoe to a deep eddy (Indian Branch) across the river opposite the fort and, tying the canoe to a rock, began fishing. A dozen or so Indians crept up and shot Samuel three times in the side. Valentine was also hit, and tumbled into the river and sank; his body was never recovered. The Indians swam to the canoe and, finding Samuel still alive, scalped him—because the youth's hair was so full and long, the Indians took two scalps. Upon hearing the gunfire, Scott and several others hurried down to the bank. Across the river Scott saw his son in the water, still alive. Samuel yelled to his father not to come across because the Indians were waiting. The elder Scott started to jump into the water to swim over to his son, but his men restrained him. Young Scott soon fell under the water. Scott stayed at the river's bank until late at night, talking to many persons who passed back and forth to the fort, expecting an Indian attack. The next morning one of Scott's men, Jacob Lipse, swam across the river and brought back Samuel's body.

A party went after the Indians. Swimming their horses across the river, they traced the Indians to beyond several pioneer homes. The Indians had paused to butcher a hog at Lillard's farm. Although "one mark of an old indian chief whose track was known wherever he went" was found, none of the murderers were captured. The loss of his second son (at age nineteen or twenty) was as terrifying as it was heartbreaking—to see him die a cruel death and not being able to save him. Pierced with three holes, Samuel's roundabout, which he had been wearing, was a sad memento which the family kept for a long time.[17]

Staying busy helped Scott to avoid melancholia over his son's death. He strived to make his location on the Kentucky River a source of profit. He and his men built a warehouse at the mouth of Craig Creek—now to be known as Scott's Landing. Scott and his neighbors successfully petitioned the Virginia legislature to designate the site as a place for tobacco inspection. The petition had called attention to the landing as being at the only location for some distance on the river where the banks were not too steep. Briefly Scott served as a tobacco inspector. As Kentuckians now turned to tobacco as a money crop, however, there would soon be a number of such inspection stations. Scott himself helped to survey the Lexington road near his landing. He did not pay much attention to farming—cultivation of what land that had been cleared was left to his sons and slaves. In 1788 Scott was listed with eighteen tithables.[18]

For several years Scott's Landing developed into a thriving little entrepôt. Wilkinson and his business connections formed an association to collect such items as tobacco, tallow, butter, cured bacon and ham, lard, and smoked briskets of beef at Scott's Landing, whence these commodities would be shipped as far away as New Orleans.[19] Wilkinson was already assured by the Spanish authorities of an exclusive arrangement to use the Louisiana port.

In early 1789 the *Kentucky Gazette,* in Lexington, advertised that John Rhea had just opened a store "at Scott's Ware House on the Kentucky," which carried "a very general Assortment of Dry Goods, Hard Ware and groceries, for which cash, Tobacco, ginseng, Furrs, viz. Beaver, Racoons, Foxes, Wild cats and Otter skins will be taken in payment." Also announced at the same time was the opening of John Duncan's new store, opposite the courthouse in Lexington, that would sell dry goods, groceries, Indian corn, tobacco, butter, tallow, and lard. Any of the "described Country Produce will be received at General Scott's, where a Receipt will be given that will qualify the bearer to receive Goods in Lexington." John Nancarrow planned to open a malting business and brewery at Scott's Landing.[20]

In addition to making the landing a commercial center, Scott was ambitious to convert his property into a nucleus of a new town, to be called Petersburg. He staked out lots on his land, and by November 1788 forty-five persons arranged for purchase of lots at £2 and £4.10. Among the prominent investors were Judge George Muter, James Wilkinson, Abraham Buford, Daniel Trabue, and a future governor, Christopher Greenup. About 225 lots were laid out, with numbers 104, 105, and 112 reserved for churches. One-half of the lots were eventually purchased.[21] Evidently there was a contingency stipulation that a town would have to materialize. Scott would find that others—notably James Wilkinson, who owned land where Frankfort would be built—were more adept than he in town-site speculation and development.

Just about every man in Scott's vicinity was a Virginian and a veteran. A close neighbor was John ("Jack") Jouett, who had become famous for his ride to warn Jefferson and members of the Virginia legislature of the advance of Tarleton's dragoons in June 1781.[22] Even strangers were assumed to have been in some way connected with the war. One story has it that while Scott was sitting in a log tavern, "a tolerably well dressed Stranger" from New England came in and called for a half pint of whiskey. The proprietor informed him that he did not sell whiskey in such small quantities.

"Stranger I will join you and pay half," intervened Scott. "Therefore landlord, give us a pint of your best." The whiskey was brought, and Scott, who drank first, addressed the stranger: "Colonel, your good health."

"I am no Colonel," replied the stranger.

"Well then," said Scott, "Major, your good health."

"I am no Major," replied the New Englander.

"Then your good health, Captain."

"I am no Captain, Sir," said the stranger, "and what is more, never held a commission in my life."

Amused, Scott explained, "Well then by heavens, you are the first man in Kentucky that ever wore a cloth coat and was not a commissioned officer." [23]

Scott possessed that combination of virtue and vice respected on the frontier. He had dignity and presence of character, and his integrity was unimpeachable. On the other hand, his two outstanding vices, drinking and swearing, had not diminished. Herman Bowman, who was Scott's adjutant in 1793, wrote that Scott was "the most agreeable companion. . . . Never told a vulgar lie. . . . Genteel, handsome, dark skin, regular neat figure, dark hair and beard, neat in person always. . . . I never heard any man that could swear pretty, except Genl. Scott." One frontier vice Scott stayed away from was dueling. Years later, when he supposedly was challenged to a duel, Scott neither acknowledged nor accepted the summons. When the challenger said that he would brand Scott a coward, Scott replied, "You only post yourself a damned liar, and everybody will say so." [24]

While other settlers might have felt starved for culture, Scott did not care much about patronizing or subscribing to the various cultural and improvement endeavors that rapidly appeared in central Kentucky. In 1787, however, he did become one of the thirty-seven subscribers to the Kentucke Society for Promoting Useful Knowledge. The first undertaking of the society was to procure textile machinery from Philadelphia. [25]

In October 1788 Scott met a most unusual visitor: Dr. John Connolly, who in 1775 had been commissioned by Lord Dunmore to lead a tory uprising in the backcountry of Virginia and Pennsylvania, only to be captured and imprisoned. Connolly, after being exchanged, moved to Canada. It seems that Connolly was not only interested in investment in Kentucky but also in stirring up resistance to the United States on the frontier. At that time James Wilkinson and the "court party" (so named because prominent judges were involved) were putting forth the idea of the separation of Kentucky not only from Virginia but also from the Union, perhaps to be secured by a Spanish alliance. In Kentucky, Connolly "conferred with no more than four men of importance—Scott, Thomas Marshall, George Muter, and Col. John Campbell. These men were numbered among the "American" or "country" party, opposed to Wilkinson's pro-Spanish schemes and independence.[26] Harry Innes, a prominent lawyer and later a U.S. District Judge, wrote Washington that Connolly during his visit "touched the Key to Fomentation" and offered assistance should westerners march on New Orleans in order to secure navigation rights on the Mississippi. "How his Machinations are to be counteracted is the great object." Connolly apparently was playing both sides of the fence. If Kentuckians invaded Spanish territory they would be at odds with the federal government, and in the end such action might further an independence movement. By supporting an attack on Spanish territory, such persons as Scott might unwittingly aid the cause of separation from the Union. Of course, Connolly met the immediate opposition of the court party because of the proposed hostility toward the Spanish government at Louisiana, and Wilkinson boasted that he scared Connolly out of Kentucky. From Detroit, on April 6, 1789, Connolly wrote Scott that "I am inclined to think your serious reflections will urge you to pursue such measures as may appear most likely to advance your own interest & that of the Country of which you are now an Inhabitant."[27] Scott had some second thoughts and realized that Connolly was his same old self—serving principally British rather than American interests. He would not have anything further to do with the expatriate former tory.

For Scott, who wanted to cultivate an image above partisan politics, involvement with any foreign intrigue, especially with the British, was all the more unwise. At age fifty, he had the esteem of the officers and men of the Revolutionary War who settled near him. The idea of serving in public office increasingly occupied Scott's mind. A staunch unionist, he also favored the separation of Kentucky from Virginia and statehood, although he did not participate in the numerous Kentucky conventions. Nor did he get involved in the contest over ratification of the U.S. Constitution, although as a former Continental army officer who expected more concrete rewards from the federal government, he undoubtedly offered no support to the substantial Anti-Federalist movement in Kentucky. He also avoided getting involved in the purely local arena—for example, he refused to accept the appointment of county lieutenant.[28]

To try the political waters, Scott allowed his name to be offered as a candidate for the Virginia House of Delegates in April 1789. He and John Hawkins were elected to represent Fayette County.[29] The new Woodford County, where Scott lived, would be represented one more year by Fayette delegates.

Scott attended the October 19 to December 19, 1789, session of the General Assembly in Richmond, Virginia. He most likely traveled the Wilderness Road. He served on the standing committee of privileges and elections and on special committees: one to draft a bill on transferring a public lot in Lexington, Kentucky, to the Presbyterian Society and another to compose an address to President Washington on the Indian problem in Kentucky. The message to the president cited Indian barbarity and recommended that war might be the solution. Scott and eight other Kentucky delegates petitioned President Washington to supply a military guard so that a saltworks could be established at Big Bone Lick, along the Ohio.[30]

Scott met with Patrick Henry, and he was included in Henry's Virginia Yazoo Company as a stockholder—apparently because he promised military service against the southern Indians, who could be expected to resist intrusion on their lands. In 1789–90, also, it looked as if war might be imminent with the Creek Indians. Scott expected to be named commander of a southern Indian expedition, or, at least, that was what he purportedly told Kentuckians when he returned from legislative duty. Wilkinson noted: "Old Scott has just arrived here & informs us that two regiments are to be raised in this district; he adds that the President has offered him the command, & that the destination of the corps is against the Creeks, via the Muscle Shoals."[31] The southern war scare soon faded when a Creek delegation visited the Senate chamber in New York in 1790 and signed the first treaty under the new Constitution.

Yet there was still the Indian problem in the Northwest. Marauding Indians were regularly terrorizing settlers on both sides of the Ohio River and those traveling downstream. Federal military authorities had no success in getting the tribes themselves to put a stop to the violence and thievery.[32] While President Washington hitherto had discouraged and even tried to prevent filibustering expeditions by the Kentucky settlers, the population had grown so greatly in the Kentucky district, and along with it political clout, that demands for ridding the Indian menace by any means could not be ignored.

Brig. Gen. (by brevet) Josiah Harmar, who commanded the American regulars stationed on the Ohio, invited Scott to bring Kentucky mounted volunteers to Limestone, where Harmar would meet him with 120 of his troops. Their mission would be to drive about 200 Shawnee and other Indian marauders from their camp on the Scioto River. On April 18 Scott with 200 volunteers joined Harmar's regulars, and the next day the combined force crossed the Ohio. By April 25 Scott's and Harmar's troops had proceeded fifty miles from the mouth of the Scioto. Then, making their way southward, they came upon the deserted Indian camp. A fresh trail of moccasin prints of four Indians was discovered, and Scott sent out a party of thirteen after these Indians. One set of tracks was particularly recognizable— that of old Reel Foot (a Shawnee so named because of two club feet), who had the reputation on the frontier of having taken scalps wherever his tracks were found. Fifteen miles away the party surprised the four Indians at their camp on Eagle Creek. Reel Foot, who was cutting a pole when Col. John Grant and his men surrounded the camp, was immediately dispatched by a bullet through the head, and the three others were also killed. The Indians never fired a shot. No other Indians were found, and on the twenty-seventh the troops were back at the mouth of the Scioto. Scott's Kentuckians crossed the river, and Harmar led his troops the sixty-five miles to Fort Washington.

All that Scott and Harmar had to show for the expedition, which, in the round trip, had covered nearly 130 miles, were four scalps and several beaver traps. "Wolves might as well have been pursued," Harmar reported to the secretary of war. The militia had wearied early and, with the shortage of provisions, had become eager to get home. "Many of them would have gone off but for the influence of Genl. Scott," commented Washington in his diary. Washington thought the troops could have found the Indians whom they were looking for on the other side of the Scioto River.[33]

Indian depredations did not cease. In June 1790 Secretary of War Henry Knox, therefore, under instructions from the president, ordered Harmar and Governor Arthur St. Clair of the Western Territory to prepare an expedition into the Indian country. The secretary of war also recommended that mounted Kentucky militia join the regulars for a march to the head of the Wabash River. It took several months to organize a campaign. Kentucky militia joined Harmar's regulars at Fort Washington in August. Harmar had hoped that Scott would command the Kentucky troops, but neither Scott nor two other often mentioned possible commanders—colonels Benjamin Logan and Isaac Shelby—stepped forward. Scott had another duty, having been elected a delegate from Woodford County to the Virginia General Assembly. He had no interest in the command because he did not have a commission, and he also knew that the militia wanted to serve under Col. Robert Trotter, a veteran of Logan's campaign in 1786. Although Maj. John Hardin received a commission to command the militia from the Virginia executive, the men would only serve under Trotter, as Scott predicted. Harmar's solution was to fragment the Kentucky troops once they joined his army. The expedition would be the largest yet sent against the Indians of the Ohio country—700 Kentuckians, 500 Pennsylvanians, and 300 regulars. The Kentucky militia who showed up at Fort Washington were raw and inexperienced; a regular army lieutenant suggested that their "whole object seemed to be nothing than to see the country, without rendering any service whatever."[34] Scott would be thankful later that he did not join this ill-fated venture.

As Harmar's army readied for the Indian campaign, Scott set out on the Wilderness Road on his way to Richmond. He was so short of cash, without even a dollar in his pocket, that he sent his son Charles to visit George Muter to get an advance on the £4.10 that Muter owed him for a lot in Petersburg. Scott also expected "to git one Guinea from [Jack] Jouett which is all my Dependence after I start."[35]

One traveled the Wilderness Road at one's own peril—subject to being bushwhacked and murdered by renegades, red and white. For protection, travelers assembled at Crab Orchard (a crabapple grove along the Dix River in present Lincoln County) and proceeded as a group. When Scott arrived at Crab Orchard, a Baptist preacher was ready to get started. Scott warned him to wait until more people came. The preacher paid no heed to the advice, went on, and was killed. Except for 40 miles of rolling hills, the trail of some 190 miles between Crab Orchard and the Block House (in Virginia on the southeast side of the Cumberland Gap) was hardly more than a bridle path following the streams through the mountains. One had to cross five wide rivers and numerous creeks. From the Block House, Scott passed through the upper (south) Shenandoah Valley and through a gap in the Blue Ridge Mountains, from where it was easy going over the low hills northeast to Richmond.[36]

As a member of the House of Delegates for the October 18 to December 29, 1790, session, Scott again served on the committee of privileges and elections and was appointed to the most important and prestigious of the half dozen standing committees—the committee of propositions and grievances, through which most of the business of the house originated. He sat on several special committees: to draw up bills for establishing a town in Bourbon County, for conferring on county lieutenants in Kentucky authority to order militia to guard duty, and for empowering the court of appeals in Kentucky to act on a divorce petition of Lewis Robards. The latter assignment had a remote bearing on the life of Andrew Jackson. Jack Jouett, also a delegate and Robards's brother-in-law, had introduced the Robards petition for a divorce from Rachel Donelson. The General Assembly granted Robards the right to sue in the Kentucky courts for divorce, which Robards failed to do; under the misconception that the divorce was actually granted by the legislature, Rachel and Andrew Jackson married illegally. While in Richmond, Scott attended the annual meeting of the state's Society of the Cincinnati, held at the Eagle Tavern on October 26–27,

1790. The society was not very popular in Virginia, and only twenty-one officers were present.[37] Although keeping up his dues for a while, Scott never had much interest in the organization.

While Scott was in Virginia, the expeditionary force under Harmar met disaster—and Scott had another son scalped by the Indians. Merritt Scott, captain in the militia from Woodford County, was in a militia detachment sent out by Harmar. Ambushed, many of the militiamen threw away their weapons and fled, while Merritt was one of the few who stood their ground. Mortally wounded, he was picked up by his Kentucky neighbor, Ens. Robert Mosby. "Let me down Robert," said Merritt. "I am to die. Save yourself if you can." When Mosby lowered him to the ground, Merritt was dead. Mosby and the other survivors escaped by hiding in a swamp.[38] Most of another detachment under Maj. John P. Wyllys was massacred by the Indians on October 22. In both engagements, 183 men (including 73 regulars) were killed and 37 wounded. The defeated army returned to Fort Washington. Scott's son was buried with the other fallen soldiers in the low bank of the ford of the Maumee (present-day Fort Wayne, Indiana). His scalp was among those in the "piles of scalps, together with canteens, sashes, military hats, &c.," that were taken to the Indian villages.[39]

During 1790 and early 1791 Scott and other prominent westerners flirted with the harebrained scheme of Dr. James O'Fallon, a reckless adventurer who was agent for the South Carolina Yazoo Company. This company was one of three which obtained nearly sixteen million acres from the Georgia legislature for $200,000 in cash, to be paid over a two-year period. Patrick Henry's Virginia Yazoo Company and the Tennessee Yazoo Company were the other two. The plan called for 3,000 Kentucky, Cumberland, and Franklin (eastern Tennessee) armed settlers to plant a colony at the mouth of the Yazoo River on the Mississippi (Vicksburg). O'Fallon visited Lexington in April 1790 and may have made Scott an offer then; in September, O'Fallon wrote Scott, officially inviting him to come into the scheme. Scott, who would be given free land, was to lead 500 settlers from Kentucky.

O'Fallon originally anticipated backing from the Spanish authorities in Florida and Louisiana. When that failed—and it looked as if Great Britain and Spain might go to war over the Nootka Sound crisis—O'Fallon developed the idea of a conquest of Louisiana, with the help of the British navy in the Caribbean. This switch alienated an early backer of O'Fallon, James Wilkinson, who already was deeply involved in a Spanish conspiracy. As Wilkinson noted, "The ignorant and low class of people with a very few respectable characters, such as Marshal, Scott & Muter, are hostile to Spain." Scott probably also now lost interest because of the suggested British involvement. In any event, O'Fallon's scheme soon fell through. The South Carolina Yazoo Company defaulted when the Georgia legislature added the requirement that the land had to be paid for in gold and silver; furthermore, President Washington, on August 14 and 26, 1790, issued proclamations enjoining United States citizens from violating treaty rights of the southern Indians, implying that force would be used if necessary. Although O'Fallon himself enrolled a battalion of 650 Kentucky militia, under John Holder, for the project, Scott gave no assistance. Scott received good advice from Arthur Campbell, frontier leader in the North Carolina backcountry and speculator: "The Yazous and other Georgia adventurers are much reprobated in Philadelphia. I wish much that you may in future decline all kind of countenance to that undertaking and change your views to over the Ohio."[40]

Scott heeded this advice. He soon learned that the federal government again planned to seek a military solution to the Indian problem and was preparing to make full use of the Kentucky militia. As the senior Revolutionary War officer residing in Kentucky, Scott could expect a call to military command. There was added motivation to even the score with the Indians for having killed his two sons. Indeed, for the next several years, Scott's view would be over the Ohio, in the quest to end the Indian depredations once and for all. He could expect to relive the glory of former years in leading troops into battle—only, much like his experiences in the French and Indian War, the enemy and the glory would be elusive.

"No Friend to His Country
Can Now Be Idle"

To Charles Scott and other Kentuckians, their militia forces were quite sufficient to convince the northern Indians to end their depredations. Western citizens also insisted that since they knew the frontier problems the best, any operations into the Ohio country, including the use of regular army troops, should be commanded by one of their own. Harmar's defeat lent credence to this argument. President Washington and Secretary of War Henry Knox did not agree but were willing to compromise. Knox, however, did appreciate the wisdom of employing mounted militia separate from regular troops. The administration approved temporary offensive actions against the Indians by mounted volunteers and also a ranger-guard system using militia. Congress voted the funds. This reliance on militia and volunteers would merely be a stopgap measure until the federal government could mount a full-scale military offensive itself.

Pursuant to the compromise policy of recognizing a role for the militia in military action in the Indian country, Congress in January 1791 established a Board of War for Kentucky, to consist of Scott, Harry Innes, John Brown, Benjamin Logan, and Isaac Shelby. The board had power to call out the militia into service of the United States whenever necessary to fight the Indians and to act in conjunction with the regular army. Furthermore, in line with the new federal policy, the Virginia legislature on December 20, 1790, authorized Governor Beverley Randolph to establish a ranger-guard system made up of militia. On

December 29, 1790, the governor appointed Scott brigadier general and commandant of the Kentucky district.[1]

Scott's primary duty for the moment was to supervise about eighteen ranger-guard stations along the Ohio. The county where each station was located furnished the rations, and the men entered into this service on a two-month tour of duty and received the same pay as the soldiers of the federal army. Scott ordered the men at each station to build a blockhouse and maintain communications between posts. If a large party of Indians appeared, runners should be sent to the nearest settlement. In February, Scott met with the commanding officers of the various counties at Collins's Tavern in Lexington to work out further details of the ranger-guard system. The Board of War on March 9 called for a draft of 326 men for this service.[2]

Indian hostility returned in intensity to the Ohio Valley. On January 2, 1791, Indians killed fifteen whites at a blockhouse on the Muskingum—the Big Bottom massacre—and a large body of Indians attacked Dunlop's Station on the Miami, west of Fort Washington—a siege that lasted twenty-five hours, with two whites killed. One small party of Indians came down the Kentucky River to the forks of Elkhorn Creek, near Scott's home, and stole horses.[3]

On March 3 Congress voted to add a new battalion, not including officers, to the U.S. Army and to call out 2,000 militia volunteers. While it had been rumored in Philadelphia that Scott, being a veteran Continental army general, would be named the commanding general, the overall command went to Maj. Gen. Arthur St. Clair, governor of the Western Territory and also a veteran general officer of the Revolution. Scott, in accordance with the policy of temporary reliance on Kentucky troops, was to lead mounted volunteers in a preliminary campaign to the Indian towns on the Wabash (near present-day Lafayette, Indiana); St. Clair would later direct the main attack against the tribes about the Maumee River. On March 9, 1791, the secretary of war ordered Scott to have the Wabash expedition (authorized strength of 750) ready to move by May 10.[4]

The Kentucky Board of War met on May 2 and, concluding there were enough volunteers, set the rendezvous for the troops at Frankfort on May 15. Each volunteer had to supply his own arms, a horse, and enough provisions to last until the troops crossed the Ohio. For the march beyond the Ohio, Scott contracted provisions for thirty days at public expense.[5] Scott's pending Indian campaign was widely popular, as reflected in the *Kentucky Gazette,* which urged its readers to give their full support.[6] It was evident that the prospect of Indian war kindled a martial spirit across the frontier.

In viewing the departure of the mounted volunteers from Frankfort on May 15, Board of War member Harry Innes observed that "a more choice body of men could not be raised in the United States—young—healthy—well armed—well mounted." The response to the call for volunteers had been overwhelming; more men applied than could be accepted, and 852 men took to the field instead of the authorized 750. Such was the enthusiasm that John Brown, a member of the Board of War, went out as a private. Just before Scott's call for volunteers, John Belli had toured Kentucky, paying the volunteers who had served in the previous Harmar expedition, and now the service was offering federal compensation at 66⅔ cents per day for privates. General St. Clair provided Scott with 500 pounds of rifle powder, 1,000 pounds of lead, 1,500 flints, and tools for making rafts to cross the Ohio. Scott's expedition of volunteers, "calculated expressly to gratify the people of Kentucky," wrote St. Clair, who visited Danville and Lexington the week before, "disgusted some who are supposed to be influential characters"—namely colonels Benjamin Logan and Isaac Shelby. Both men had wanted the command, and neither would accept a lesser position. Shelby, however, "has done everything to forward the business, while Logan has thrown much cold water upon it."[7]

Scott's expedition had as its objectives the Indian villages along the Wabash River in the vicinity of present-day Lafayette, Indiana: namely, Ouiatanon, a small stockaded town of the Wea band of the Miami, across from it a Kickapoo village, and farther up the Wabash at Eel Creek (near the junction of the Tippecanoe and Wabash Rivers), Kethtippecanunk, at the time inhabited by a miscellany of Weas, Potawatomis, and perhaps some Kickapoos, which was close to the later site of Prophetstown and the battle of Tippecanoe in 1811. The chief Miami villages (the Crane band, called Twightwees by the British) were located northeastward on the Maumee River.[8] United, the two groups of Indians could put a formidable force in the field.

On May 23 Scott's mounted volunteers crossed the Ohio at Battle Creek, five miles below the mouth of the Kentucky River (near present Madison, Indiana). Scott's army made speedy progress the next seven days, even though trudging over steep hills and fording swollen streams (including four branches of the White River). It rained heavily every day. On June 1 the volunteers passed through a gap in a densely timbered ridge of the Round Top Hills; northward stretched the Wea Plains, dotted with little groves and exuding a brilliant patchwork of late spring blossoms.[9]

Scott calculated that he was now 155 miles from the Ohio. He learned from his guides (one of whom, unknown to him, had a wife in one of the Indian towns)[10] that Ouiatanon was about four miles in his front, behind a small woods. As Scott and his men paused, a lone Miami chieftain, reputedly Captain Bull, appeared in the distance on horseback. A soldier fired his rifle at him, and the chieftain hurried back to Ouiatanon to sound the alarm.

Scott sent Col. John Hardin, who was itching to redeem himself from his defeat in the Harmar expedition in October, with sixty men, to assault two small temporary Kickapoo hunting encampments on the left. The Kickapoos mounted their horses and galloped toward a ford eight miles down the river—the only crossing nearby with a rock bottom. Both the Indians and Hardin's troops made it over the river. Hardin caught up with the Kickapoos at Pine Creek and fought a brief skirmish. Six warriors were killed, and some women and children captured. Picking up more Indians whom he had left behind, Hardin, when he returned to Scott's camp at 6 P.M., had fifty-two prisoners.

Meanwhile, Scott led the main body of troops toward Ouiatanon, finding as he came closer to the little village that it was not at the edge of the prairie, as his guides had told him, but on bottomland on the bank of the Wabash. On the way Scott ran across a lone cabin, which Captain Price and forty men "stormed," killing two warriors.

When Scott got to the top of a hill close by the Wabash, he saw some Indians below hurriedly trying to escape over the river in canoes. Scott ordered Colonel Wilkinson and the first battalion to stop them. Wilkinson and his men arrived at the bank of the river just as the last canoe had started to cross. A brisk fire came from the Indians at the Kickapoo village on the opposite bank; Wilkinson's riflemen killed all the Indians, who were crowded into five canoes. Because the Wabash was unfordable at this location, Scott sent a detachment under Wilkinson upriver and another below under Maj. Thomas Barbee to attempt crossings in order to get to the Kickapoo town. Barbee's men, by canoeing and swimming, forded the swollen river, only to discover that the Indians had abandoned their village.

At Ouiatanon, Scott spotted a white flag on a hill. Thinking it to be a flag of truce, he sent an old squaw whom he had captured to the Indians with the message that if they surrendered their towns would be spared. Nothing came of this. Actually the white flag marked the burial place of a chieftain (a customary practice of both the French and Indians in marking graves of prominent persons).

The next day, June 2, Scott sent Wilkinson to destroy Kethtippecanunk, eighteen miles from Scott's camp. Only 360 men of the 500 assigned to this mission were able to go because many of the men and horses had been "crippled, and worn down" by the strenuous activity of the day before. After an all-night march on foot, without halting, Wilkinson's men entered Kethtippecanunk just before dawn. The enemy, amply warned, had all escaped in canoes across Eel Creek, which was unfordable. From the other side of the stream, the Indians fired on the Kentuckians, but Wilkinson's marksmen returned such a heavy volley that the Indians quickly fled from the bank. The volunteers had only three men wounded. Wilkinson looted and burned all the seventy cabins in the stockaded town and destroyed provisions, furs, cattle, and several acres of corn. By evening Wilkinson was back at Scott's camp.[11] Scott in his report noted that many of the inhabitants of Kethtippecanunk were French "and lived in a state of civilization; by the books, letters and other documents, found there, it is evident that place was in close connexion with, and, dependent on Detroit."

Not having a reply to the truce proposal sent out by the old squaw, Scott on June 4 ordered the burning of Ouiatanon, although he left one cabin standing for sixteen of his most weak and infirm prisoners, whom he released.[12] He then issued a proclamation to the Wabash tribes and gave copies to the released prisoners, expecting that the proclamation would find its way to all the Indians of the area. Addressed "To the various tribes of the Piankeshaws, and all the nations of Red People, lying on the waters of the Wabash river," the proclamation stated that the United States had been patient with the Indians, but that the Indians had persisted in hostile actions. It had been necessary, therefore, to send an army, before which the Indians had declined battle and fled. Scott assured the Indians that the United States had no desire "to destroy the red people." Should the Indians decline peace, the strength of the United States would again be exerted: "your warriors will be slaughtered, your towns and villages ransacked and destroyed, your wives and children carried into captivity," and those who do "escape the fury of our mighty chiefs, shall find no resting place on this side the great lakes." Scott informed the Indians that he was taking hostages to Fort Washington, where they would be well treated. If the Indians wished to recover the hostages, then they should go to that post by July 1, "determined, with true hearts, to bury the hatchet, and smoke the pipe of peace." Thus the Indians would live in peace and happiness, and the United States would become their "friends and protectors." But Scott warned that if the Indians continued hostilities, "the sons of war will be let loose against you, and the hatchet will never be buried until your country is desolated, and your people humbled to the dust."[13]

Most of the warriors of the Wabash tribes had joined the other Indians on the Maumee, having expected that Scott would attack there. Scott had considered bringing "terror and desolation to the head of the Wabash" in addition to the attack on the central Wabash towns; but, although he thought he had enough men, this plan was ruled out because of the poor condition of

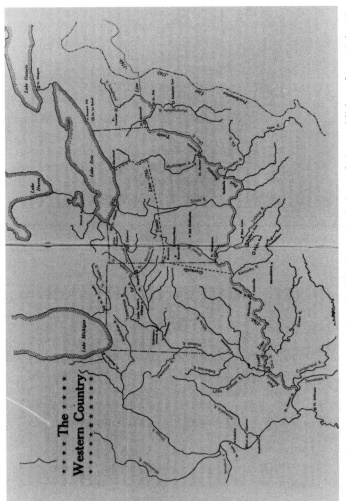

The Western Country. (Reprinted with the permission of the publisher from John D. Barnhart and Dorothy L. Riker, *Indiana to 1816: The Colonial Period* [Indianapolis: Indiana Historical Bureau and Indiana Historical Society, 1971])

the horses and the shortage of provisions. As the mounted volunteers started their journey home on June 4, 500 warriors came down the Wabash and followed the Kentuckians for a while, but did not start a fight for fear that the hostages would be harmed. Scott had taken the prisoners, intentionally mostly women and children, because he had been ordered to do so by the secretary of war's instructions of March 9.

In effect what Scott had done was to defeat the Indians in detail. He probably did not realize how close he had come to battling the combined strength of the Wabash and Maumee tribes. The success of the expedition was small—burning three Indian towns, killing thirty-two "chiefly warriors of size and figure," and taking fifty-eight prisoners (seventeen of whom were released, including the old squaw); the Kentuckians had none killed (although two drowned in the White River on the return trip) and only five wounded. Yet the demonstration of the force of arms in the heart of the Indian country was significant in itself. Unfortunately, though, Scott's excursion provoked the Indians to combine for further resistance.

Scott was proud that his troops committed no act of inhumanity; "even the inveterate habit of scalping the dead, ceased to influence." Reports, however, were heard to the contrary. According to a Moravian missionary, the Kentuckians killed an old chief, whom "they treated barbarously and worse than the Indians." Probably in reference to the same instance, British agent Alexander McKee learned that "a war chief of the Ouias [Weas] who was killed at the first village they literally skinned." Scott also burned all the goods belonging to a French trader, valued at £500.[14]

The return march through thickets and bogs further fatigued the troops, and provisions were almost depleted. Many horses had to be abandoned. Scott sent on ahead a sergeant and twelve men with a report for General St. Clair, by way of Lexington, where his son Daniel, accompanied by the escort, would deliver it to Fort Washington. On June 15 the army reached Fort Steuben (Clarksville), where forty-one prisoners were turned over to Capt. Joseph Asheton of the First U.S. Regiment, who would take them to Fort Washington. The next day the volunteers crossed the river to Louisville and were immediately discharged. Some 300 volunteers accepted the invitation of Col. John Campbell to join him at his Louisville home for beef and mutton and all the grog they could drink, and the tables were kept spread for those who lingered on for a few more days.[15]

General St. Clair congratulated Scott and also the Kentucky Board of War on the Wabash campaign. Since the president's instructions to Scott, through the secretary of war, in March had allowed for another such expedition, St. Clair ordered the Kentucky volunteers, not to exceed 500 men, to attack the upper Wabash Indian towns.[16] The expedition would be a testing of Indian strength, preparatory to the major offensive to be led by St. Clair, which was still in the planning stage.

Because he was ill, Scott declined to lead the second expedition. The Board of War, meeting in Danville in early July, in his stead, therefore, appointed James Wilkinson the commander. Scott thought 500 men for the expedition too few and opposed removing all the frontier ranger-guards in Kentucky, which St. Clair had directed, until the results of the campaign were known. The Board of War duly ordered all guards discharged except for those in Bourbon County guarding the ironworks and the Woodford County militia at Big Bone Lick. As Scott notified the Virginia governor, the board could keep guards at these two posts if it wished because it served under the authority of the Virginia government (Kentucky would not become a state until June 1, 1792) and the matter was not one of federal jurisdiction. Scott pointed out to Governor Randolph that he kept twenty-five men at Big Bone Lick in order to protect the saltworks and a settlement that was in the making there. St. Clair yielded and informed Scott that he approved keeping a guard at Big Bone Lick at federal expense until August 15. Scott claimed that he had spent much time, "Riding almost Constantly," in the "business" of the guard stations.[17]

Meanwhile, Scott, while winding up his duties as commandant for the District of Kentucky, consented to a request from Col. John Edwards of Bourbon County that he be allowed to lead 300 men up the Scioto to break up the Indian bands that had been stealing horses on the Kentucky side of the Ohio. The militia assembled at Maysville (Limestone) on July 19, 1791. Crossing the Ohio, they penetrated deep into the Ohio country, within thirty miles of Sandusky, but found only deserted towns. Unknown to them, they barely avoided ambush by a large Indian force. Because of its futility, this jaunt was dubbed the "blackberry campaign." [18]

Wilkinson finally collected his troops and left Fort Washington on August 1, with the chief objective, as dictated by St. Clair, the Indian town of Kikiah, near the junction of the Eel River with the Wabash. Wilkinson destroyed Kikiah, which the Indians had evacuated, as well as other small villages, including Ouiatanon, to which the Indians had returned, and a Kickapoo town of thirty houses on the prairie. He killed six warriors and by mistake two squaws and a child and took thirty-four captives, mostly women and children. "Falling into General Scott's traces" on the return march most of the way, the volunteers were back at Fort Washington on August 21. Luckily, too, Wilkinson did not meet up with a combined force of the Indians. As did Scott's expedition, Wilkinson's foray stirred the wrath of the Indians. The next time they would get their revenge. Nevertheless, the destructiveness of the Scott and Wilkinson campaigns was a major factor in the decision of the Weas, Kickapoos, and the other Indians of central Indiana and Illinois to sign a treaty of "peace and friendship" with the United States the following year; the Kickapoos would soon move on into Illinois and Missouri. [19]

At last the federal government's Indian expedition was getting ready. General St. Clair called for 500 Kentucky militia to join his regulars and spent August 20–23 in Danville discussing the prospect with Scott and other members of the Board of War. Those who had gone out as mounted volunteers were reluctant to serve under a federal commander. In spite of his own doubts that a regular army commander had any authority over the militia, Scott immediately assumed responsibility for raising the quota, pledging that the troops would be ready by September 25. The Virginia governor sanctioned the militia call. Scott pressured the delinquent county lieutenants; by orders of the governor, he arrested and court-martialed Col. James Barnett, county lieutenant of Madison County, for dereliction of duty. [20]

So few persons volunteered that Scott took it upon himself to issue a draft from the militia. To make sure there would be enough men, he requisitioned 1,200 militia to rendezvous on September 25 at Craig's Mill in Georgetown. Only 300 men showed up, and Scott sent them immediately to Fort Washington. To make up the deficiency, he ordered a second draft for October 4, which apparently never materialized.[21]

The Kentucky militia caught up with St. Clair's army at Fort Hamilton. Following directly northward (along the Ohio side of the present border with Indiana) the army's next halt was to build Fort Jefferson. Delays of the contractors in bringing up supplies, the shortage of horses, lack of forage because of the season of the year, poor discipline, and inadequate reconnaissance were among the problems that faced St. Clair. The Kentucky militia were contemptuous of the raw recruits among the regulars. Some militia deserted within a few days after joining the march, and on about November 1, sixty of the Kentucky militia went off at one time; this forced St. Clair to send one of his best regiments after them to prevent them from plundering the stores in the rear. On the evening of November 3 the army encamped in a small clearing on both sides of the shallow St. Mary's River, unaware that 1,000 Indians were in the vicinity. Col. William Oldham, who commanded the Kentuckians, was in charge of sending out a patrol but failed to do so. At dawn (November 4), the surrounding woods rang with bloodcurdling war whoops. The Indians darted from among the logs and trees and, seldom seen, caught the Americans in a deadly crossfire. After nearly three hours of fighting, the troops broke and ran for their lives, discarding their arms, cartridge boxes, and regimentals, making the twenty-nine miles back to Fort Jefferson by nightfall. The Indians made no immediate pursuit, being content to revel in victory at the scene of the battle. In all, 632 Americans of the 1,400 man force were killed, including Brig. Gen. Richard Butler, the second in command, and Colonel Oldham.[22] It was a shuddering reflection for Scott, when he considered that he had come close to facing a similar combination of Indians and that his force had been half the size of St. Clair's.

As soon as Scott received word of St. Clair's defeat, he sent a circular letter to the county lieutenants. He pointed out that Fort Jefferson was under siege by the Indians and also that "many, many brave wounded gallant men are now left on the road, unable to travel, and without any provision but the flesh of the pack horses." Scott asked that volunteers, completely equipped and with twenty days' provisions, assemble at Craig's Mill on November 15. "The circumstances require the greatest dispatch and no friend to his country can now be idle," he said. Those volunteers who could not reach the rendezvous in time were to follow as soon as possible. Scott hoped that the response would be so great that he would have 1,500 men.[23]

Disappointingly, only 200 men showed up for the rendezvous; Scott led them to Fort Washington. Meanwhile, the Indians had lifted the siege of Fort Jefferson and dispersed. When it became apparent there would be no major offensive, due chiefly to the winter season, Scott and the volunteers, after only several days at Fort Washington, returned to Kentucky. St. Clair had predicted that Scott's "project will blow up." Wilkinson blamed Scott for the poor turnout of the volunteers: Scott so "perplexed & bewildered the subject with his desultory eloquence the idea is dropped."[24]

St. Clair visited Lexington about December 10 to confer with Scott and Wilkinson. Wilkinson accepted an assignment to lead a small party of regulars and Kentucky mounted militia to the site of St. Clair's defeat, to inter the bodies. Leaving Fort Washington on January 24 and reaching the battleground on February 1, Wilkinson and his men dug huge pits through the three feet of snow and frozen ground, giving the decomposed corpses a mass burial. This was a dangerous mission, but the Indians made no effort to attack.[25]

St. Clair's defeat strengthened the Indian confederacy. Neutrals, including the Delawares and the powerful Wyandots, were ready to join the Miamis, Shawnee, and other hostiles. Even then, the Indians could not hope to succeed without British assistance. British agents promised arms and supplies, which the Indians were already receiving through the fur trade. Scott had found ample evidence of British assistance to the Wabash Indians during his 1791 campaign. British policy at the time aimed at a revision of the Treaty of Paris so that an Indian barrier state would be created, which would protect the Canadian fur trade emporium. Hence the British held on to the northwest posts that were to be surrendered by the treaty.[26] What the United States was now facing was an organized Indian and foreign threat at its borders.

President Washington decided to vindicate the national honor by putting a well-trained professional army in the field, assisted by militia cavalry. As Secretary of War Knox reported in December, "sudden enterprises of short duration" are "utterly unsuitable to carry on and terminate the war in which we are engaged, with honor and success." A lengthy debate developed in Congress whether to strengthen the federal army or place main reliance on the militia. New England delegates, though favoring a strong army, did not want any involvement in an Indian war. Finally, as Albert Gallatin observed, congressional advocates of "expeditions of the kind similar to Scott and Wilkinson" were "obliged to join those who have proposed the President's plan in order to oppose those who wish to forsake us altogether." Thus Congress, on March 5, 1792, created three additional regiments for the regular army—960 men each, for three-year terms of service—and provided for the completion of the two regiments and battalion of artillery already on duty: a total federal force of 5,128. The new regiments could be disbanded if the Indian war ended. The army would be divided into four complete units, capable of acting independently, each under the command of a brigadier general—complying with the legionary principle of Roman times. To many citizens, particularly westerners, the new army was but the first step by the Federalists to create a permanent military establishment during peacetime.[27]

St. Clair, although cleared by a court of inquiry, had to be replaced as commander in chief of the army. Age fifty-six, he was suffering from gout, and his military reputation was in shambles. The nomination could be expected to go to a Revolutionary War veteran. Scott had a chance, except that now he was directly involved with the militia, a fact which might have worked some prejudice against his commanding the regular army. Several candidates, notably Governor Henry ("Light-Horse Harry") Lee of Virginia and Anthony Wayne, both with powerful political allies, lobbied extensively for the position.

In December 1791 Washington drew up the "Opinion of the General Officers," a memorandum for the purpose of a cabinet discussion on a replacement for St. Clair. The document, considered at a cabinet meeting on March 9, 1792 (Hamilton, Knox, and Jefferson present), mentioned twenty generals and had capsule character evaluations of sixteen generals "now living, and in this Country." Not included were "those who it is conjectured would not from age, want of health, and other circumstances come forward by any inducements." Washington was remarkably candid, and for almost everyone on the list he mentioned at least one negative quality. Washington commented on Scott: "Brave and means well; but is an officer of inadequate abilities for extensive command; and, by report, is addicted to drinking." Although Washington made known his preference for Lee for commander in chief, he deferred to the judgment of his cabinet that an appointment of Lee would offend other officers, for Lee had attained only a rank of lieutenant colonel. Washington said that he had more embarrassment over this appointment than any other. Wayne won out, and on April 12, 1792, a commission was sent him as "Major General and of course commanding officer of the troops in the service of the United States." James Wilkinson was appointed a brigadier general.[28]

In addition to establishing the new federal army, Congress passed the Militia Act on May 8, 1792, providing for an uniform system of militia. The states were to appoint a major general for each division and a brigadier general for each brigade; the measure also gave the president the power to call out the militia to enforce the laws, suppress insurrections, and repel invasions. On June 5, four days after statehood, the first governor of Kentucky, Isaac Shelby, appointed Scott major general of the Second Division of Kentucky militia (north of the Kentucky River); Benjamin Logan was named major general of the First Division (south of the river).[29]

The campaigns of Scott, Wilkinson, and St. Clair in 1791 thus had a profound effect on the shaping of a military establishment. The events of 1791 also contributed to a tradition that military preferment could be gained from leading a quixotic mission against an inferior enemy. Scott's Ouiatanon expedition broadened his image as not only an old war hero but also an Indian fighter. Among the legacy of the Indian war of 1791, certain ideas were reinforced in the national consciousness: a whole people could be punished indiscriminately for the outrages of hostile individuals and bands; a foreign country (in this instance territory belonging to the Indians) could be invaded because the actions of a group or element in that country threatened American national security; power makes right; manifest destiny, in the sense that Americans are the carriers of freedom and civilization, gives the right to use force against a noncontiguous people within the American sphere of interest to make them enlightened; the defense of the frontier, hitherto largely maintained by the frontiersmen and locally by the states involved, would be the responsibility of the federal government; and a professional army—if not an enlarged permanent establishment—was necessary. 1791 was a year of victory and disaster; its events constituted one step on a long road toward the conversion of a majoritarian democracy to acceptance of military solutions for crises of nation and empire and eventually a pervasiveness of militarism in the national psychology. The Militia Act of May 1792, which increased the war powers of the president more than any single measure has since, alone testifies to the significance of the Indian confrontation of 1791.

Meanwhile, because of the intrusion of military affairs, Scott neglected his property and business interests, with which he had problems because of lack of working capital and cash. He let his tobacco warehouse, still simply a loosely fitted log cabin at the mouth of Craig Creek, fall into disrepair and disuse. Other such establishments on the river, including Wilkinson's at Frankfort (built in 1792), siphoned off much of Scott's business. The Woodford County Court in September 1791 issued a summons to Scott to show cause why he had not fully completed his warehouse, as required by law, and also to account for money he had received for procuring weights and measures. For several years thereafter, Scott answered summonses for not having installed the required standard weights and scales. Scott had his son Daniel, during a visit to Virginia, make arrangements with David Ross for securing the equipment. The county court took action in October 1793 to have the sheriff confiscate and sell tobacco, belonging to five persons, which had been left in Scott's warehouse for two years "and not Demanded."[30]

Scott's son Charles, Jr., established a ferry, known as Scott's Ferry, a half mile above the farm. Scott planned to build a water gristmill on his property near the mouth of Craig Creek. Although he sought a court order to acquire an acre of land opposite the creek belonging to David Sutton, it seems the mill was not built—in May 1795 the matter was still before the court.[31]

Early in 1792 Scott considered moving to Big Bone Lick and taking over the supervision of the saltworks there. David Ross, the main investor, lived in Virginia and found it too expensive and difficult to keep an eye on the project. He gave Scott and George Muter powers of attorney to do with the saltworks what seemed best for Ross's interest. Ross wrote that if Scott would move to the vicinity of Big Bone Lick, he could "accomodate" Scott "with a small piece of land." The saltworks could not have been a very profitable venture—only about one bushel of salt could be obtained from 400 gallons of water, which had to be boiled in small containers for the best results[32]—although there was a lot of demand because of the plentifulness of game and extensive hog raising on the frontier. Scott declined Ross's offer. Life on the Ohio River would have been too isolated, away from the mainstream of affairs in central Kentucky. In addition, at the time, Scott still hoped that his proposed town of Petersburg would be a success.

Scott was not alone as a town-site speculator. Throughout Kentucky there was extensive city speculation. Many immigrants coming to the frontier preferred urban settlement. Scott considered his location as ideal for a town and envisioned a waterfront commercial district, backed up on the higher ground by a residential section. But, like so many other projected urban sites, Scott's proposed town was not getting beyond the survey stage. With nearby Lexington booming (1,000 population and

300–400 houses at the time)³³ and other towns developing along the Kentucky River, Scott realized that about the only chance for Petersburg to take off as a town was for it to be designated the new state capital. Scott figured that this was not an unreasonable expectation; after all, back in Virginia, the capital was located centrally and at the end of the navigable part of a major river, just as his land was situated.

Scott's disappointment was not long in forthcoming. Among the first business of the summer 1792 session of the new state's General Assembly was the selection of a site for the capital. Many localities besides Scott's competed—Frankfort, Leestown (on the outskirts of present-day Frankfort), Boonesborough, Lexington, Louisville, and even Delaney's Ferry on the Kentucky River were in the running. Boonesborough, with 120 houses (in 1789), made the most attractive offer of 18,550 acres and £2,630 English sterling. Nineteen subscribers to Scott's Petersburg petitioned the legislature in August 1792, pledging a total of £204. The assembly appointed a committee of five persons to select the location of the capital. Initially twenty-one persons were nominated for the committee, with Mercer and Fayette counties each allowed to strike out a name in turn until only five persons were left. The issue came down to Lexington and Frankfort. Robert Todd, a committee member who had large real-estate holdings in Lexington, sought to avoid the appearance of a conflict of interest and cast the deciding vote (making it three to two) for Frankfort, which itself had offered a considerable inducement.³⁴ Thus Scott's Petersburg became neither the capital nor a town.

Creditors in Virginia and elsewhere were pressing Scott to pay some debts that were still outstanding. In the fall of 1791 Scott sent his son Daniel to Virginia with his power of attorney to do what he could to straighten out his financial obligations. Also, Scott had given Edmund Thomas some of his military lands to dispose of, and these had not been sold. Scott had practically paid off his loan from Edward Carrington, but there were still other debts. One of Scott's creditors demanding payment had to sell his own house and slaves. The estate of Charles

Woodson, deceased, also sought payment on an advance that had been given on Scott's wheat crop many years before, which Scott claimed he had repaid.[35]

While in Powhatan County, Daniel married Martha ("Patty") Mosby on November 16, 1791. Scott wrote Daniel on January 17, 1792, that he had learned of Daniel's marriage and would have everything ready for him and his bride when they returned to Kentucky, including finishing a house for them. Having lost two sons to the Indians, Scott cautioned Daniel to be careful in coming down the Ohio River. A bit of family news was that Daniel's sister Polly had been wooed by one Hughes, who "Supposed himself engaged and told everyone so," but he was "rong," and Polly was making a fuss about this.[36]

Charles, Jr., wrote Daniel on February 24, 1792, that he heard that Daniel was married but wished that Daniel had written him. Daniel's corn had brought a good price, but "if I had of followed your directions it would unevitably all of Bean Stolen." Daniel's mare and colt were "in as Good Order as can be Expected Concerning the hard Winter." He asked Daniel on his return to pick up "the nicest Boots" he could find in Winchester "and likewise a good piece of Cloth for a Great Coat." By the same conveyance, their father advised Daniel that the severe winter had delayed the completion of his house. Scott entreated Daniel: "Pray for gods sake make the best collection for me You can as it is Much Wanted." He reminded Daniel to get the weights for his warehouse from David Ross. Scott said that "we Hourly expect orders from government to take the field with the Volenteers of this country & to Continue for the whole Campaign unless the work is Sooner don." Scott wished that Daniel would be back in Kentucky by early spring, and again he warned about the danger along the Ohio River.[37]

Charles, Jr., did a little active courting himself and was distressed that Daniel heard a rumor that he had fathered a bastard child. On July 10, 1792, he pointed out to Daniel that this was an old affair. A friend had advised him to marry the girl, but it turned out the girl was not pregnant, and Charles, Jr., was able to "Get Clear of her Intire." He had, in fact, acted on Daniel's suggestion that it was about time to strike out on his own and had contracted with one William Neal for three years, presumably to run a farm. With all his "things pact up to start," he had decided to talk to their father "concerning of my Bargain and he told me that he could not Spare me." Charles, Jr., had tried to reason with Scott and "told him that I was doing some thing for myself." But "the Answer that he Gave me was that if I wou'd stay with him and see after the plantation affairs I was the only son that he had that would stay with him he wou'd Give me some thing Extra ordinary more than any of the Rest and If I Chose to leave him I might depend upon it that I shou'd not Get a farthing." So Charles, Jr., stayed on the farm. Apparently quite contented, he was hoping to harvest nearly 500 barrels of corn and "some of the Best wheat that ever was made." On other news, he informed Daniel that the General Assembly had named new militia officers, and he was a captain. Interestingly, he reported that their father was planning to run for Congress, and "I believe there is no doubt but what he will be Elected." It seems, however, that Scott did not find much enthusiasm for his candidacy. But he did have enough support in 1792 to be appointed a presidential elector.[38]

Scott's letter of October 4, 1792, questioned Daniel about his delay in returning and the difficulty in clearing up his debts. He had been unable to find the receipts that would resolve the Woodson debt, presumably because he had destroyed them with other "old papers" when he moved to Kentucky. Scott mentioned to Daniel that he had lost six blacks. Otherwise, "Our family has been very well patsey has had her leg broak but is Walking about again." In spite of the worst drought that he had known, his wheat and corn were of the best quality.[39]

While the Scott family seemed to be drawn more closely together—even with Daniel far off in Virginia—military affairs were still very much on Scott's mind. His military duties for 1792 and early 1793, as a division commander of the militia, were confined largely to employing parties of militia as scouts and guards. He had the same difficulty as before in securing muster returns from the various counties. At least as to future command of Kentucky militia in another Indian campaign Scott only had to worry about Benjamin Logan as his competition, for

Wilkinson had joined the federal army. Scott's having fallen out with Wilkinson, however, did offer an impediment. As Arthur Campbell wrote in February 1792, "General Scott's influence is lessened" in Kentucky "through the Contrivance of Wilkinson, whose intrigues are well known."[40] Nevertheless, Scott could count on a major role in future military operations.

"Blood of the Hydra"

It took longer than Scott had expected before there was another offensive against the Indians. Gen. Anthony Wayne's federal army, officially known as the Legion of the United States, first had to be trained, and negotiations with the Indians would have to be exhausted. Not until April 1793 did the Legion move down from the Pittsburgh area to establish a camp, named Hobson's Choice, a mile below Fort Washington. Here the army would undergo strenuous training, awaiting notification from the War Department to advance into the Indian country.

All the while, Indian depredations returned to the banks of the Ohio and occasionally even into Kentucky.[1] War parties roamed the Ohio country. In May 1792 Col. John Hardin and Maj. Alexander Truman were murdered on a peace mission. In July fourteen persons were killed. In the fall the Miami chief, Little Turtle, and several hundred warriors boldly attacked workmen outside Fort Hamilton and a convoy at Fort St. Clair (halfway between Fort Hamilton and Fort Jefferson). One good-will gesture—the release of Indian prisoners whom Scott and Wilkinson had taken in 1791 from the Fort Washington stockade in July 1792—did not have any effect in improving relations.[2]

Scott did not expect that the Indians could be brought into a treaty. Since the Washington administration had let it be known that militia could operate in the field in conjunction with the federal army, Scott informed General Wayne of the availability of Kentucky militia and of himself. Wayne replied that although the law that established the western army "only contemplates mounted Volunteers," he would welcome such troops to go into the field jointly with the Legion or to act separately as the situation might require, but all operations would be under his direction. Wayne invited Scott to come up to Hobson's Choice, where "you'l meet with a sincere welcome from an old brother officer." The federal commander also informed Governor Shelby and Benjamin Logan of his desire to enlist the aid of the Kentucky militia. In his report to the secretary of war, Wayne stated that a "strong jealousy" existed between Scott and Logan, which he hoped "to turn to public advantage, by holding up an idea of two distinct Operations at a proper time & season"; each would, therefore, compete with the other in raising their quotas, which should stimulate recruitment.[3]

Governor Shelby convened a council of the Kentucky militia general officers at Lexington, on June 24, 1793, to shape plans for calling out 1,500 mounted volunteers; present were major generals Scott and Logan and brigadier generals Thomas Kennedy (later replaced by Thomas Barbee) and Robert Todd—Benjamin Harrison and Robert Breckinridge were absent. The council unanimously served notice that militia officers should not be reduced in grade while in federal service and that the volunteers in the field should be employed against the enemy separately from the regular army whenever possible.[4]

Scott then spent a week at Hobson's Choice, where he and Wayne worked out details for the participation of the Kentucky volunteers. It was agreed that the Kentuckians would march in supporting distance of the federal troops but never closer than two miles except in time of battle, when they would be assigned a combat role separate from that of the regulars. Scott informed Governor Shelby that these terms, which were in accordance with the president's instructions, were the best that he could get. Wayne wanted the Kentucky troops to cross the Ohio by August 1. Scott also reported that he learned from Wayne that the Indians were avoiding treaty negotiations and that the president had alerted the Legion to be ready to take to the field.[5]

For the impending expedition, 750 volunteers were to be raised from each of Scott's and Logan's divisions. Governor Shelby appointed Scott to the command of the Kentucky troops.

Scott complained that some prominent citizens (meaning Logan especially) were "throwing Cold water on the Volenteer Business." Wayne told him, however, that was to be expected of men of "disappointed ambitions," and the best policy was not to take any public notice of their obstructionism.[6]

It was especially displeasing to Wayne that Governor Shelby and other Kentucky officials were insisting that the volunteers operate widely independent of the federal army—in hopes that the Kentucky troops would confront the Indians first and receive the glory of a victory. Wayne vented his wrath over this prospect to Secretary of War Knox and also to Governor Shelby, to whom he said that to allow the volunteers free rein from the army "in order to burn a few wigwams and to kill or capture a few women and children" would "be an object unworthy of gallant mounted volunteers." Scott was caught in the middle. He told Wayne: "I am Truly unhappy that Your letter by me to the governor was not pleasing. . . . Your Mention of the Wigwams & Squaws that would be only found, has angered him considerably. I wish You had given him other reasons."[7]

Actually the call for volunteers had gone out too soon, since peace negotiations with the Indians dragged out longer than expected, and there could be no military action until their conclusion. Because of the delay in scheduling field operations, Scott felt that enthusiasm for enlisting in Kentucky was waning, and as he wrote Gen. Thomas Posey of the Legion, "I tremble for fear the fever will be over."[8] Meanwhile, Scott requested authority from Wayne to fill vacancies among his line officers (subject to ratification by Wayne) and to name his staff officers; Wayne approved. Scott still complained of opposition to recruitment in Kentucky. "Various Reports are flying thro the Country," he wrote Wayne, "to Injure the Service which Keeps me in Continual motion to put things to rights, for Godsake Say something to me about the Movements of the army or We Shall be ruined." Wayne advised Scott that the Indian negotiations would soon be over and that he could not believe that the "extravagant Claims of the Savages" (chiefly now the insistence on the Ohio River as the Indian boundary) would be accepted by the peace commissioners. In the meantime, "patience is a good virtue &

we must endeavor to exercise it untill official information is received of the result of the pending treaty."[9]

Secretary of War Knox's letter of September 3 signifying the end of treaty negotiations reached Wayne on September 11. Immediately the Legion commander ordered Scott and the volunteers to be at Fort Jefferson by October 1. Scott set the rendezvous for the mounted volunteers at Georgetown: September 20 and 30 for the brigades north and south of the Kentucky River, respectively. Upon receiving Wayne's order, Scott wrote Governor Shelby that he was "fearful the fier in the Volentiers (from the Unavoidable Delay) has in Some Degree abated," but with "proper Exertions it may be Kindled again & this Year be Crown with Victory." Scott again asked Shelby to use his influence to encourage recruiting. "Our little new Country is Blasted if the men dont Turn out." Scott was irked that there had not been much response south of the Kentucky River and that he was not kept sufficiently informed of the progress of recruitment there.[10] As one means to lure recruits, Scott had Wayne's letters, which appealed to patriotism and praised the bravery of the volunteers, extracted in the *Kentucky Gazette*.[11]

At the Georgetown rendezvous, the southside brigade arrived at only two-thirds of strength, and many officers were missing. After a parade of the troops down Main Street on September 24, at the local tavern Scott convened a board of officers, which filled the officer vacancies. With time running short, Scott again called upon Governor Shelby for help in raising troops; Shelby obliged by sending out circular letters to field officers and prominent gentlemen south of the Kentucky River, asking them to use every power of persuasion they had to spur enlistments. Scott also asked Wayne to call for a draft of the Kentucky militia; Wayne complied by writing to Governor Shelby, who on September 28 ordered a draft from the militia to fill up the Kentucky quota, promising the draftees they would be considered volunteers if they equipped themselves and joined the army at Fort Jefferson by October 15.[12]

Wayne's letter of September 26 to Scott, published in the *Kentucky Gazette* on October 5, helped further to stimulate public interest in the war effort. The challenge was not a "little predatory war, made by a few tribes of Indians," declared Wayne; "it is a confederated war, forming a chain of circumvallation round the frontiers of America," and "unless the fire Kindled at the *Miami of the Lake* [Maumee River] is extinquished by the blood of the *Hydra* (now a little way in our front) it will inevitably spread along the frontiers" from Pennsylvania to Georgia. "One united & Gallant effort of the Legion and mounted Volunteers will save the lives of many, very many thousands of helpless women & children." By this same letter Wayne ordered Scott to advance with all the men he had collected, leaving enough officers to bring forward the draftees.[13]

On September 29 Scott sent on 591 volunteers from George-town, and a week later he led another contingent across the Ohio. He briefly linked up with Wayne at Fort Hamilton on October 7. Wayne continued his march, while, for the time being, the Kentuckians stayed at the fort. On the seventeenth Gen. Thomas Barbee arrived at Fort Hamilton with nearly 400 men—350 short of his quota. The mounted volunteers now consisted of about 1,000 troops—500 less than full strength (a return of October 26 showed 1,013).[14] Obviously the draft, though two call-ups had been slated, had not really been put into effect.

Wayne established camp six miles beyond Fort Jefferson on October 13. Here he built a fifty-acre stockade along the east bank of the southwest branch of the Great Miami and named it Fort Greene Ville (at present Greenville, Ohio). Wayne ordered Scott to have the volunteers march to the "head of the Line" and directed him to repair to headquarters, accompanied by a twenty-five-man escort. Perhaps the volunteers would have the honor of the first offensive action against the Indians. "I have in contemplation," Wayne told Scott, "to give you an Opening to strike at the enemy at a point which will be communicated to you on your Arrival." The two brigades of volunteers were marched to Fort Jefferson. Little Turtle's Indians hovered around the marches of both the Legion and the volunteers. On October 17 a band of Indians surprised a baggage and provision convoy of ninety men, of whom thirteen were killed.[15]

After returning from his conference with Wayne, on October

23 Scott led the volunteers only two miles in advance of Fort Jefferson. He sent three companies to meet a convoy under Col. John Francis Hamtramck coming up from Fort Hamilton. Wayne wrote Scott on the twenty-fourth that he felt uneasy because Scott had remained so long in one place; the "Savages must have discovered your position, and may probably be tempted to make a push for your Horses." Wayne advised extreme caution in "crossing over the S. W. Prairie, however your Knowledge and experience will be your Best Monitor on the occasion." The same day the mounted volunteers reached to within a mile of Wayne's troops at Fort Greene Ville and encamped on the southwest branch of the Great Miami. From this "Island Camp," on October 28, Scott sent sixty-three volunteers to join eighty-four federal troops under Maj. William McMahon on a reconnaissance mission.[16]

Probably knowing quite well that Scott could not accept, Wayne proposed that the volunteers alone have the honor of attacking the principal Indian villages at the confluence of the Auglaize and Maumee Rivers (present-day Defiance, Ohio). Indeed Scott thought that "the enterprize to Auglaize" was "too hazardous, for the Volunteers in their present situation" for several reasons. He did not have enough men—deducting the sick, only 900 effectives. Because of lack of forage due to the cold season, he would be short of one-third of the horses. Scott also believed "that the whole combined force of the hostile Indians N. W. of Ohio are collected to watch the motions of your Army or assembled at Auglaize; in either case we shall be struck at powerfully." Furthermore, he had no guide familiar with the country to lead the troops other than by the "usual road."[17] This latter point seems a little odd, since Scott's volunteers included a company of scouts under the famed frontiersman Simon Kenton; but this western part of the Ohio country was still relatively unfamiliar to Kenton and others like him, whose past experiences with the Indians were more to the eastward. Also, evidently the day of the woodsman was passing, replaced by that of militia-farmers.

The Legion itself had supply and forage problems. The contractors, Robert Elliot and Eli Williams, had delivered only one-fourth of the required rations at Fort Jefferson. Scott, however, undoubtedly overestimated the Indian strength. In September the Indians had dispersed for the winter, and with the defection of the Chippewas, Ottawas, Potawatomies, and Mingoes from the hostile confederacy, the Indians probably could not have put more than 500 warriors in the field.[18]

Wayne answered Scott that "the proposed interprize against AuGlaize was an object that I had much at Heart however it may yet be affected in due Season by a *Detachment* from the Legion." Since a major operation by the volunteers was "out of the question," Wayne proposed, "as a Secondary object," that Scott's troops attack the hunting camps of the hostile Indians and a small Delaware village on the White River, forty to fifty miles southwest. This was "the quarter from which frequent predatory parties of Indians make inroads into the frontier Settlements of Kentucky; and plunder capture & Massacre the helpless Inhabitants with Impunity." This suggestion echoed Wayne's previous contemptuous remarks about the Kentucky volunteers—that this kind of operation was what the Kentuckians desired in the first place.

Wayne's chief scout, William Wells, would guide the volunteers to the hunting camps and to the Indian town. Wells certainly was qualified, though he, too, like Kenton, lacked recent and close familiarity with the Indiana country. Captured as a boy by the Miamis and adopted as a son by Little Turtle, whose daughter he married, Wells had returned to the white man's civilization; his brother was one of Scott's volunteers. Scott was to destroy the Indian camps and town and kill or capture all the hostile warriors whom he could find. Once this mission was accomplished, the volunteers would head for Fort Washington to be discharged. Should any of Scott's men desert or be absent without leave before the muster at Fort Washington, Scott was to strike their names off the rolls, whereby they would be deprived of pay. "With a full reliance upon your long tried fortitude, Judgment & experience," Wayne told Scott, "I have only to wish you compleat success and that you and your command may return to Kentucky crowned with Laurels."[19]

Early on Sunday, November 3, 989 volunteers began their

march. At nightfall, about half of the men (501 troops) suddenly decided to head for home by way of Fort Washington. The mission they had been sent on hardly seemed worth the trouble, especially with the continuing heavy rains, and the major offensive campaign had been abandoned for the season; the ultimate destination was Fort Washington, for discharge from the service, so the troops might as well go there directly. Wayne reported to the secretary of war that "this dereliction is by no means chargable to Genl Scott or any of his General or Field Officers—on the Contrary, I am well convinced that every exertion in their power was used to prevent it." The "dereliction" did not particularly bother Wayne, for he thought the remnant of Scott's force—488 men—was sufficient for their objective.[20]

The continuing rains prevented Scott from "chastising the enemy" as he wanted to do. His troops merely broke up a small Indian camp of five men, all of whom escaped. "They wear on a Stout branch of White river on the opposide from us it Being Very high & difficult to cross it gave the Scoundrels an oppertunity of gitting off with the loss of one horse, the property of Elliot & Williams [the contractors] a fiew Blankets . . . & Several little things. My Spies got but two Shoots at them a Cross the Creek." There were "a Number of paths but none this fall   my Guards knew nothing of the Country we wear in." Already having traveled fifty-two miles to the southwest, Scott and the volunteers headed for Fort Washington, where they arrived on November 10; the volunteers were mustered out the next day. By shortening the time in the field, Scott figured he had saved the government $3,000.[21]

The abortive Indian campaign of 1793 added fuel to the growing resentment in Kentucky toward giving the federal army the primary responsibility for subduing the Indians, with the Kentucky troops merely serving as an adjunct to the Legion and taking orders from its commander. Moreover, sides were being taken according to the emerging national division in politics—Federalist versus Democratic-Republican. Criticism of the use of federal troops in the Indian country provided a means to attack the Washington administration, purportedly dominated by Alexander Hamilton. The existence of the Legion itself violated the tradition against standing armies. The ill success thus far of the federal army underscored not only the incompetence of the administration but also the waste of expenditures. Opposition rhetoric appealed to the ideals of the Revolution and the preservation of states' rights. To the Democratic-Republicans, the militia was the least expensive and most effective way to deal with the Indian situation. Democratic-Republican societies were being formed throughout Kentucky. Also among westerners, the national government had not been forgiven for not securing the opening of Mississippi navigation, and some Kentuckians, such as George Rogers Clark and Benjamin Logan, were willing to join a French-sponsored expedition to seize Spanish Louisiana without any sanction from the United States government.[22] Adding to distrust of federal power was the hated excise tax on whiskey (at least one distillery in Scott's neighborhood closed its doors), and there were rumors that a federal force might be used to quell insurgency against the tax in western Pennsylvania.

Given the resentment among some Kentuckians toward the use of a federal army instead of militia exclusively in bringing the northwest Indians to terms, possibly Scott could be made a scapegoat as collaborator with federal military authorities as well as an inadequate military leader. As it was, Scott almost had to contend with a legislative inquiry of his conduct. He wrote Wayne on December 17 that he had heard that he would be asked by the legislature to account for "my conduct whilst commander of the Volunteers under your Order. What use they intend to make of it I dont know." Although he heard more rumors of the same nature, Scott refused to step forward to report to the legislature and was not required to do so. He expressed his dislike for some reports in the newspapers critical of Wayne and the federal government.[23] Public opinion, however, would soon shift more favorably toward Wayne and the federal army in Ohio—and hence also toward Scott.

While the Kentucky troops were at home, Wayne built Fort Recovery, twenty miles above Fort Greene Ville upon the site of St. Clair's Indian defeat. Six hundred skulls of the American dead, which had been dug up and strewn about by the Indians, were reinterred. Not only was it sensible strategically to have a strong fort deeper into the Indian country, but the building of Fort Recovery had symbolic and emotional impact. To the Indians the battle site had become sacred ground. The battle had inspired them to persist in making a stand against the white man, and its memory was celebrated in Indian lore and dance. Now both sacred ground and pride were desecrated—a blow to Indian morale. To the Kentuckians, Fort Recovery was also symbolic. Not only did it show the determination of Anthony Wayne, but it also conferred honor on the fallen heroes, many of whom were Kentuckians. Wayne sent an extract of the general orders governing the dedication ceremony at Fort Recovery to Scott—"every Sentance in which," Scott wrote Wayne on January 25, 1794, "gave me great pleasure, as also Your friends in this Country."[24] General Wayne gained respect in Kentucky.

During early 1794 Scott anxiously looked forward to the next campaign into the Indian country. He again published extracts of Wayne's general orders in the newspapers, saying that he himself could not forget "the insolent Savages who has Spilt the Blood of my self & country in Various places with impunity." Not that Scott regarded the Indian war as one of personal vengeance, but he did have a score to settle over the killing of two of his sons. At age fifty-five, he realized that what should be the last Indian campaign in the Ohio country would also be his last military service in the field. "The hand of time is on me," he told Wayne, "before the Wheel turns again I may be off." He was anxious, therefore, to be in the next expedition and was already making tentative plans to put the Kentucky volunteers in the field by June 1.[25]

Yet Scott had to face some discontent over his leadership. "Both Officers & privates are giting very Clamerous about their pay," he wrote Wayne in early January, and "begin in Plain Language to Charge me with neglect in this Business." After much prompting by Scott, including sending his paymaster to Wayne's headquarters to straighten out the muster rolls, the War Department released $41,200 to the volunteers in January. Still, some of the pay had been withheld. The War Department had not received the final muster rolls; and this was complicated by the fact that one-half of Scott's troops had gone home before they should have. Wayne had recommended forfeiture of pay for the some ninety volunteers who had missed the muster at Fort Washington. Scott was planning a trip to Virginia and decided that he might as well visit Philadelphia to help straighten out the matter of pay and also to confer with the secretary of war on arrangements for getting the volunteers into the Indian campaign.[26]

Scott did not stay long in Virginia—if he went there at all. While in Philadelphia (where he lodged at the Conestoga Wagon Tavern) from April 10 to about May 18, he spent much time at the War Department, which then consisted of a single office for the secretary of war and one or two clerks. Secretary of War Knox wanted to learn all the firsthand information he could about military affairs in the west. President Washington was also curious and met with Scott three times—their first visit in sixteen years.[27] Secretary of War Knox's final determination on the pay question is not known—whether or not all were paid.

Reports critical of Wayne's leadership circulated in Philadelphia. A rumor that the Legion commander had denigrated the volunteers in a letter to Knox also greatly disturbed Scott. Nevertheless, he went to Wayne's defense at the war office. He emphasized that when he visited Wayne in June 1792 Wayne was of "great sobriety" and gave his full attention to the affairs of the army, as he had when Scott was with him in the field. Scott, however, did admit that he found some discontent in the army; "whether it was owing to the Change of Discipline, the Difference between Garrison & Field the Hardness of the Duty or his Unequivocal orders inforsed, I cannot say." As far as he was able to judge, "taking every Difficulty into view the army was conducted with great propriety, never loosing sight of the public good or the honor of the arms of the United States." Scott told Knox that he believed there was not an officer who served with him under Wayne's command but would gladly serve Wayne again.[28]

Most complaints against Wayne originated with James Wilkinson, who, as soon as he became brigadier general in the Legion, began to bother Knox with alternative policies and strategy. Wilkinson wanted an independent command at Fort Washington. Increasingly Wilkinson's hatred of Wayne became venomous and public. He prepared charges, alleging fraud and financial malfeasance, to be presented to the Senate. Wilkinson carried with him some officers, thus splitting the officer corps and threatening the effectiveness of the Legion. Wilkinson's vendetta against Wayne would also include Scott. But there was no doubt as to where Secretary Knox stood; Knox kept Wayne informed of all the charges and told him that he would protect him from all misrepresentation. Wayne could also expect, the secretary of war pointed out, "cordial co-operation" from Scott.[29]

While in Philadelphia, Scott secured from Knox an endorsement of his command, as major general, of the volunteers and a lengthy set of instructions, which President Washington approved. Scott was authorized to raise 2,000 volunteers (if Wayne by his instructions from the War Department of March 31 had already called for volunteers, then that number should be deducted from the total). The Kentucky troops were to be engaged for four months (unless dismissed sooner); the two regiments of each brigade were to be converted into three battalions each, and each battalion was to consist of four companies (eighty-three noncommissioned officers and privates each)—therefore twenty-four companies in all. Furthermore, Knox's instructions required that Scott, Governor Shelby, and militia brigadier generals Robert Todd and Thomas Barbee form a board of war for appointing all field and company officers and determining the rendezvous.[30]

Before leaving Philadelphia, Scott wound up some personal business involving Edward Carrington's accounts. Returning home by way of Pittsburgh and down the Ohio, Scott was accompanied by a newly appointed Legion officer, Ens. Thomas Bodley, whom Knox had ordered to assist him with recruiting in Kentucky. Scott and Bodley arrived at Fort Washington on June 5. Scott sent a copy of his instructions from Knox and other dispatches to Wayne; the pay for the Legion, which he had brought from Philadelphia, he turned over to Maj. William Price.[31]

When he arrived at Lexington, Scott learned that Wayne had

already issued a call for 1,000 volunteers for thirty days and that these should be considered part of the 2,000 "contemplated" in Knox's instructions to Scott. Wayne directed Scott to complete raising the full quota. The Kentucky military board, meeting on June 23, appointed officers and set the rendezvous for the volunteers for July 10 and 14. Scott had a handbill published, citing a British-Indian conspiracy, and he noted that it stimulated recruiting.[32]

Meanwhile, General Wilkinson, always a conniver, asked Wayne if the impending entry into service of Scott and the volunteers meant that Scott, and not Wilkinson, would succeed Wayne should he become disabled. Wayne simply replied that Scott, as the senior general, would probably insist upon his right to command while the Kentucky volunteers were operating in the field with the Legion. Wilkinson also heard from Knox that he should minimize any personal animosity toward Wayne and Scott.[33]

A military offensive could not begin too soon. On May 13, 1794, the Indians attacked an escort to a supply train, killing five of the six of the advance guard. On June 30 over 1,600 Indians, led by the Shawnee chief, Blue Jacket (Little Turtle had been deposed as war chief), attacked a supply convoy of 140 men just outside Fort Recovery. A large number of Canadians, costumed as Indians, and three high-ranking British officers, in full uniform, watched the action at a short distance. Nineteen Americans, including the convoy's commander, Maj. William McMahon, were killed, and nineteen wounded. The Indians attempted several times to storm the fort but were repulsed. Running out of food, the next day they withdrew. At the attack, it was estimated there were 160 each of Shawnee and Delawares, 130 Wyandots, 100 Iroquois, 40 Potawatomies, 170 Tawas (Shawnee), 700 Chippewas, 78 Miamis, and 86 Eel River Indians; and another 650 Indians came up afterward.[34] This was the largest gathering of Indians since St. Clair's defeat. The battle of Fort Recovery—the failure of an immensely superior number of Indians to reclaim St. Clair's battlefield—proved to be a tremendous blow to the hostile Indian confederacy, much more so than the subsequent brief encounter at Fallen Timbers.

At Georgetown, between July 10 and 16, Scott mustered 1,594 volunteers—each man dressed in a hunting shirt and leggins and carrying a rifle, tomahawk, knife, pouch, and powder horn. On the twelfth, 760 troops from the north side of the Kentucky River—under majors William Price, William Russell, and Notley Conn—marched for Fort Washington. Scott, with several of his staff (Maj. Cornelius Beatty, quartermaster general; Samuel Postlethwait, aide-de-camp; and Ens. Thomas Bodley) set out with the southside troops on July 17. Wayne urged Scott to get the volunteers as quickly as possible to Fort Greene Ville. Although Scott was pleased with the turnout of the volunteers, he was disappointed that he had not collected the complete quota of 2,000. "My enemys as also Yours [Logan and his supporters]," he wrote Wayne, have "thrown every possible Difficulty in my way."[35]

Making camp for a few days near Fort Washington, the volunteers did not favorably impress some of the regulars at the garrison. Col. Winthrop Sargent, who was also secretary of the Western Territory, commented that the volunteers were "riotous and disorderly while in this town and seem not to be capable of fulfilling public expectations." Scott told Sargent that the volunteers were "damned fighting Fellows" and "the best Party that ever came out of Kentucky." Sargent did not agree, observing that most of the volunteers seemed to be either boys or old men. In reporting his visit with Scott to the secretary of war, Sargent said he and Scott both acknowledged the "Want of Harmony between Wilkinson and Wayne," and he added that Wilkinson spoke of Scott "in Terms dishonorable" and considered Scott a "habitual Drunkard." On this point, Sargent said that he himself had good reason "from the Information of very respectable persons at the different Settlements upon the Ohio" where Scott had stopped on his way down from Philadelphia to believe that Scott too often drank to excess, "though it is but Justice to observe that when he assisted me yesterday morning [July 22] he was perfectly sober and collected." From Fort Washington, Scott reported to the secretary of war that although he was disappointed in not raising the full quota of volunteers, the quality would compensate for the deficiency. Furthermore, "there is the highest possible harmony between my Corps and the heads of departments, of the Federal Army—Strike out one person [Wilkinson] and all would go well."[36]

With supplies arriving, including whiskey, the volunteers marched out of their camp near Fort Washington on July 22 and 23. Scott, under escort, rode on ahead in order to confer with Wayne at Fort Greene Ville about the disposition of the volunteers. The volunteers encamped two miles east of Fort Greene Ville on the twenty-fifth. Two days later they paraded through the fort on their way to take up a position a mile north. The Kentuckians, in woods attire and riding leisurely or walking their horses, made a sharp contrast with the regular troops, immaculately uniformed in blue coats (trimmed with the color representing their sublegion) and white-plumed and black-horsehair-tufted hats.[37]

Shortly after dawn on July 28 a signal gun was fired from the fort, and the march to the upper Indian country began.[38] The volunteers served as covering support for the Legion: Todd's brigade on the left flank and Barbee's in the rear. At the head of the Legion was a battalion of volunteers commanded by Maj. William Price: 200 yards farther ahead were the scouts.

Reaching the St. Mary's River on August 1, the army paused to build Fort Adams, a small stockade with two blockhouses. While the troops worked on the fort, a large tree was felled near where Wayne was standing, and he was severely injured by some of the branches. He was already suffering terribly from gout. After the accident Wayne was not the same, supposedly often "deranged & incoherent," and had to be lifted on and off his horse.[39] Wilkinson now assumed most of the regular field duties of the commander in chief.

The army reached the confluence of the Auglaize and Maumee rivers on August 8. The Indians had abandoned their populous settlements in the area. Here Wayne built a log house, surrounded by pickets, and named it Fort Defiance. Moving down the Maumee, the army on the eighteenth reached Roche de Bout, a small craggy island. Six miles down the river was the British Fort Miamis. Wayne sent several flags to the enemy, asking the Indians to come to peace terms, insisting, however, that the American force should have freedom of mobility in the area. The chiefs replied that several days were needed in order to hold a council. The Indians began a fast, as was customary before battle, and prepared to ambush the American force, about three miles up the river from the British fort—using the fallen trees amid the thick brush as barricades. At Wayne's encampment overlooking the rapids of the Maumee, Fort Deposit was built for storing the baggage.

Wayne met with Scott, Wilkinson, Colonel Hamtramck, and several other officers on the eighteenth. Wilkinson proposed a plan of attack, which would include sending Scott and about 500 volunteers to the front to force the Indians into battle. One officer at the session, whose identity is unknown, recorded that "some fears were started by Genl Scott about bringing a general Engagement—the C. in C told him with an heavy Oath, that he did not understand him! that this should not be by God! . . . he wanted to know the nature of the intermediate ground, and the position of the enemy—things were repeated 20 times," and Colonel Hamtramck "when they left the tent swore '*the Old Man* [Wayne] was mad!'"

Maj. William Price and 100 select Kentucky mounted volunteers reconnoitered down the river and discovered where a large body of Indians had been. On the nineteenth Wayne prepared to engage the enemy. The Indians, now compelled to give up their fast, sent out parties in search of food; their fighting strength had been reduced from 1,300 to 800. Wayne's army— the Legion and the Kentucky volunteers—numbered 3,800; the rest of the Legion manned the forts that had been established.

At 7 A.M. on August 20 the army left Fort Deposit and marched down the Maumee. Of the Kentuckians, Price's "Corps of Observation" went on ahead; Todd's brigade held the left flank; and Barbee (with Scott) was in the rear. Wayne ordered Scott when the fighting began "to gain and turn the right flank of the savages with the whole of the mounted volunteers."[40] At 8:45 A.M. Price and his volunteers reached the area "of fallen Timber and thick brush with Hoop and black Ash bushes which rendered the place difficult to see a Man 10 yds." Shots rang out from the thicket, and the Indians rushed out from their concealed positions. Price's volunteers had time to get off only a quick volley and hastily retreated the half mile back to Wayne's army. Wilkinson's and Hamtramck's regulars charged with fixed bayonets and then fell back. The Legion dragoons, aided eventually by some of the mounted volunteers, rode into the woods—the dragoons swinging their swords and the volunteers firing their rifles. Scott and the main body of the volunteers took a circuitous route to the left in order to catch the enemy in the rear. The dense brush and trees made riding difficult. Scott had Todd's brigade dismount, while the other volunteers attempted to skirt the woods farther to the left. The enemy, however, had no heart for battle and after the initial engagement retreated about a mile. The whole American force halted and, except for few of the dragoons, did not pursue the enemy. Commented one soldier: "This looks more like unto a drawn battle than a victory." Actually only about 900 of the American force participated in the action, 300 of whom were the Kentucky volunteers, chiefly Price's men and those volunteers who got a shot at the Indians in the woods.

The American troops remained stationary for several hours and then moved to a mile of the British fort. During the action that never quite became a battle, the Americans lost about 30 killed and 100 wounded—a dozen of the casualties from among the volunteers; the Indians lost 30 to 40 killed. Scott apparently, as with the federal officers, did not have the benefit of a definite battle plan. One officer (pro-Wilkinson) pointed out that Wayne's lack of a battle plan could have resulted in disaster: had the enemy advanced in tight formation, close upon Price's retreating scouting party, the extended American front line would have been breached. The battle could have become an indisputable victory, also observed the officer, if the Kentucky volunteers had gained the rear of the enemy soon after the Indians began the attack; then "we should had the pleasure of seeing every Head of this dreaded *Hydra* at our feet."

The British commander of Fort Miamis, Maj. William Campbell, refused to open the gate of the garrison to the Indians or to offer them other protection. Wayne and Campbell exchanged demands that each withdraw from the area; the British force

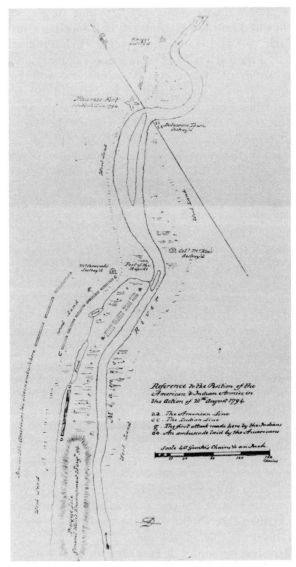

"Reference to the Position of the American & Indian Armies, in the action of 20th August 1794." (Original in the Public Record Office, London, MPG469).

was too small to take any action, and neither side wanted the responsibility for starting a war. Wayne systematically razed all the storehouses, homes, gardens, and cornfields in the vicinity, within one hundred yards of the fort. Some of the volunteers were sent eight miles below the fort, destroying all British and Indian property in sight. The main army, meanwhile, returned to Fort Deposit, and on August 24 headed back to Fort Defiance, arriving the twenty-seventh.

After the battle of Fallen Timbers, the volunteers had special duty assignments. General Todd and 400 of the volunteers from August 29 to September 10 were on a mission to bring supplies from Fort Recovery. Barbee's brigade had the same duty on September 11–20. Because of a shortage of packhorses, the volunteers had to use their own horses, which, they claimed, were injured by having the 100-pound kegs of flour strapped to their sides, without saddles.

The army moved to the Miami villages up the Maumee, at the junction of the St. Mary's and St. Joseph's rivers, on September 17, and Wayne began the construction of Fort Wayne. Scott had his hands full with the morale problems of the volunteers. With the prospect of fighting over, they did not take to garrison duty. The volunteers complained of the food. The flour that Barbee brought up was musty from the heavy rains. There was a scarcity of salt, and many horses died eating only the lush bluegrass. Whiskey had run out, and all that was available was sold for $8.00 a gallon by visiting sutlers. For a while there was a shortage of beef. The volunteers also complained of the too frequent fatigue assignments, particularly in working on the forts.

Discipline was more lax among the volunteers than among the harshly trained Legion. One time the army was alarmed by the firing of rifles in the volunteer camp—actually Scott's men were only "cleaning" their weapons. As much as possible, Scott avoided meting out severe punishment. Once he remanded a sentence of corporal punishment, being "extremely distressed to see a Volunteer receive Corporal punishment particularly those under good Character." Scott did have a major arrested for insubordination, and several others for abandoning their posts. The appearance of a new chaplain for the Legion, David

Jones, at the end of September attracted some of the volunteers to religious services in the Legion camp. Overall, Scott had the respect of his men, as much as anyone could have with the kind of troops he had, notwithstanding Wilkinson's comment: "The worthless Old scoundrel Scott has become an object of pity. He is the contempt of the whole army, except his Brother Regular and Irregular."[41]

One last convoy assignment for the Kentuckians nearly resulted in mutiny. On October 1 an order for General Barbee's brigade to bring up supplies from Fort Recovery led to protest among both officers and men, and a cry around the camp went up—"home home!" The next day petitions were submitted, pointing out that the volunteers of Barbee's brigade had already carried flour from Fort Recovery and that they had been promised by their officers that they would be discharged. Scott called several of the officers together and told them to tell the men that the Legion was busy erecting the fort, the volunteers' terms of service had not yet expired, and he expected them to perform their duty. If there was the slightest delay in getting the convoy train started, Scott said, the delinquents would lose their pay and be reported to the war office as "revolters." About 8 P.M. "a great nois and Quarreling" sounded among the troops of Barbee's brigade. Whiskey was passed out to the discontented troops, and many got drunk. Scott had his aide, Samuel Postlethwait, make the rounds and take the names of those who would not go on the mission. Some of the volunteers thought this was a trick of some sort and refused to identify themselves. At 1 A.M. Wayne visited the troops and assured them that they would be discharged after obtaining the supplies; this had the effect of quieting the protest. The mission accomplished, Wayne on October 13 notified Scott that the mounted volunteers could now go home. They would be mustered out at Fort Washington by Capt. Edward Butler, who would accompany them.[42]

Scott and the volunteers left Fort Wayne on October 14 and arrived at Fort Washington a week later. At the "critical" muster at Fort Washington, on which pay was to be based, the major problem was whether or not the Kentuckians would be paid for horses they themselves disposed of. Wayne had said no if the horses had been sold, but Scott managed to have consideration given for those volunteers who had to sell their horses because the animals were injured or sick. One soldier was smart; he sold his horse to Postlethwait, but the latter could not claim it until he got to Lexington—hence it could be counted for pay purposes. Unfortunately, pay to the volunteers was delayed because of the danger of sending it from Philadelphia through western Pennsylvania for fear of the whiskey insurgents.[43]

Scott received plaudits for his part in the campaign of 1794 from Kentucky and the nation. The House of Representatives passed a resolution thanking him and Wayne and the Legion and volunteers in general.[44] The battle of Fallen Timbers, as time passed, would increasingly be regarded as a great victory; in reality, it was hardly even a battle, but the campaign had succeeded in its purpose of breaking the power of the northern Indian confederacy. In the minds of many, it vindicated the federal government's resort to arms. More importantly, the Indian campaign of 1794 demonstrated the ability of the new government under the Constitution to defend the nation's borders and overall to employ coercive force.

While Scott's military image and popularity had improved, the same could not be said for his rival and competitor, Gen. Benjamin Logan. A Mississippi expedition against the Spaniards that Logan had labored for came to naught as a result of both the collapse of the Genet mission, to which the planned military action was connected, and a presidential proclamation ordering Kentuckians to cease and desist in preparations for the expedition. In the late summer of 1794 about 100 Kentucky volunteers had invaded the towns of the Chickamauga (band of the Cherokees) Indians and killed and scalped many Indians. Logan, considering that this was not enough punishment, sought to raise an expedition against the Chickamaugas in October 1794, but the stubborn actions of the governor of the Southwest Territory (Tennessee), William Blount, thwarted this attempt.[45] Logan retained a political following and was almost elected governor by the state's electoral college in 1796, but it was Scott who had the military laurels.

The northwest Indians buried the hatchet. In January and

February 1795 all the hostile tribes, including the Shawnee under the infamous Blue Jacket who were the last holdouts, sued for peace. Wayne issued a proclamation forbidding anyone to enter the Indian country with hostile intentions and also from "killing insulting or injuring" any Indians belonging to the Wyandot, Chippewa, Potawatomi, Miami, Shawnee, or Delaware tribes. Although the British made some effort to keep alive an Indian confederacy, the Indians were demoralized and disorganized.[46] Jay's Treaty (although not taking effect until the summer of 1796) forced the evacuation of Fort Miamis as well as two other British-held forts in American territory, Detroit and Michilimackinac. Concluding negotiations with the Indians took a while, but finally, on August 3, 1795, the Treaty of Greene Ville was signed.

Meanwhile, in the spring of 1795, Scott made another trip to Philadelphia, chiefly to sort out the records so that the volunteers would get their final pay. He also was concerned about the wild charges against Wayne and himself that Wilkinson was hurling about more recklessly than before. He also held the faint hope that the secretary of war might give him a role in the final peace-making ceremonies with the Indians, along with Wayne. Scott, however, found he was rather coolly received by the new secretary of war, Timothy Pickering, who was more officious and diplomatic than his predecessor, Knox, who had usually seen things militarily, the same way Scott did. Scott complained of the "perplexity" and "the tedious delay in the business of paying the men." After "much reasoning Rehearing & reconsidering," however, Scott got the pay settled to his satisfaction, except for an extra 25 cents a day for Major Price's "Corps of Guards & Spies," since Congress had not provided for extra-duty pay. Price's men had performed most of the hazardous duty during the 1794 campaign. Since even a small bonus could not be allowed by law, Scott petitioned Congress to vote the compensation, and he asked Wayne for his support.[47]

Although Scott was unable to obtain any particular information at the War Department pertaining to Wilkinson's and others' criticisms of the Indian campaign, he was assured that any such complaints were not taken seriously. As he wrote Wayne:

"the report had not the Smallest weight with the principle Characters & Wheels of Government—a proof of this is Your Standing Solas" in the pending treaty with the Indians, "a Circumstance that has given me great Pleasure." Furthermore, "the reports respecting myself is treated With Silant contempt to the great Mortification of our enemys." Scott could hardly hide his disappointment in not being able to join Wayne for the treaty making, but he realized that his presence would have been irregular.[48]

Scott stayed in Philadelphia from April through July. On his return down the Ohio, with Lt. Ebenezer Denny as his pilot, Scott debarked at Limestone, where he wrote Wayne on August 5 that he expected soon to pay him a visit. Wayne, too, was eager to see Scott and assured him of the "most Sincere Welcome & of the best entertainment that Head Quarters can afford not only for yourself but such of your friends as may want to accompany you." Scott was delighted and wrote on the fourteenth that he would make the journey with several of his friends. But Scott never made the visit to Wayne. He postponed the trip to November, which date he was also unable to keep.[49] In December, Wayne was off for a six-month triumphal return to Philadelphia; six months later he was dead. Charles Scott had bid farewell to arms—if not to war.

"On the Soldier's Brow, a Civic Garland"

Charles Scott's last years coincided with the quickening rise of nationalist sentiment in America. The Jefferson victory, the "Revolution of 1800," signaled a new political unity and a rededication to the principles of the Revolutionaries of 1776. As the new generation cast about for American identity, it was recognized that an American national consciousness had begun with the assertion of freedom against tyranny and that the shared experiences, through the force of arms, in the defense of independence had given meaning to the American national character. In the quest for national identity, Americans had to go back no further than the American Revolution. To the "first celebrators of nationality," writes a modern-day historian, the "memory of military conflict held a central place in their efforts. And it founded America not just on principles but also on the passions of bloodshed."[1] Furthermore, as Americans justified the nation's past by the deeds of its heroes, so did the old Revolutionaries loom larger than life; Scott, among his fellow Kentuckians, would emerge as a quintessential hero and patriot, irrevocably identified with America's own birthright as a nation.

During the early years of the Republic, successive crises regularly stimulated patriotic and military fervor, recalling the original commitment to defend American freedom by force of arms: the Indian campaigns of the 1790s; the near war with France, 1798–99; potential slave rebellion; possible war with Spain over Louisiana in 1803; the Tripolitan War, 1801–5; and the confrontations with Great Britain over American maritime rights, leading up to the War of 1812. A new generation of young men, remembering the war experiences of their fathers, were equally desirous of proving themselves and of vindicating American honor in arms; they would carry on where their fathers had left off. While the new America sought to define its identity, the "Spirit of '76," out of the immediate past, became America's heritage and the summons to defend its freedom and independence.

Meanwhile, it seemed in the mid-1790s that Charles Scott, the old soldier, would fade away. There was no longer excitement and adventure: the challenges of settling the frontier and fighting in the Indian wars had ended. Scott even lost interest in his mundane ventures—farming and commerce. The county court had to keep after him to keep up the maintenance of his tobacco warehouse, one of forty-two in the state. In 1796 Scott was ordered to "repair & make Close" the warehouse and secure it with "Strong Doors hung with Iron hinges and with Strong Locks or bolts." He eventually made the repairs but was negligent in obtaining the hinges, which the court in 1800 noted were still lacking. Yet the warehouse still had limited use; for example, in 1799, 204 hogsheads of tobacco were inspected at the site.[2] Scott, however, realized only a small profit from the brief storage of the tobacco.

Scott's life was saddened by the loss of his two remaining sons. Daniel, who had settled in Virginia after going there to straighten out his father's finances, died in 1797. In a letter to Daniel's widow, Patty Mosby Scott, on December 14, 1797, Scott asked that she send him all of his papers that were "in the possession of My poor Danl. at his death"; even though these might appear to be "only Small Shop notes," they were necessary to settle some of his affairs. Scott told Patty that his wife, "the old Ladie," desired him "to offer You her unfeigned Esteam & Reguard as dose also the little twinn Nancy, the rest of our Family is not at home—all is well." Charles Scott, Jr., married Frances Cook (daughter of John Cook) on February 23, 1795, and, at last, moved off his father's farm to Fayette County; in late 1799 or early 1800 he also died.[3]

Helping to distract from the family bereavement, social and public affairs held interest for Scott. He frequently visited with old comrades in Lexington and Frankfort. In Lexington, the state's center for commercial and political activity, there was always a warm welcome at the prestigious tavern on the corner of Market and Mulberry (Limestone), which his son-in-law John Postlethwait operated from 1797 to 1804 and again later. Until 1799 Scott continued to serve nominally as major general of the Second Division of militia.[4] He declared himself a Jeffersonian Republican, which, of course, was a safe decision, for the Republicans were in the great majority in Kentucky. From later indication, it seems that he spoke out against the Alien and Sedition Acts. Scott, however, did not take an active role in opposing these "gag" laws—the questions of civil liberty and states' rights were better left to the lawyers and legislators. In 1799 Kentucky adopted a new constitution taking effect June 1, 1800, which provided for popular election of the governor (James Garrard was reelected in 1800) and presidential electors. Scott stood as a candidate for elector in 1800, pledging himself "to vote for a republican President." In his district he defeated Caleb Wallace of Versailles by a vote of 75 to 44. The four electors from the total northern district met on Wednesday, December 3, at Frankfort and cast all their votes for Jefferson and Burr.[5]

Independence Day became increasingly popular in Kentucky. Military parades and barbecues were held throughout the state, and the eloquence of politicians enchanted the masses—indeed the Fourth of July was not only the nation's jubilee but also the state's "political sabbath." The numerous toasts exhibited a consensus on the national issues and gauged the popularity of leading citizens. Frequently the toasts called for a fortitude embodying the "Spirit of '76" as a means of preserving America's freedoms and guarding against transgressions on American sovereignty. Such patriotic festivities—with Scott and other Revolutionaries (mostly deceased) being the subjects of many of the toasts—gave Scott high visibility as the old military hero.

In 1803 it looked as if the military spirit might be tested. The Spanish government protested the American acquisition of

Louisiana on the grounds that it violated the French pledge not to turn the territory over to a third power, a promise made when Louisiana was retroceded to France. The transfer of the territory had not yet been accomplished, and it seemed that Spain would refuse to give up Louisiana; moreover, the right of deposit for American goods at New Orleans had been withdrawn in 1802. A Kentucky Revolutionary War veteran, Francis Preston, wrote in November 1803 that there was "nothing now in the mouths" of Kentuckians except talk of war. The president of the United States called upon the Kentucky governor to have 4,000 volunteers ready to march into Louisiana; eight regiments were raised in the state.[6] At the time, at age sixty-four, Scott did not seek a military command. But if a real crisis had developed, he undoubtedly would have offered his services.

Yet Scott did manage to be involved limitedly in military affairs. In 1803 he received a special assignment from the secretary of war. Congress had passed a law for the establishment of a new fort (to replace Fort Washington in Cincinnati) somewhere between Maysville and Louisville on the Ohio. Secretary of War Henry Dearborn requested Scott and Governor Garrard to examine different locations and submit their opinions. James Taylor, the leading proprietor of Newport, Kentucky, offered five or six acres at the town (for which he expected land in Cincinnati in exchange). Garrard and some Frankfort residents, however, insisted that the fort be located at Frankfort. At a large barbecue in Frankfort, an address was drawn up in favor of this site and presented to Garrard and Scott. Scott, who thought a federal post should not be situated in the interior of the state and that the hilly terrain around Frankfort was unsuitable, refused to attend the barbecue. He sought a conference with Governor Garrard but could not find him. He asked his son-in-law George M. Bibb, a prominent Lexington lawyer, to meet with Garrard. After waiting several days for an appointment, Bibb gave up. Scott, therefore, took the assignment solely on himself, which Secretary of War Dearborn approved. Scott decided upon Newport and selected the sites for the arsenal, powder magazine, and barracks; on behalf of the federal government he executed a deed from the trustees of Newport for the land offered by Taylor for the price of one dollar. Scott spent fifty-two days at this work, charging the War Department six dollars per day for his expenses and those of several others who assisted him.[7]

Scott occasionally inspected the progress in the construction of the new federal post, which was finally completed in 1807. James Taylor recalled later that Scott, when he stayed with him in Newport in 1805, "was of middle size and well proportion," with "dark hair Hazle eyes, black beard, fine high forehead . . . a very handsome man, remarkably neat in his dress, a very pleasant companion, & gave great interest to every thing."[8]

In the summer of 1804 Scott feared that Kentucky might have an insurrection of slaves. The successful slave uprising in Santo Domingo could prove contagious, and already there was a restlessness among blacks in the state. Capt. Thomas Eastland of Woodford County raised a troop of horse, which he told Scott was in readiness to march anywhere in the state upon an emergency. Scott requested the War Department to supply the side arms of the company, for which the men would give security. "I can assure you," Scott told Secretary of War Dearborn, "that ther is Strong reasons to believe that we Shall have Some trouble ere long with the Blacks, Since the fate of Sendingo they have given themselves Extraordinary airs and some whites among us are not too good to Join them."[9]

Relative harmony and prosperity marked the election year of 1804. Christopher Greenup, as a Jeffersonian Republican, won the governorship unopposed. Scott again stood as a candidate for presidential elector for the northern district. "Gen. Scott is so well known," said one writer in the *Kentucky Gazette* on May 8, 1804, that "no illustration of his abilities will be expected; but let it suffice that he is an old patriot, worn out in the use and service of his country and a tried republican." Scott sought to familiarize himself more with the electorate. On May 12 a number of gentlemen dined at Scott's farm; the toasts included: "Maj. Gen. Scott—May his past services be gratefully remembered by the present and future generations, for centuries to come." Scott probably joined a large number of people, also in May, at an "American Jubilee" at nearby Great Crossing in Scott County, held to commemorate the acquisition of Louisiana. Toasts were drunk and cannon fired; "every countenance beamed benevolence and patriotism—every eye seemed to flash the electric spark of '76." In November, Scott, virtually unopposed, won the election as a presidential elector.[10]

Casting a grim shadow over the year for Scott, however, was the death of his wife on Saturday, October 6, 1804. "This amiable woman," said the *Kentucky Gazette*, "has left a great number of respectable connections and friends to mourn her loss. In all the relations of wife and mother she was distinguished by the kindest manners, and most endearing deportment—In that of a neighbor, great benevolence of disposition marked her conduct through life."[11]

By a will of July 11, 1804, made primarily to dispose her slaves, "being the same which were in the said Indenture [prenuptial agreement, 1762] and their Increase," Frances ("Frankey") gave her husband "the use and loan" of slaves Joe, Scipio, Sarah, and Ned "during his Natural life." Twenty more slaves were left to three daughters—Martha, Polly (Mary), and Nancy. A male slave was given to the children of deceased son Charles, Jr., and was to be hired out, with the proceeds to be applied to their support. A black child "to be Taken from among the descendants of my Slaves, Nanny, Silvia and Sall," who had been left with Littlebury Mosby in Virginia, each was to be given to granddaughters Betsy Trueheart (daughter of Littlebury Mosby, Jr., and Eliza Scott Mosby) and Judith S. Scott (presumably daughter of son Daniel). All three daughters would have an equal share in ownership of Nanny, Silvia, and Sall. Mary Ratliff and Polly Ware (both illiterate), along with Sally H. Mosby and Fanny Mosby, witnessed the will. Charles Raily and George Brooke were named executors.[12]

With Frankey gone, Scott was now all alone. All four sons had died. Martha had married George M. Bibb on May 19, 1799. Bibb would have a distinguished career as jurist, U.S. senator (1811–1814), and, briefly, secretary of treasury under President Tyler. The Bibbs settled at Cornland in Daviess County and had eleven children. Martha died on April 12, 1829; Bibb subsequently remarried. Nancy Scott, who soon left the homestead and who apparently never married, also died in 1829.[13] Polly (Mary) was married to John Postlethwait.

After his wife's death, Scott most likely moved in with the Postlethwaits in Lexington. James Taylor commented that Scott in 1805 did not keep house. Scott's farm had become attached by a suit brought against him by Jack Jouett, as assignee of Daniel Weisiger. John Postlethwait and his brother, Samuel Postlethwait, bought the farm at a sheriff's auction in 1802 for £162.3.2. Scott stayed on the farm until his wife's death, and then, from October 1804 to February 1805, he advertised it in the *Kentucky Gazette* for sale or lease. The land was estimated at 256 acres (although the deed says 270 acres, more or less), 80 to 100 acres of which was cleared. In addition to the house, there were an "excellent pasture" near a "very fine range," outhouses, a spring, springhouse, garden, a variety of fruit trees, a ferry, warehouse, "and two other houses and out-tillages, capable of accommodating families." Prospective buyers could apply to Scott on the premises or to John Postlethwait in Lexington. George Yellot, who had just arrived from Maryland with his family, purchased the farm from Postlethwait in October 1805 for $2,000.[14]

While adjusting to changes in his personal life, Scott was gratified at the public recognition he was receiving as an old hero. The various patriotic festivities of 1805 and 1806 extolled his name. At a barbecue in June 1805 at Cave Run, four miles from Lexington, two of the toasts were "The Spirit of '76" and "Gen. Charles Scott." A month later Scott attended a large Fourth of July celebration in Lexington and was among those reviewing the military companies. The gathering, as was customary, moved to Maxwell's Spring for dinner and was treated to the oratory of Jesse Bledsoe and Henry Clay. Scott was elected president of the celebration. The Kentucky volunteers in attendance offered toasts to Scott "the Patriot and the Soldier" and "general Charles Scott; a soldier of '76, a terror to our enemies, and Friend to his country." The group then returned to Lexington for a ball at John Downing's Traveler's Hall on Main Street.[15] For Independence Day 1806 Scott received similar attention.[16] Typically the Fourth of July orators worked their way up to a final pitch that every true patriot should emulate his Revolutionary forebears and be willing to defend American liberty with his own blood. Scott presided over an "elegant Barbecue" and dance on August 20, 1806, at the Olympic Springs, commemorating the anniversary of the victory over the Indians at Fallen Timbers in 1794.[17]

The patriotic celebrations contrasted with a divisiveness in Kentucky politics. A southside party, representing mainly rural interests, contended with the Bluegrass-Lexington faction of merchants and men of wealth. A leading issue was the private Bank of Kentucky, which was finally approved by the legislature on December 27, 1806. Opponents of the bank charged that it was inimical to republican principles and served the special interest of Lexington merchants at the expense of the public good. For a while the southside party gained momentum in its antibank war. Efforts to destroy the bank failed, however, as did attempts to secure an alternative—namely establishing a state bank or bringing in a branch of the Bank of the United States. Thereupon, the Bluegrass faction dominated Kentucky politics through the War of 1812.[18] Scott was only loosely aligned with this faction, led by Henry Clay.

Especially with the growing nationalism and discrediting of separatism, accusations of foreign intrigue and even treason charged the political atmosphere. Joseph Street's *Western World* in 1806 accused prominent Kentuckians, chiefly Harry Innes, judge of the U.S. district court, Senator John Brown, and Benjamin Sebastian, judge of the Kentucky court of appeals, of involvement in a "Spanish conspiracy," dating back before Kentucky became a state. Proved to have been a pensioner of Spain, Sebastian resigned. Humphrey Marshall and other Federalists made this a big issue, to discredit the Republicans. The Aaron Burr "western conspiracy" also led to countercharges among the politicians. The *Western World* accused the former vice-president of actions tantamount to treason—attempting to raise a military force to be used against the western Spanish territory and even seeking to establish a separate western empire. Burr visited Lexington and Louisville several times and was quite popular in Kentucky. The newspaper's charges led to

Burr's being brought before a Kentucky grand jury. Although Burr was exonerated, the case bitterly divided Kentuckians. Scott avoided the strife, although self-styled Republicans such as he were prone to take offense at the prosecution (or persecution) of Burr. Burr's arrest by federal authorities on the charge of treason shortly after his "acquittal" in Kentucky, however, disillusioned his Kentucky supporters.[19] As for Scott, the political animosities and the struggle for power in Kentucky politics, with a new generation of politicians seeking to wrest power from the old, left him in a position to be the unifier—above politics and the unquestionable patriot. The coming of the War of 1812 could also be viewed in this context in Kentucky as a cause to overshadow the internal dissensions.

Scott began to consider the possibility of running for governor in 1808. Being the senior Revolutionary officer in Kentucky, he well knew, gave him an advantage. Kentuckians usually preferred to elect candidates with a military background. Two men of military reputation announced two years early for the next gubernatorial election. Col. Thomas Todd and Gen. Thomas Posey advertised their candidacies in the summer of 1806. Posey's hopes soon dimmed. He had been elected lieutenant governor by the state Senate to fill the vacancy left by the death of John Caldwell but then lost an election for his seat in the state Senate. The debate that ensued over whether he had a right to be lieutenant governor, not being a member of the state Senate according to the constitutional requirement, did not enhance his gubernatorial chances; also, although he claimed to be a Republican, his enemies had some success in labeling him a Federalist. Todd removed himself by accepting an appointment as justice of the U.S. Supreme Court in 1807. Early the next year a local grass-roots movement sought to create interest in drafting Isaac Shelby for another term as governor.[20]

The factors would immensely influence Scott's decision: would Shelby run, and to what degree would there be patriotic fervor? If Shelby were a declared candidate, Scott would have difficulty in defeating him. Shelby enjoyed a reputation as a Revolutionary War hero, particularly from the battle of King's Mountain; he had a key role in drafting the Kentucky Constitution and had been the state's first governor. Contending for the governorship with Shelby could well prove embarrassing for Scott, some of whose own military record was best be left unexamined—notably the retreat at Monmouth.

In 1807 a wave of intense patriotism spread through Kentucky. Although Kentuckians had often been reminded of the violations of America's neutral rights by the belligerent powers, outright hostility against Great Britain erupted over one episode. On June 22 the British man-of-war *Leopard* fired on the *Chesapeake* and forced it to strike its colors and submit to a boarding party, creating tremendous repercussions throughout the United States. In Kentucky there was a clamor for retaliation—embargo and war. When the embargo on all exports to foreign countries came, Kentucky was one of the few areas in the country that gave it full support. To the Kentuckians' way of thinking, the British and French had brought such a measure upon themselves by interfering with American rights on the high seas. Even the depression in prices for Kentucky's commodities, beginning in 1806 and continuing through the War of 1812, did not change their minds. Furthermore, the embargo (and afterward the Non-Intercourse Act), so it was reasoned at the time, provided the opportunity to develop industry and agricultural diversity within the state.[21]

During the *Chesapeake-Leopard* crisis, Scott applied to Governor Greenup for permission to raise a troop of mounted volunteers. This would be in accord with the instructions the governor had received from the president to enroll volunteer militia under a national quota of 30,000 troops, as voted by Congress. The Militia Act of 1792 had provided for one volunteer troop of horse for each militia division. Greenup, therefore, authorized Scott to raise a cavalry unit, to be entered into the Fifth Division of militia. Although there were indications that volunteers would be plentiful in the Lexington area, Scott, largely due to a happy event, desisted from further military activity.[22]

On July 25, 1807, Scott married Judith Cary Bell Gist, fifty-seven-year-old widow of Col. Nathaniel Gist, and moved to the 3,000-acre Gist plantation, Canewood, in northwestern Clark County, straddling the Bourbon County line. Colonel Gist, who had served with Scott during the war and who had also been a prisoner of war at Charleston, had died in 1797, age sixty-seven. He was the reputed father of the famous Cherokee chief Sequoyah, whose American name was George Guess (the pronunciation of "Gist" at the time was "Guest"). Nathaniel and Judith Gist had eight children (two sons and six daughters, one of whom died as a child). At Canewood there were still the three younger Gist children: Anna Maria, age sixteen, Eliza Violet, age twelve, and Maria Cecil, age ten.[23] Canewood was known for its elegance and hospitality. One person who found "beautiful Canewood" especially charming during visits many years later was Rebecca Gratz (then sister-in-law of Scott's stepdaughter Maria), the model for the Jewish heroine Rebecca in Sir Walter Scott's *Ivanhoe*.[24]

Scott, at sixty-eight, had a new wife and family, and once again a home of his own. His acquired status as country gentleman afforded credibility to the role of a Cincinnatus. So long begrudged by some for his earthiness and vulgarity, he found that the instant patriciate gave him a touch of class. It is said that the new Mrs. Scott thought that Scott was headed for the governor's mansion and wanted greatly to be Kentucky's first lady. Be that as it may, the marriage certainly had political benefit.

As Scott expected, Americans were of bellicose temper in 1808 because of resentment over the *Chesapeake* affair and other violations of American neutral rights. Incidents involving Indians in the Northwest Territory were exaggerated in Kentucky, and it was believed that the Indians were aided by the British in Canada. There might be a new Indian war.[25] Certainly there was no better climate for Scott's candidacy for governor. The times, so it seemed, called for men of military experience. As Kentucky's highest-ranking Revolutionary War officer, Scott was one of the few generals of the Continental army still alive. No one in Kentucky than he better represented the "Spirit of '76." There was talk that Scott should be elected governor—not only because of his experience but so that thereby Kentuckians could express their gratitude to the Revolutionary War generation and symbolically renew their faith in the principles of American liberty.

The major obstacle to Scott's candidacy was removed; Isaac Shelby was willing to step aside. To seek the governorship would give Scott great satisfaction. The chief magistry of the state would crown a long career as citizen-soldier. With office bestowed by the people, Scott would find vindication of his military record. He had no pressing demands on his time, nor did he have political obligations that needed to be repaid. Above political strife, he thought that he could represent unity and patriotism in the state. Scott had always harbored some political ambitions, but in the past, with so many lawyers and grandiloquent orators around, he had not stood much of a chance. The political field was open in 1808. The mood was militarist and patriotic.

Scott's candidacy for governor became official with an announcement at Frankfort on February 11, 1808. John Allen also declared his candidacy,[26] and a month or so later Green Clay did the same. Gabriel Slaughter (a future governor), Edward Bullock, and Samuel Caldwell entered the race for lieutenant governor. Scott, sixty-nine years old, had as his chief opponent Allen, who at age thirty-six was a brilliant lawyer and was expected to have a spectacular political career.

Scott surprisingly would show himself an astute politician, although all that he had to do was to remind people of his long patriotic record. Allen, having served as a counsel for Aaron Burr, had to fend off attacks on his patriotism. Green Clay, although purporting to represent the dirt farmers, was the largest slaveowner in the state and had the reputation of being a greedy speculator.[27]

With patriotic fervor running high, no one dared in an open forum to attack Scott's character and patriotism (though normally both would be fair game in the free-for-all frontier style of Kentucky politics). It helped Scott, in the sense of avoiding political animosity, that he had not run for elective office other than as presidential elector (not much of a risk, with the majority of the state favoring the Jeffersonian Republican party) and as delegate to the Virginia assembly, when Kentucky was in its infancy and the job, which required long distances of travel, went almost for the asking.

Besides the high pitch of patriotism and anti-British feeling among the electorate,[28] several other factors aided Scott's candidacy. His campaign manager, Jesse Bledsoe, undoubtedly was one of the most remarkable politicians in Kentucky's history. Bledsoe's talents, however, were best behind the scenes than openly in his own behalf; he was the "kingmaker" and Scott's alter ego. Bledsoe wrote newspaper pieces for Scott during the campaign. He had the superb ability of casting Scott's patriotic appeal in resounding rhetoric. Henry Clay said of Bledsoe that he was the most natural orator he had ever known. Equally as fiery-tempered as the former senator, who was now Speaker of the Kentucky legislature, Bledsoe almost fought a duel with Clay in 1802, but the circuit court advised both men that they were friends and men of honor, and the duel was never fought. On occasion Bledsoe was known to get disgustingly drunk.[29] Nevertheless, he had the intellectuality, classical training, canny judgment of a lawyer, creativity, and rhetorical flair that made him the ideal complement to General Scott.

Though it was a role that was somewhat a liability as well as an asset, Scott assumed leadership of the veterans' lobby in Kentucky, which consisted largely of officers who had sold their bonus certificates before the Funding Act of August 1791 and who now were petitioning the federal government to reimburse them for their losses. Scott, as the senior Revolutionary War officer in the state, called a meeting of all the old veteran officers, to be held in Frankfort on August 15, 1808 (two weeks after the election). Word also got around in the spring of 1808 that Virginia had granted "a fresh Bounty of Lands" to its Revolutionary War officers, and this, in a sense, tied the present to the past, in addition to buoying the hopes of poor farmers and speculators alike.[30] Also abetting veteran identity was the revival of the old Kentucky volunteer spirit. This was evident in Governor Greenup's decree that those militia who had volunteered for service during the crisis of late 1807 could wear a black leather cockade, adorned in the middle with a small white metal button.[31]

By the end of May the campaign began in earnest. To Scott's advantage his two opponents became the subjects of a vicious newspaper war waged between their proponents and detractors. One letter, opening the fray, published in the *Kentucky Gazette* on May 31, questioned the propriety of having John Allen, Green Clay, and two of the lieutenant governor candidates run for executive office while still serving in the legislature. Joseph Street's *Western World,* with many of the articles reprinted in other newspapers, persistently indicted Allen for having served as counsel to Burr before a Kentucky grand jury and having been privy to the "Spanish conspiracy" of Judge Sebastian and others. Allen was even accused of having been bribed by the Spaniards. "A Farmer," in the *Reporter,* July 23, 1808, emphasized that Allen should have disclosed his knowledge of Sebastian's being a pensioner of Spain and also claimed that Allen did not have sufficient knowledge of military affairs or practical politics that the times called for. To support Allen would be saying that "public virtue which leads men to prefer their country to their friends, and even to themselves" was "a mere farce, fit only for the vulgar and the ignorant" and "that he who conceals conspiracy and treason, and he who detects it, at whatever hazard are all alike."[32]

A distrust of lawyers also worked in Scott's favor—especially of those who practiced at Frankfort and Lexington, close to the moneyed interests. Allen was now a Frankfort lawyer. Commented "A Plain Dealer" in the *Kentucky Gazette,* "I have found him to be the uniform promoter of the local interest of Frankfort," and, although "it is admitted he is a great practicing lawyer," he "lives retired and secluded from intercourse with the common herd of mankind." Should such a man be made governor, "who has every thing but *law* to learn?" asked the writer. "No, citizens, no. A firm veteran of another cast [Scott] offers,— no lawyer, indeed! but one who, when Mr. Allen was puling in his mother's arms, was defending his country, not only against the tomahawk of the savage, but also against the disciplined troops of a tyrant."[33]

Henry Clay went to lengths to defend Allen, writing under the pseudonyms of "Regulus" and "Scaevola," though his anonymity did not last long. Clay, the politician, was not about to take on Scott directly. One candidate, he said, "from his impor-

tant services and his venerable years spent in obeying his country's calls, has an exclusive claim upon her gratitude. Whether
that claim ought to be satisfied by the honours of the first office,
in the gift of the people," was a question on which he would be
entirely silent. Clay argued that at the time of the Burr case most
Kentuckians were pro-Burr, and it was unjust to single out Allen. Clay emphasized that Burr was never charged with treason
in Kentucky and that he was found innocent of promoting an
expedition to Mexico. Clay also argued that it was Allen's duty
to appear as Burr's counsel. Of course, in defending Allen, Clay,
who was Burr's co-counsel, also had his own reputation at
stake.[34] Dr. Anthony Hunn, who published *The Lamp,* a newspaper in Lincoln County, launched a venomous personal attack
on Henry Clay for the "Regulus" and "Scaevola" letters, and
Clay replied in kind. As for his opposition to Allen's candidacy,
Hunn argued chiefly that Allen was a creature of the aristocratic
cabal at Frankfort.[35]

Allen, however, had substantial support from many prominent Kentuckians. Among letters backing him published in
the *Reporter* were those from Samuel Hopkins, R. M. Gano,
B. W. Ballard, Joseph Winlock, John Thompson, Lewis Craig,
Thomas Johnston, William Steele, George Madison (later governor), and Nathaniel Hart.[36]

Scott's other opponent, Green Clay, had a limited power base
among the settlers south of the Green River. Virginia had provided lands in this area to satisfy military warrants. But many of
the lands were not proved out by the original military grantees,
and the Kentucky legislature, therefore, had offered such lands
for sale. Although the purchase price was low, the settlers, who
had squatted on the lands, asserted that they were unable to pay
because the lands were not very productive. By 1808 the arrears
were substantial. Clay favored debtor relief for the settlers south
of the Green River, an opinion which did not set well with the
early settlers north of the river, whose accounts with the state
were fairly straight. Green Clay accused Scott of not realizing
that there were two sides of the Green River.[37] Green Clay's supporters, like Allen's, published testimonials in the newspapers,
which stressed Clay's integrity in business relations and, in order

to counteract Scott's hero image, Clay's service in George Rogers Clark's expedition against the Shawnee in 1782.[38] But Clay, who had extensive landholdings and was involved in numerous commercial ventures, could not shake off his image as a fortune hunter.[39]

Because of all the furor over the candidacies of Allen and Clay, it seemed that the easy thing for a citizen to do would be to vote for Scott. One "Humphrey Dubs" of Madison County, with homespun logic, tended toward this conclusion in a letter to the *Reporter*. Dubs said he had gone to the courthouse to talk with people about the election. Some persons were for Allen because he knew everything about the law; but no one could tell Dubs where Allen stood on issues. Others supported Clay because he was from the same country and could be counted on for giving out whiskey, bacon, and turkeys at the election. A citizen pointed out that Clay was a military man and could command troops in war if necessary, but "nobody could give me a reson why I should buye a nighbours horse if he was a bad one when I could buye a strangers which was good for less muny." Then Dubs asked about General Scott. Some of the Allen and Clay supporters "abused him very much." Dubs talked to an old veteran who had been with Scott in the Revolution and the Indian wars. Scott, it was pointed out, had often served on dangerous missions, and "he had never deceived his countrymen"; Washington "lovd and confided in him." Dubs also heard that Scott "was a staunch whig and opposed to gag laws and excises— and had voted for Jefferson when an elector—and was a good republican to this very hour and no one could say but he was an honest man and lovd his country and never would injure us." Dubs therefore decided to vote for Scott.[40] The letter, of course, was no doubt supplied by one of Scott's campaign workers.

Scott himself had not planned to use the public prints during the campaign, nor had he encouraged his supporters to do so. By mid-June, however, he changed his mind. People began to write regularly to the newspapers on his behalf.[41] Scott released an announcement on June 16 to the press, published in the *Kentucky Gazette* on June 28 and the *Reporter* on July 2. Addressing "The Free Men of Kentucky," he said he wanted to lay to rest the rumor that he had neither a wish for nor an "expectation" of the governorship. "I am too old to be ambitious," Scott said. "My country called me into public service—I have ever obeyed her calls, and to the last hour of life will obey it. That country which knows my services is the best judge whether I am to be trusted with the office of governor." If a life "devoted to her present service might merit her suffrage, I shall not be forgotten by my fellow citizens, particularly by my old fellow sufferers in war, in spite of my enemies or the enemies of *my* country." Scott said he would serve the state with the best of his abilities if elected. "I know it has a better choice, not a better friend."[42]

The Independence Day celebrations, only several weeks before the election, gave a lift to Scott's candidacy. At a barbecue at Maxwell's Spring near Lexington, for example, one of the toasts indicated the interest in the veterans' movement for further compensation, which Scott was heading. Elsewhere in Fayette County "a small party of Genuine Republicans" met for a barbecue. One toast hailed "Charles Scott our friend and brother, who stood by his country and saw it immersed in blood at the awful moment that tried men's souls."[43] Similar tributes to Scott were expressed at other celebrations.[44] While picnics and barbecues had been standard fare for better acquainting the electorate with the candidate (a custom tracing back to Virginia politics), Scott did not have to attend to be present at the Fourth of July festivities across the state.

Two weeks before the election Scott placed one more letter in the Kentucky newspapers, addressed to *"the Honest Freemen of Kentucky,"* which showed his toughness and indicated that he could be adept at gut politics. In defense of the meeting of war veterans that he had called, Scott pointed out that many old officers were destitute and merely wanted justice done by receiving the full value of the five years' pay which had been given to them in depreciated certificates. To those detractors who accused him of wanting a pension and promoting "the Cincinnati business, and an order of nobility, &c.," Scott let his temper go. "Those men who were dirtying their little clothes when I was fighting for my country," he declared, "ought to have more grace, than to spit lies in my face, because I have helped to purchase the privilege of their doing so. They may sit in the shade and lie as much as they please." Scott said he wished to be elected governor by honest men; "and whether elected or not, I will console myself, there is not a majority of rascals." While "some are very busy in persuading the people I am old, infirm, and in my dotage, I am ready to confess, I am not quite nimble enough to mount every stump, and tell the people a long tale in my own favour, and I thank God I have still sense enough to keep me from it." The people, "I should hope by this time of day, know me. I expect to live poor, but to die honest."[45]

Scott presumably gave a few campaign talks. According to tradition, he and Allen both were present at a general muster. Allen spoke first. When it was Scott's turn, he began by praising Allen as a fine example of a native Kentuckian (actually Allen came to Kentucky with his parents from Virginia at age eight). Scott mentioned there were many in the audience who had come to the Kentucky wilderness at the time he did. "We hardly expected," he said, nodding toward Allen, "that we should live to see such smart men raised up among ourselves." He said that the old settlers had no time for education or books but had to be constantly armed and on guard. Because the country was protected, "now every one can go where he pleases, and you see what smart young fellows are now growing up to do their country honor." Scott then said it would be a pity to make Allen governor; rather, it would be better to send him to Congress. "I don't think it requires a very smart man to make a governor," Scott noted, "if he has sense enough to gather smart men about him, who can help him on with the business of the State. It would suit an old worn out old wife of a man like myself. But as to this young man I am very proud of him; as much so as any of his kin, if any of them had been here today listening to his speech." According to a reminiscence, "Scott then descended from the stump, and the 'huzzas for the old soldier' made the welkin ring."[46]

Scott always had a knack for aphorisms; his uttering a few of them during the campaign probably convinced people that he had not reached senility. One of the most famous, according to tradition, was: "The people, when they got wrong, had to get damned wrong before they could get right."[47]

Two long letters in the *Reporter*, one signed "An Old Soldier" and the other an "old man in Jefferson county," rehearsed sentimentally Scott's long career, not all too accurately, a fact which may indicate that a person of the younger generation had a hand in writing the letters, perhaps Bledsoe. The first letter concluded by saying this would be the last opportunity the people would have to reward Scott's services fully. "Let us add to the wreath of laurel, which wears so well on the soldier's brow, a *civic garland*," urged the writer. "Long live the citizen soldier, and the soldier citizen. Let us give, in general Scott, an example of the gratitude of real and genuine republicans. And so shall we teach our sons to *serve their country*, by shewing them that their country will *never forget their services*." The second letter drifted into an attack on Allen. Against the charge that Scott was too old, the writer said that Scott had never been too aged to serve his country and would not be now. Furthermore, Scott's experience, knowledge of people "and things," patriotism, private and public virtues, and his being a farmer made him more qualified to be governor "than the eminent lawyer, whose experience of man has been acquired in the school of contention, and in the sinks of vice."[48]

Voters filed to the courthouses on Monday, August 1. Kentucky elections were often raucous affairs. By the Constitution of 1799, the state returned to the Virginia style of elections—from the written ballot back to viva voce voting. A cultured English traveler, observing the election day in Paris, Kentucky, noted that voting was very simple. The county clerk sat at a table in the courthouse, and as citizens came in he recorded their names and those for whom they voted. At Nicholasville, the Englishman found about one hundred horses tied to trees at the courthouse. "I was induced to hasten past this place," he commented, "as the voters in that sterile part of the country did not appear quite so peaceable and orderly as those I had seen in the morning at Paris." He "was not sure but some of them might have been moved by the spirit of whiskey to challenge me to run a race with them, or to amuse the company with a game of rough and tumble." The election returns were slow coming in, but Scott led from the beginning. The complete results of about two weeks after the election showed: Scott, 22,050; Allen, 8,430; and Green Clay, 5,516.[49]

Scott kept his promise to hold a meeting of the old Revolutionary War soldiers. The veterans of the Virginia line assembled at Richard Taylor's house in Frankfort on August 16, and Scott was unanimously named chairman, with Christopher Greenup as secretary. Two committees were formed: one to petition the Virginia legislature to direct that public money held by the surveyor of lands for the Virginia Continental line should be applied to the establishment of factories and public institutions in Kentucky, and the other to correspond with veteran committees of other states concerning petitioning Congress and to consider generally matters of veterans' interests. Scott was authorized to start a Kentucky chapter of the Society of the Cincinnati and to name its president and other officers (this, however, was contrary to the national organization's discouragement of chapters outside of the original thirteen states).[50] Meanwhile, Scott wrapped up other old business as he prepared for the inauguration.

On their way to the inauguration, Scott and his family arrived in Lexington on Tuesday, August 30. The next morning, at 9 A.M., a company of light infantry, two rifle companies, and a Lexington cavalry troop paraded on the public square in honor of the governor-elect. At 10 A.M. the Scotts left Lexington under military escort, followed by a large number of citizens. At Daily's Inn, where the procession stopped in the afternoon, cavalry from Frankfort arrived, and "a regular encampment" was made for the evening. Early the next morning, September 1, Scott reviewed a military parade and emotionally addressed the troops. Joined by the Frankfort light infantry company, the procession entered Frankfort, with bells ringing and weapons firing. After pausing for refreshments at a local inn, the "cavalcade" moved to the Capitol, where Scott took the oath of office. A public din-

ner in the House of Representatives chamber—with Jesse Bledsoe, who would be Scott's secretary of state, speaking on Scott's
behalf—concluded the inaugural events.[51]

The newspapers carried a brief address given by Scott some-
time during the inaugural proceedings. After expressing his
gratitude, Scott concluded: "May heaven shower its choicest
blessings upon you—My last prayer will be for my country's
happiness, and yours individually. To promote the prosperity of
my beloved countrymen, will be the unceasing object of my
life."[52] The talk brings to mind an anecdote, which, if there is
truth in it, most likely applies either to this brief speech or to
Scott's references to providence in his annual messages as governor. As the story goes, Bledsoe had completed a message and
gave it to Scott for approval. Scott read it carefully, and then
gravely looked up at Bledsoe and said: "Well, Mr. Bledsoe, I
know you think you are a d——d sight smarter than I am, and
so you are in many respects; but this message as it is now, won't
do at all; I'll be d——d if it will."

Bledsoe was astonished. "Well, Governor," he said, "tell me
what is the matter with it, that I may see if I can make it to
suit you."

"Why, d—n it to h—l," said Scott, "why don't you put a good
solemn prayer at the end of it, and talk about Providence, and
the protection of Heaven, and all that? Why General Washington never wrote a Message nor a Proclamation in his life, but
what he ended it with a prayer." Bledsoe rewrote the message as
instructed, and Scott then gave it high praise.[53] The fact is, however, that Bledsoe presumably had his own way in omitting a
specific prayer when writing Scott's annual messages, for the
printed versions include only general references to the Almighty.

Among Scott's first actions as governor was to provide executive clemency in two cases, acting on petitions from a great
many citizens. He pardoned Moses Walker, under sentence for
hot stealing, because the jury prejudicially overvalued the hogs.
He reprieved, and then pardoned, a slave by name of Nancy,
sentenced to be hanged by a Scott County court of oyer and
terminer, on grounds that illegal and hearsay evidence had been

admitted at her trial. In November, Scott was again elected a presidential elector for the northern district.[54]

In mid-November, Scott issued an address, published in broadside and in the newspapers, to the "Freemen and Soldiers of Kentucky," in order to stimulate the enrollment of Kentucky's quota of 5,005 militia volunteers under a federal requisition, set by Congress in March 1808. Significantly, he based his appeal for volunteers upon the threat to national sovereignty and rights rather than simply the interference with American commerce; not only would this view attract recruits, but it also reflected Kentuckians' interpretation of the controversy with Great Britain. Scott declared that America, "menaced from abroad by the enemies of our liberty and independence," had the choice only "of submitting to become the humble slaves of their will, or stand firm upon our own dear bought soil of freedom;—prepared to meet and repel with our lives, their aggressions on our rights." Volunteers were preferable to draftees. "Men who are reluctantly forced to defend a treasure, do not care so much about the loss of it." Scott advised that "no idle clamours against the government" should dampen one's zeal to defend his country's rights. Political differences should have nothing to do with performing one's duty. "The government is the one of your choice. Measures may be changed when wrong, by the free and regular voice of the people; but he cannot surely be a friend to his country, who would not support its constituted authorities." In closing, Scott said: "Suffer, fellow-citizens an old man whom you have highly honoured for his wish to do well, to tell you that there is no recollection sweeter than that of having encountered every hardship and looked every danger in the face to assist in purchasing the independence, or in defending the liberties of our country."[55] Recruitment, however, was to lag over the next months as Anglo-American tensions eased.

On December 13 Governor Scott attended a joint session of the Kentucky assembly to deliver his first annual state of the commonwealth message. A committee of the Speaker of the house and members of the Senate escorted him to the Speaker's chair. Bledsoe also accompanied him, and it was he who read the address. Scott's speech, in warning of potential war, called for a strong military defense. While Americans only wished to enjoy the fruits of liberty for which they had struggled hard and not to become involved in "the calamities of those conflicts which agitate the European world," the history of mankind, however, "furnishes a sad and continued example, that with a great portion of the nations of the world, *right* is but another name for *force*—The best way therefore, to avoid aggression is to be prepared to repel it." The violation of American rights by both Great Britain and France left "but one alternative, to submit to be the passive instrument of their pleasure at the expense of all we hold dear, or to make that resistance which the God of nature has put in our power. On our *own* soil, if we are united and vigilant, we have nothing to fear. But surely we should not sit idly until the approaching storm overtakes us." Although in a republican government standing armies in peacetime should never exist, the militia should be well organized and ready for service. Scott prodded the legislature to provide equipment for the volunteers. He strongly supported Jefferson's embargo and urged the state to promote domestic industry.

Moving on to other internal affairs of the state, Scott called for legislative reform to give debtors respite, and he lamented the shortage of moneys in the treasury. In order for the state to have "regular funds" to draw on, taxes should either be raised or be better collected. There had been too much reliance on bank credit. In concluding his long message, Scott declared "that whatever clouds may overcast our political horizon, or whatever difficulties may await us: whether we are called upon to defend our shores against a foreign foe, or resist savage invasion . . . when we look back to the times of '76; when we contrast our resources now with our apparently defenceless situation then, we are confidently led to exclaim, 'under a benevolent providence we must Prevail.'" Both the Kentucky Senate and House of Representatives passed resolutions endorsing Scott's support of the embargo and his recommendation for economic self-sufficiency, positions which in turn were taken up by the state's congressional delegation.[56]

During the winter of 1808–9, Scott slipped on the icy steps of the governor's mansion; whether he broke any bones is un-

known, but thereafter he was lame and had to use a crutch.[57]
Increasingly he became more physically infirm, but his administration as governor would witness a vigorous use of the functions and the authority of the executive office and an
extraordinary sense of public responsibility. Even if we grant the
ever-presence and assistance of Jesse Bledsoe, Scott undeniably
had full possession of his rational powers, and he exhibited a
highly disciplined yet probative mind. A half century of duty
made him the able commander, and the patriotism of '76,
adapted to a new age, had no better exponent.

IX

"The Spark of '76 Flashes from His Eyes"

The isolated and placid setting of Kentucky's capital belied the challenging tasks facing the new governor, in peace and war. The serenity of the town of some ninety residences was owing to its situation within a bend of the Kentucky River, on its northeast side, confined by two steep hills. In addition to the Capitol, other important edifices were a courthouse, four large taverns, and the state penitentiary. The Scotts and the three stepdaughters settled in at the governor's "Palace," a two-story Federal-style brick house. The family entertained frequently, and any fellow war veteran from Virginia was especially welcomed.[1]

Perhaps the most routine and delicate of the governor's duties was the filling of numerous civil and military positions, many of which were solicited. Scott had difficulty in making some appointments. Two nominees to the Court of Appeals refused to serve. John Boyle turned down a circuit court judgeship and was then given a seat in the Court of Appeals.[2] When the state Senate rejected Scott's appointment of Dr. Walter Brashear as lieutenant colonel commandant of the Second Regiment of militia, whom Scott had commissioned during the recess of the legislature, Scott persisted with the nomination and lectured the Senate on constitutional principles. Since Brashear was the best man for the position as far as Scott was concerned, he told the senators that he assumed they would not want him to make a worse nomination.[3]

The use of executive clemency sheds light on the severity of the local courts in judging slave cases. Scott pardoned a slave boy, age sixteen, who was convicted of burglary, on the grounds that others had put him up to the crime. Several other slaves sentenced for burglary were also pardoned; a slave convicted of murder was spared, on the basis of insufficient evidence. Two fourteen-year-old slave boys, belonging to Green Clay, who had been sentenced to hang for burning a factory belonging to John W. Hunt in Lexington, received their pardons "whilst under the gallows."[4] One white man, Zeba Campfield, sentenced to four years for manslaughter in killing a mulatto boy, his own slave, was pardoned after having served three years because the evidence had been "only presumptive and light." Several other whites were pardoned, one because he was so ill that it seemed likely he would not survive his prison term. A Garrard County man indicted for murder seems to have been pardoned before his trial.[5]

Scott exercised his veto power cautiously, but in three instances he demonstrated a resolve that showed his full understanding of his constitutional responsibility. He vetoed an act which would free claimant-occupants from liability for rents and profits that would accrue to a prior claimant until the time a court judgment settled ownership and which also provided that occupants who made improvements equal to three-fourths of the land value could purchase the land for the price of evaluation without the improvements. Scott thought the legislature acted too hastily, without giving the people an opportunity to be heard, and he also had doubts as to the measure's constitutionality. The veto was overridden. The legislature, however, was in agreement with Scott's proposal, in his previous annual message, for the need for debtor relief. A replevy law was passed, which stayed execution on debts for one year, providing debtors gave bond and security.[6]

The governor vetoed a law that would immediately create Harrison County. Scott cited several objections: the haste, petitions he had received opposing the act since it was passed, the need to hear further from Bourbon County constituents since the jurisdiction of that county was being reduced, the wish of some legislators who had voted for the act to have it reconsidered, and the lack of any provision in the act for gathering taxes in the new county for the present year. The legislature, nevertheless, repassed the measure over the veto.[7]

Scott locked horns again with the assembly when he vetoed an act repealing an earlier statute that had granted an annuity to George Muter, former chief justice of the Court of Appeals. Muter was approaching senility and had been persuaded to resign in late 1806. A Scottish merchant before the war and Virginia's first commissioner of war in 1780–81, Muter early moved to Kentucky and had received his judgeship from Virginia when Kentucky was still a district of that state. He had used much of his salary as judge to pay off his prewar British debts. Scott's lengthy veto message was a genuine expression of conscience and a determined plea on behalf of a suffering brother Virginia officer. Scott argued that it could not have been the intention of the framers of the Kentucky constitution to prohibit the legislature from giving relief to such a person as Muter in his destitute condition. "Humanity forbids to abandon an aged animal," said Scott, "which has faithfully labored for us, and which has been worn down from the prime of life in our service, upon the bleak commons, to live upon the scanty blades he can pick up, or to die." It "could never have been intended by reasonable men with humane feelings to deny that support to one of the distinguished of our fellow-creatures, which every honorable sentiment would lead us to extend to a horse or a dog."

The legislature had passed the repealing act because the constitution forbade compensation except for public service. But Scott said that the assembly had taken too narrow a view. The state constitution had sought only to abolish exclusive privileges, such as amenities attached to nobility and the like and "the abominable practice of pensioning favourites, who have deserved nothing of their country." State governments should "be as competent to legislate on state subjects as the United States on federal subjects"; especially, the state should legislate on "cases happening under our own eyes.... surely none would think of sending a citizen worn out in state service, to the City of Washington to be supported." In essence, the legislature, by having given Muter a pension, had established a contractural relationship with him; furthermore, Muter, who had lost most of his small plantation, would become a charity case if his allowance was not renewed. But if Muter were rich, Scott argued, "it could not alter the nature of his claim, which appears to me as much a vested right, as a patent could convey. And if it was impolitic or wrong to make the engagement to pass the law giving him 300 dollars a year, it appears to me doubly wrong to take it away." Scott urged the legislature not to "run the risk of destroying all confidence in our Government, on a mere point of policy or construction, by taking away bread from an old man just tottering on the brink of the grave, when your feelings and your sense of justice must be opposed to it." A decision for Muter, Scott added, would be supported by the electorate "when they shall be correctly informed." In concluding this remarkable paper, Scott said that while he did not mean to impugn the motives of those who had voted for the repeal, he himself would not die in peace if he had approved it.

Indeed Scott's veto message provided interpretative commentary on the state constitution as well as a profound personal statement. Although the legislators esteemed him for the force of his convictions, they overrode the veto. After all, they would face election again, and Scott would not. Even a small pension for Muter at this time was just too aristocratic a measure. Muter's only support until his death would be from Thomas Todd, who had replaced him on the Court of Appeals in 1806 and who then became a justice in the U.S. Supreme Court.[8]

Scott considered Indian diplomacy exclusively a federal responsibility. Although he conceded to the request of the federal government that he appoint a commissioner to join in a treaty with the Chickasaws for further extinguishing their claims to lands within Kentucky, he balked at the idea that the state should pay the expenses of the treaty and the price for the Indian lands within the state.[9]

It was Scott's view that the office of governor should exert political influence. During the August 1809 legislative election campaign, he used his prestige to try and defeat Humphrey Marshall as a representative from Franklin County, so offending

Marshall that, after he had lost the election by seventy-six votes, he published a piece in the *Western World* (reprinted in the *Kentucky Gazette*) ridiculing Scott. Contending that Scott had said that all those who voted for Marshall were tories, Marshall retorted, "Why, so we were last year, when we voted for you Governor!" Furthermore, "We have heard of men's living in *glass* houses, and in tender mercy we caution this gentleman not to begin to throw stones." Scott, "a phenomenon in physicks," continued Marshall, "whom the people of Kentucky put into office as the *antipode,* to Spanish Conspirators, Burrities, &c. is seen to unite very kindly with them in the late election. The effervescence, so common in chimerical experiments where heterogeneous bodies are thrown together, seemed to be altogether thrown on their adversary." Then came the unkindest cut: "Did Governor Scott exhibit himself, on the first day of the last Election, at the Court-House, with the laudable purpose, for which the old Grecians, used to expose their slaves, *drunk*—as a subject of derision, and a caution to their young men? If so, it must be admitted that the picture was to the life," and the governor "merits the thanks of his country, as he did those of Gen. Washington at the battle of Monmouth!" The writer then borrowed a passage from John Marshall's *Life of Washington:* that Scott "mistook an oblique march of an American column for a retreat; and in the apprehension of being abandoned left his position and repassed the ravine in his rear."

"An Old Soldier" (almost certainly Bledsoe) replied in kind, denouncing Marshall's hypocrisy. "You are the man who dare to threaten Gen. Scott," said the writer, "by insinuating that you know more than you have yet told—'that the General's house is built of glass.' The people of Kentucky despise your insinuation as much as they contemn you. His fame will be found treasured up 'inter penetralia,' in those sacred recesses where your unhallowed feet will never tread." Scott's reputation was unreproachable, and "there is not a man on earth whose heart is more easily read than Gen. Scott's. Brave, generous, and candid, he never disguised a feeling of his heart." Scott "challenges you to charge upon 'his glassy house.' But you will never do it. Poor fainthearted wretch! You would tremble before the lightning of his eye, tho' his withered arm portends no danger." The author called up memories of Scott as patriot and Indian fighter and further denounced the fraud and deception practiced by Marshall. Regarding the reference to the battle of Monmouth, "Was not Gen. [John] Marshall, the author of that quotation personally Scott's enemy?" The writer did acknowledge that Scott "does sometimes take a glass too much with a friend." But should this "blot out all his virtues and cancel all his services? Shall this single failing cloud virtues which would have given lustre to a Roman in the days of Italian prowess?" Scott "has gone through fire and water for us," and "if merit is thus to be insulted and the people do not respond to it with their warmest indignation, when there are other calls and other tyrants may invade our shores, I fear we shall not find other Scotts, who will hazard all for a doubtful return of fame." Should Scott "stand as a monument of slighted merit, a spectacle to frighten virtue from our shores" and meet "in his declining years the scoffs and taunts of his country, well may he say with Wolsey in the language of disappointment, 'Had I but served my God with half the zeal / I served my "country" he would not in mine age / Have left me naked to mine enemies'" [10] This letter, with the classicisms and the ending quotation pointing very much to Bledsoe, concluded the exchange.

Throughout 1809 the prospect of war seemed to lessen. The federal government canceled the order to have 5,005 Kentucky volunteers in readiness to march, and Scott in May discharged those troops who had been raised. The *Kentucky Gazette*, which printed Scott's orders, said it had information that Governor William Henry Harrison of the Indiana Territory did not consider an Indian war a possibility. Yet a martial spirit was in the air, and as usual it received encouragement from the many Fourth of July celebrations throughout the state. Scott attended the day-long festivities at Lexington. At Cave Springs, near Versailles, there was a toast to Scott: "Intrepid and undaunted in the field: may his reputation as our chief magistrate descend unsullied to posterity"; also, "The spirit of '76; it's busy among the people, we feel its influence." [11]

In the state of the commonwealth message on December 4,

1809, which summed up public opinion that had been expressed in the newspapers and at public gatherings, Scott had little hope that England and France would honor American maritime rights. No credibility could be placed on British promises, he felt, and any further negotiations with the British government would be useless; Scott even recommended severing all diplomatic and commercial relations with European countries. Although war was a means by which the United States could defend its rights, he was glad that it had not come to that. Scott considered that economic isolation represented a form of resistance to interference with American rights and independence and not a position of weakness by the abandonment of American maritime rights. By continuing to pursue a course of economic isolation, Americans would have "to give up only the luxuries of other nations for the sweets of independence and self government," and "the people who could not do it with the country and resources we possess, are unworthy the divine birthright of freedom."

In this address Scott also advised the legislature to build up a capital fund in the Bank of Kentucky, to which the state had just repaid a loan in full. Agricultural and industrial self-sufficiency needed more encouragement in Kentucky. Moreover, Scott told the legislators to listen to the people, who "when properly informed are never wrong," though sometimes temporarily misled. Taxes should bear as lightly as possible on the poor, by "exempting articles of the first necessity." Scott concluded by saying that he regretted that he could not attend the legislature in person to deliver the address because of his injury the previous winter. The message was extremely well received. The house informed Scott that it agreed with his recommendations and praised his leadership.[12]

For the next two and half years of Scott's administration the country steadily drifted toward war. The Erskine Agreement of April 1809, by which the British were to withdraw the Orders in Council and which led President Madison in June to lift nonintercourse with the British, had been repudiated by the British government Madison reinstated non-intercourse with Great Britain. In September 1809 a new British minister, Francis Jackson, arrived and soon proved so contemptuously anti-American that he was declared persona non grata; it would be two years before there would be a new British minister.[13] Such impairment of diplomacy contributed to the coming of the War of 1812. The militancy of the West continued to sustain a war fever. While resentment existed against France, to westerners the failure of Great Britain to make concessions on maritime rights; the revival of an Indian resistance movement, with alleged collaboration from the British (reminiscent of the 1790s); and a concern, in spite of the support of the temporary economic sanctions, for establishing a world market for western produce tended to make the British the more culpable. There was disgust that American coercion had weakened, as evidenced by the Embargo Act's being replaced by the Non-Intercourse Act of March 1809 and by Macon's Bill No. 2 of May 1810. Young western leaders, the war hawks, gaining influence in the states and in Congress, after 1810 were demanding war, to restore national honor and to recover freedom of American commerce, whereby economic prosperity would return to the West. Republicanism—and the Republican party itself, as a recent interpretator of the causation of the War of 1812 has written—was at stake. A government that could not defend the economic interests of its citizens did not deserve the respect of its people. "If Republicans foresaw party dishonor in submission," notes Roger H. Brown, "would not disgrace also fasten itself to the form of government that permitted such weakness? Ever since the Revolution American leaders had been conscious of the unproven capacity of their republic to function effectively in the jungle of international life."[14] What Scott and the old soldiers had won would now be asserted by the new soldier defenders of the Republic— independence.

While Kentucky's war hawk in the Senate, Henry Clay, was exciting old Revolutionary antagonisms against Great Britain,[15] Kentuckians at home were impatient for action by the central government. A letter, "A Spark from the Altar of '76," in the March 13, 1810, issue of the *Kentucky Gazette,* condemned Congress's attitude of neutrality and apathy in facing up to the foreign crisis. The writer of this piece, to be inspired by a little true patriotism, had spent an evening with Governor Scott. Scott was expecting word from the president to activate the militia. "Bless his old revolutionary soul!" exclaimed the correspondent. "Whenever a war with Great Britain is mentioned, the spark of '76 flashes from his eyes as pure and as *terrible* as when it first descended from *heaven*"; but, unfortunately, "we may, say of the *General* with *melancholy certainty,* what corporal Trim said of poor Le Fevre: He will never march again but to the grave!"

Like Scott, William Henry Harrison anticipated war, and he wrote two long rambling letters to Scott (March 10 and April 17, 1810), offering advice on the organization, discipline, and maintenance of the militia. Harrison, a territorial governor expecting that he would soon need the assistance of the Kentucky militia to help enforce treaties that had taken millions of acres from the Indians, was more enthusiastic in extolling the value of the militia than he might have been in a different situation. In the two letters to Scott, Harrison traced the history of militias from the Old World to the New, citing thirty-two military leaders from Theban Epaminondas to Anthony Wayne. In closing his second letter, he pointed out that Kentucky had an advantage over other states in having three distinguished Revolutionary War officers "to direct the efforts of its citizens in the attainment of military information"—namely Scott, Samuel Hopkins, and Thomas Posey. The efforts of these men could establish a disciplined militia, "a system that would soon pervade the continent, which would vindicate the American character for having neglected that to which Rome and Athens were indebted for their glory, and without which no republic can long exist." It was Harrison's prayer that Scott would be "amongst the last of those who may be called to enjoy in another world the happiness you have deserved for contributing to emancipate a nation in this."[16]

Scott kept a low profile in 1810, undoubtedly due in large part to his growing infirmity. The state of the commonwealth message on December 4, however, thoroughly examined the progress as well as the liabilities of the state. Scott praised the improvements in agriculture, including the large production of hemp and livestock, which were finding markets in other states. But he regretted the extravagance, inattention to resources, and "decay of public spirit." He cited the need for men of higher quality to serve in government; adequate compensation would further this goal. For militia reform, he proposed the establishment of a youth corps. Training should be provided for at least one period annually. The elder militia might still be kept enrolled and called up when necessary. Such a system would provide a "disposable military force," ready for any emergency, and it would do away with the burdensome general musters, thereby saving time, labor, and money (which could be applied to the training expenses of the new youth corps).

Also in this address Scott derided the dual administration of the county and the circuit courts in maintaining public roads. He recommended a special tax for keeping up the roads and giving citizens the option of paying the tax or performing road service themselves. On general taxation, Scott deprecated the state government for frequently having to borrow money to meet its ordinary expenses. "We must either be bad financiers, or the collectors of the public money are too wise for us, or both." A few extra cents on each 100 acres of land or upon each slave would be no burden on the poor; if each head of a family paid only 50 cents in additional taxes annually, this would enable the government fully to meet its needs. Scott applauded the revocation of France's restrictive decrees (which turned out not to be the case), but he warned that there was little hope for redress from either France or Great Britain, and, therefore, Americans should be prepared to protect their rights. In closing, he called for equanimity in the treatment of both France and Great Britain. He also warned of "disunion," on which "the hopes of our enemies rest, & it is from this, and our supineness, that the destruction of the goodly fabric, we have raised with so much toil, and cemented with the blood of illustrous patriots, is most to be apprehended . . . may the centinels of the Republic, at whatever post they may be placed, always give faithful warnings of its approaches."[17]

While everyone for the past several years had been expecting Scott to slip off to his eternal reward, he held to his mental vitality and had just enough physical agility to get around once in a while. He attended the 1811 Lexington Fourth of July celebration. A military escort accompanied him to Maxwell's Spring, where he was warmly received. Secretary Bledsoe gave an oration that took a good part of an hour, in which he praised classical virtue.[18] Elsewhere there were the usual celebrations, with toasts linking Scott to republicanism and liberty.[19]

In September 1811 a controversy over use of Kentucky troops embarrassed Scott. Governor Harrison of the Indiana Territory was planning to establish federal control over lands ceded by the Treaty of Fort Wayne in 1809. While visiting Louisville, Harrison sent a dispatch to Scott simply saying that he could use Kentucky mounted volunteers, but he did not make a formal request. Eventually Col. Joseph Daviess, the prominent Lexington lawyer who had prosecuted Aaron Burr, and Capt. Peter Funk responded and raised about sixty Kentucky cavalry. However, a remark by Harrison to a Kentucky officer in Louisville that he needed some Kentucky troops was published in the newspapers and gave the impression that Harrison was avoiding the Kentucky governor. Also giving the same impression—and this was played up in Humphrey Marshall's *American Republic*—was Harrison's directing Col. Samuel Wells to recruit for the federal regiment in Kentucky.[20] Wells wrote Scott, enclosing Harrison's letter. Bledsoe opened both letters before Scott received them, and he penned a note to Scott expressing his outrage—a rare communication which indicates Bledsoe's role in policymaking.

As Bledsoe reported to Scott, Harrison's letter to Wells was "an application in a more extraordinary and irregular manner I never witnessed" and it was "highly disrespectful" to Scott. "If there was indeed no *Governor* in *Kentucky* the thing might have been excusable." But the governor of Kentucky should not be considered so inconsequential as to be communicated with "second hand." If Harrison had been authorized by the secretary of war to call for Kentucky troops, Bledsoe pointed out, "I can hardly suppose the Secy at war could intend to make him Governor and commander in chief of the State." If this "usage" should prevail, "all Civil and Military respect" would end. Bledsoe dutifully told Scott: "You however will be the best judge." This statement by Bledsoe indicates that Scott was very much in control of his administration. In a postscript Bledsoe added that "I think the Honor of the State requires a refusal without a more respectful & regular application."[21]

The *American Republic,* in exaggerating the incident, declared that the Kentucky militiamen were not yet Hessians, to be traded in war. "Could not Governor Harrison distinguish, or did he suppose Governor Scott could not distinguish, between the Territory, and the state—between the case of an invasion, and a foreign expedition. If either of the Governors have not the proper perception of the difference, it is time they were taught." It was also contended that the governor of Kentucky could not order militia to go out of the state. Scott indeed was his own "best judge"; he refused to make an issue out of the matter—if he did, this would produce the kind of "disunion" and divisiveness against which he had preached. Harrison, when he heard of the controversy, wrote Scott that since his request of Wells had been for federal recruits he "did not think that the application" was "so material." He also told Scott that "the bare idea of your entertaining a different sentiment of me is extremely distressing." No ill will developed between the two, and Scott would be a staunch backer of Harrison's rising military career. A month later, after the battle of Tippecanoe, Scott wrote Harrison: "I should be the last to throw cold water on any enterprize you were ordered to execute; for I feel a lively interest in your fame and fortunes."[22]

The battle of Tippecanoe excited the military spirit in Kentucky. There was no doubt in the mind of most Kentuckians that the attack of the Prophet and his "collection of all the vagabond Indians he could find"[23] on Harrison's force was supported by the British. The Louisville *Courier* commented: "Well, war we now have" in "the western woods," and therefore there was no further need for "protracted moderation."[24] Kentucky had new martyrs: Colonel Daviess and other leading citizens fell at Tippecanoe.

Harrison wrote Scott a detailed letter describing the battle (in which 60–100 Kentucky volunteers participated), seeking to disprove charges that he had mishandled the expedition. The Indians fired the first shot, he said, and there was no contention between himself and Colonel Daviess, as alleged. He also objected to the rumors that the army was taken by surprise and that bravery and not military skill had been the deciding factor. Harrison admitted to logistical problems, which he said were not his fault. He emphatically denied that some of the officers fought only in their shirttails. In effect, Harrison wanted Scott to help counteract such rumors.[25]

There was no doubt among most Kentuckians, as reflected in newspaper opinion, that the Indian war in the Northwest was a British war. Scott also gave credence to this view in his December address. The savages alone, he noted, would not contend "with the force of the United States, which they well know would crush them at a blow." The "hand of British intrigue is not difficult to be perceived in this thing." The *Reporter,* in the spring of 1812, commented that, although undeniably "the Indians are engaged," one might "as well call the revolutionary war a Hessian war because the Hessians were hired by the British, as to term this an Indian war."[26]

The announcement that President Madison had accepted Great Britain's offer for reparations for the *Chesapeake* affair did not change Kentuckians' desire for war. Reparations for taking the four men from the *Chesapeake* would not resolve the basic issue of impressment, with thousands of Americans having been seized by the British. In his annual address to the assembly even Scott did not mention the British offer of reparations.[27]

To Scott, unless Great Britain drastically altered its policies toward the United States, war was inevitable to preserve the national honor. In his last state of the commonwealth message, on December 3, 1811, he noted: "A Crisis, portentous of events, which immediately affect us, seems to have arrived," for "war seems to lower over our horizon—Our exterior relations have never borne a worse aspect, since our Revolution." The battle of Tippecanoe signaled "a weightier conflict" to follow. The governor of the Indiana Territory was "attacked treacherously," when, under orders, he sought to establish posts on ceded Indian lands. "The Spirit of '76 has too long slumbered. . . . Boldly to retaliate, is often to prevent greater injury," Scott declared. "We should ever bear in mind, that we have nothing so much to fear as from ourselves." But "the Storm which threatens us may have one good effect, the seperating the Chaff from the wheat, and uniting the sound parts of the Community, for we cannot but believe, there is still virtue amongst us, under a savoring providence, to save our Country." Scott prodded the legislature to purchase 5,000 stand of arms and to make the militia system more efficient, as he had before recommended. On the domestic side, the governor reiterated points he had made previously.[28]

Gabriel Slaughter, the lieutenant governor, on behalf of the state Senate complimented Scott on the address—"the last they will ever have the opportunity to receive from the same revered Source." The Senate agreed with Scott: "The American Republic ought not to be coupled with that degradation which would follow our submission. Most fervently do we invoke the Spirit of '76 to save us from it, and we join with you in the belief, that while we stand united, and have confidence in ourselves, we can have no enemy to fear." There was no doubt, the Senate felt, that the Indians at Tippecanoe were aided by the British, as evidenced by Governor Harrison's letters. The Senate endorsed Scott's recommendation to put the state in a position of defense. The message closed on a personal note: "Though from the nature of human events, you will ere long withdraw from public Service, yet a remembrance of your services will long live in the hearts of a grateful Country." The assembly, however, did not act on Scott's request that the militia laws be improved, nor did it vote for the purchase of additional arms.[29]

War fever, nevertheless, was sustained at a high pitch in Kentucky. In December 1811 the legislature passed resolutions condemning Great Britain; if compensation was not made for the wrongs, Great Britain should be resisted with the full strength of the United States. Parades and meetings were held throughout the state, calling for war with Great Britain.[30] The outcry would soon be directed to "On to Canada!" The best way to punish Great Britain was to attack the empire at one of its weakest points; making Canada a "hostage" would provoke Great Britain to honor American rights.

In March 1812 the legislature notified Scott of its pending adjournment and asked if he had any final word for the assembly. Scott sent a brief message, saying he had nothing new concerning legislative matters. "Like a traveller who has passed through a long and toilsome journey," he said, "I welcome the prospect of repose." Scott expressed his gratitude for having received the governorship and said that he wished he could have done more to aid the people's happiness. And this time he did include a prayer: "May that Almighty Power which disposes of human events, dispense its choisest blessings to you and them; and in its mercy to the last earthly hopes of the human race, may no trial be prepared for my country, which its virtuous energies shall not be able to surmount." Humphrey Marshall, who would let bygones be bygones, said later in his history of Kentucky that Scott "makes his valedictory, and retires, like a patriot, and a sage."[31]

To raise the morale of the militia and to prepare them for a call for volunteers from the federal government, Scott issued two messages in the newspapers, in February and April. At last a requisition for troops from the federal government came. On May 1 Scott received a circular letter from the War Department, sent to the governors of the states, which requested the mobilization of 100,000 militia. Kentucky's quota was 5,500.[32] Scott, again using the newspapers, immediately called for volunteers, 1,500 of whom would march to the aid of Gen. William Hull on the northern frontier. Scott told the prospective volunteers that the causes of the impending war "are to be found in the blood of our unoffending brethren—in the groans and stripes of thousands of our countrymen, impressed and confined at this moment in the floating dungeons, forced to turn their arms against the country which gave them birth, and friends and relatives dear to their hearts. Rise in the majesty of freemen—regard as enemies the enemies of your country. Remember the Spirit of '76."[33] When central Kentucky received the news on June 26 that Congress had voted for war on Great Britain (June 18, 1812), patriotic demonstrations were held in Lexington and elsewhere, with cannonading and musketry lasting throughout the night. As *Niles' Weekly Register* reported: "The news of war was hailed as a second decree of Independence in Kentucky."[34]

William Henry Harrison received a royal welcome at Frankfort on Saturday, June 27. He honored Scott in a toast: "The Militia of Kentucky and the Governor of Kentucky. May the mighty spirit which animates the feeble frame of the veteran hero, diffuse itself amongst the military sons of our country, and enable them to tear from the ramparts of Quebec the last emblem of British power in America." Scott responded: "Governor Harrison and the brave officers and soldiers who were engaged in the action of Tippecanoe." Harrison gave a short speech, generally praising his troops at Tippecanoe. He then visited Lexington, arriving July 1. At the tavern of Scott's son-in-law, which John Postlethwait had reopened in 1809, 120 people feted the hero of Tippecanoe. Harrison's toast was: "Kentucky Patriotism—Evinced by the marching of her *ploughmen,* to avenge on the heights of Abraham, the wrongs done to the *seamen* of Massachusetts."[35] Harrison caught the mood of Kentuckians: a war for American rights—not of empire or expansion.

By the end of July Kentucky's quota of troops had been raised and organized. The Kentucky volunteers, however, had little enthusiasm for joining Gen. Hull's army. Harrison recognized this and asked Scott to inform President Madison that the Kentucky troops could just as well serve under Harrison. But a dispatch from the War Department, reaffirming an earlier request, urged Scott to send 1,500 volunteers to go with Gen. James Winchester to the aid of Hull. Winchester, at the same time, sent an express to Scott asking for 1,100 volunteers to meet him at Newport. Harrison again visited Frankfort and conferred with Scott on August 9 and 12, before and after a visit to Lexington, agreeing to let Winchester take the volunteers that he had requested. Harrison, however, expected to receive the other 400 troops.[36]

The demands and urgency of war filled Scott's final days as governor. In the gubernatorial election, Kentuckians again overwhelmingly elected an old Revolutionary War hero, Isaac Shelby, who they were confident would follow ably in the footsteps of the old soldier who preceded him in organizing and presiding over the war effort. Scott could hardly wait to return to Canewood, where he had not been since November. He even informed the governor-elect, "Pardon me my Dear sir for reminding you that my time Expires the 25th Inst [August] when

I hope it will be convenient for you to receive the Keys of the Government." Scott lost his secretary of state, Jesse Bledsoe, who resigned on July 27 in order to run for the state legislature; Bledsoe was succeeded by Scott's young personal secretary and assistant secretary of state, Fielding Winlock. Scott regretted that Bledsoe had not stayed out the final days of his administration, and he acknowledged Bledsoe's "friendly and powerful aid." [37]

From several directions there were calls for Kentucky troops. Governor Ninian Edwards of the Illinois Territory twice requested permission from Scott to recruit volunteers from southern Kentucky because of an expected Indian attack on the Illinois and Missouri settlements. Scott published a notice stating that he was allowing volunteers from the state to afford military service to the governors of Indiana, Illinois, and Louisiana territories, from whom they would take orders. He warned, however, that all such volunteers should refrain from any hostile action not ordered by the territorial governor and be careful not to involve the United States in any unauthorized hostile acts against friendly Indian tribes. Eventually Col. William Russell would lead a detachment of Kentucky troops into Illinois. Scott had already ordered out militia to range on the perimeter of the settlements south of the Cumberland, primarily to keep off straggling hostile Indians. Troops were being collected at Louisville for an expedition up the Wabash. [38]

Scott ordered the new brigade under Brig. Gen. John Payne (John M. Scott's and William Lewis's regiments) to rendezvous on August 15 at Georgetown, where the men would be armed and provisioned before marching to Newport to join Winchester's command. A day before the rendezvous, the Franklin County militia paid Governor Scott a visit at the governor's mansion. The soldiers lined up between the front steps and the fence. Two servants, one with a pail of whiskey and the other with a pail of water, passed through the ranks. Scott, hobbling along on his crutch, came out to talk to the men. With "his gray hair streaming in the wind and tears running down his aged cheeks," recalled a soldier many years later, Scott wished the men Godspeed and entreated them to be brave. After he had made the rounds of the troops, Scott choked with emotion and, suddenly turning around, hammered his crutch on the steps, exclaiming, "If it hadn't been for you, I could have gone with the boys myself."[39]

The brigade encamped on Craig's Hill in Georgetown on the fifteenth, and early Sunday morning the next day a throng of 2,000 greeted the soldiers and watched a parade, which was reviewed by Scott, Payne, and other dignitaries. Rev. James Blythe, president of Transylvania University, preached a sermon, and Jesse Bledsoe and Henry Clay also addressed the troops. Little did these militia volunteers know the fate awaiting them. Clothed only in linen and cotton, with open shirts and no coats or blankets, they were expecting merely an adventurous excursion.[40]

Scott had written President Madison on July 30, asking him to employ Harrison in "a strong campaign against the northwestern Indians."[41] Harrison returned to Frankfort on August 24 to help settle the final arrangements for the use of Kentucky volunteers. Leading citizens were requesting Scott to name Harrison commander of the Kentucky militia for the ensuing campaign. Scott and the others had no use for Gen. James Winchester, a sixty-year-old Tennessee planter and Indian fighter who, as second in command of the Northwest Army and a regular army officer, was then collecting a force to relieve General Hull at Detroit. Scott called a meeting of prominent Kentuckians who were in Frankfort both to wish Scott well as he left office and to attend the inauguration of Isaac Shelby as governor. The "caucus" was held on August 25, Scott's last day in office. In addition to Scott, present were Henry Clay, Stephen Ormsby, John Fowler, Jesse Bledsoe, Isaac Shelby, Samuel Hopkins, Harry Innes, former governor Christopher Greenup, Martin D. Hardin, William Logan, Richard M. Johnson, and Thomas Todd. Unanimously they voted that Harrison should take charge of all of the Kentucky militia on the northern expedition. Also, Harrison should be appointed a major general by brevet in the Kentucky militia. Each person attending gave his signed "written advice."

Scott immediately issued a commission of major general in

the militia to William Henry Harrison. This action aided Harrison's military career. The Kentucky appointment influenced the president to appoint Harrison supreme commander of the Northwest Army. In September, Harrison would receive a brigadier general's commission in the regular army. (Secretary of War William Eustis, a physician who was not too accustomed to military usage, had neglected to get a major generalship for Harrison, appropriate for the command; this would come, however, in March 1813.) Naming Harrison as major general of Kentucky militia raised constitutional and legal questions since he was not a citizen of the state and the militia major generalship allotment had already been filled. The commission by brevet, however, was considered sufficient technically (even though actually it was not) to obviate any constitutional or legal objection.[42]

Scott explained to the secretary of war that in appointing Harrison he had acted "solely under the Earnest and ardent desire I have for the prosperity of my Country." His own judgment was "supported by men in whom the utmost confidence is deservedly placed." The arrangements "were intended merely as provisional, and to meet the pressing exigencies of the case." Scott urged that Harrison be given command of the Northwest Army. The "confidence" of the "Western people" in Harrison "generally is almost a guarantee for his Success should he be appointed to Command there. Indeed I view it as of so much importance that the protraction or Speedy termination of the war there may depend on it."[43]

In his last act as governor, Scott, in orders dated at noon on August 25, precisely at the end of his term, directed Harrison to command the Kentucky militia "ordered to Canada to assist Genl. Hull," composed of Payne's brigade and Robert Poage's regiment "now on their march" and Lt. Col. James Simrall's light Kentucky dragoons and "such other portions of the volunteers and militia of this State, as may have been or shall be ordered to join you." This order in effect superseded Scott's earlier authorization to Winchester to have command of the major body of Kentucky troops going to the aid of the northern federal army. Scott also authorized, in addition, 500 mounted volunteers to join Harrison, should Harrison have need for them. Since the

Kentucky militia troops were raised according to an act of Congress of April 10, 1812, Harrison should expect himself to be governed by orders from the president, whom, Scott said, had been advised of Harrison's appointment. In the meantime, Harrison was to act "with the Troops under your command from this State, So as most effectually to accomplish the views of the Government, and to protect our exposed frontiers."[44] Having performed this last duty, Scott witnessed the inauguration of the new governor, and then he and his family left for Canewood.

From Lexington on August 29 Harrison, clad in a hunting shirt, set out to assume command of the Kentucky troops. On the way he learned of Hull's surrender at Detroit and of the massacre at Fort Dearborn. Winchester's troops had reached Fort Wayne—a fact that General Hull did not take into account, for whatever reason, when he surrendered Detroit. For the time being, Harrison and Winchester had more or less a gentleman's agreement, with each commanding a part of the army; when Harrison received his regular army commission, Winchester acquiesced in Harrison's having the general command.[45]

At Fort Wayne Harrison divided his army, putting 1,200 men, mostly Kentuckians, under Winchester, who, on January 19, 1813, captured Frenchtown on the Raisin River about thirty-five miles northwest of the Maumee Rapids; this was hailed as a great victory in Kentucky. Three days after Winchester's troops had taken Frenchtown, on January 22, Gen. Henry Procter, with 597 British soldiers and 800 Indians, counterattacked. His force badly beaten, Winchester accepted surrender to avert further massacre of his troops: 300 had been killed and another 27 wounded. Five hundred Kentuckians were among the captives. Thirty-six wounded Kentuckians who had been left behind after the battle, waiting for British sleds to take them away, were killed and scalped (in addition, some forty Kentuckians were slain in the battle). The body of Scott's stepson-in-law Nathaniel G. S. Hart was among the naked and mutilated corpses strewn along the side of the road, which were scavenged by dogs and hogs. Scott's able competitor in the 1808 election, John Allen, and John Brown were among the other eminent Kentuckians killed.[46] Many Kentuckians blamed Harrison for not having assisted Winchester. It was Harmar's and St. Clair's defeats all over again—Scott had missed those slaughters and, because of his age and infirmity, this one too. "Remember the Raisin!" was the rallying cry amid the fury in Kentucky. Perhaps Scott was a bit envious when Governor Shelby left the executive office in Frankfort to take command personally of the Kentucky militia volunteers in the field.

Meanwhile, Scott enjoyed the easy pace at Canewood. Only his youngest stepdaughter, Maria Cecil, was now at home. Two stepdaughters had married while Scott was governor—Anna Maria to Hart in 1809 and Eliza Violet to Francis Preston Blair on July 21, 1812. Maria would marry Benjamin Gratz on November 24, 1819. Scott became quite attached to Maria. Years later Maria wrote her mother (then Scott's widow), recalling the first letter she had written her, from Lexington, when she was twelve years old. "I was so thankful for your care and love for me," wrote Maria. She wished she could remember the words she used then, "for they got me the first praise I ever heard on my letter writing. I shall never forget the compliment General Scott paid me.—in the first place because I was astonished at his thinking I had written a good letter, and in the next because I was a little ashamed that any one except yourself should get an insight into my heart."[47]

Eliza Violet was eighteen when she married Francis Preston Blair. Scott was not too pleased with the match. He thought Blair, who was very underweight, with stooped shoulders, was consumptive and would die young. "You will be a widow in six months, Violet," Scott supposedly said. Violet replied, "I would rather be Frank's widow than any other man's wife." So they were married at the governor's mansion—and Scott's prediction was wrong by sixty-four years. Violet's cooking and the family lung medicine (herbs, honey, and whiskey) obviously were effective.[48]

Blair was to become editor of the *Globe,* in Washington, D.C., and a staunch supporter of Andrew Jackson. Blair would draw parallels between Jackson and Scott. In writing to his sister-in-law Maria Gratz in 1831, he said that Jackson was "very much like old General Scott. Benevolent and kind to a fault to those whom he loves; frank, affectionate and full of hospitable feeling. In this last, he goes beyond our old Kentucky General." When Jackson spoke about his enemies, "he puts one also much in mind of old Scott when he spoke of Humphrey Marshall."[49]

Scott's health failed rapidly in the late summer of 1813, and "after a lingering illness of some months," he died on Friday evening, October 22, 1813. The funeral procession "of citizens and volunteer corps," scheduled for the next Friday, was delayed by inclement weather until Tuesday morning, November 1, at 11 A.M.[50] Scott may have had a last satisfaction—one that in a sense closed his own career—to learn of Harrison's revenging the defeat at the Raisin with a crushing victory at the battle of the Thames, in which Kentucky volunteers had a major role, on October 5, 1813.

Among the newspaper tributes, the *Kentucky Gazette* on October 26, 1813, said that "the unbounded philanthropy of Gen. Scott, united with that social disposition which so strongly marked his private life, will cause his memory to be held in sacred remembrance by his numerous friends and acquaintances"; and his services,"which he performed for the Republic" in the Revolutionary War, Indian wars, and as governor, "have erected for him a monument in the recollection of his countrymen as durable as the Republic itself, and more magnificent than brass or marble." The *Reporter* commented: "The inestimable worth of this veteran soldier and patriot is recorded upon material more durable than marble; he will live in the memory of his country as long as history or tradition shall hand down to posterity the epoch of her liberty." *Niles' Weekly Register* of February 25, 1815, reiterating the Kentucky notices, stated that Scott "retired from office amidst the plaudits of the State, not till he had roused her choicest sons, and awakened that Spirit for the prosecution of the Existing war in defense of our rights, which has shed blaze of glory on the world. With the firmness of a hero, he had the affections of a child. He lived only for his country and his friends. He died poor, covered with honor."[51]

Scott's career spanned the "epoch" of American liberty and was indelibly wedded to that epoch. It coincided with the era of winning the Revolution and the Trans-Appalachian west—from the French and Indian War to the War of 1812. The two periods of distinction in Scott's career were those of the Revolution and the War of 1812. In one, Americans won their freedom from Great Britain, and in the other, in the view of Scott and other Kentuckians, independence would be fully consummated. As one historian of the Ohio country has put it, "The War of 1775–1783 between the United Colonies and Great Britain was Revolutionary; the War of 1812–1814 between the United States and Great Britain was the War of Independence."[52]

The significance of Charles Scott and the second War for Independence can best be measured by the enthusiasm mounted by Kentuckians for the war in 1811 and 1812 and their tremendous eagerness to serve in the military campaigns during the initial year of the war. While Scott himself did not exert his leadership for war beyond public opinion, he sustained patriotic ardor by his eloquence (with the help of Bledsoe). Scott's most important contribution to the coming of the war was to adhere consistently to the theme of national honor. In his messages to the legislature and appeals to the public, though holding the British in greater contempt, Scott defined the threat to American liberty in the violation of American rights by both Great Britain and France and European powers generally. To defend American sovereignty against one European nation would instruct the others. Military enthusiasm was so great during 1812 that most of the Kentuckians who enlisted in the regular army during the war did so at that time. The state provided 11,114 regulars, militia, and volunteers in 1812, while in each of the subsequent years of the war only a few hundred enlisted. Kentuckians paid the highest price in lives; of 1,876 Americans killed in battles during the war, 1,200 were Kentuckians.[53]

Granted that Charles Scott was both a product and a beneficiary, even if somewhat accidentally, of the times, the qualities of perseverance, common sense, simplicity, and sense of duty stood him well in his military and political life. As an orator for the occasion of the reinterment of Scott's remains from Canewood to the Frankfort cemetery in November 1854 remarked: "To a man of his stamp and mind, every incident in life is a lesson, every opportunity a teacher, and every day brings some wisdom.

For there was about him a natural judgment which made him take a right view of things, and shaped always his general course aright."[54] In public service, Scott was the dutiful and enterprising officer through the thick of the Revolution and the Indian wars and, in the end, an able administrator. Entering military service in the aftermath of an inglorious defeat and dying in the year of another, he nevertheless witnessed and contributed to the triumph of American arms, for better or worse, in the establishment of the American Republic. On Virginia's last frontier, he helped to tame the wilderness and to create a new community. A Daniel Boone or a Simon Kenton he was not, nor did he have their wanderlust or their fascination for the unknown. Nor did he have the shrewdness of an Andrew Jackson or the polemic skills of a Henry Clay. When Scott arrived in Kentucky, some 30,000 pioneers were there before him. But for a while he lived on the fringe of civilization and experienced the dangers and hardships as did other frontiersmen. Moderate in attitudes, although sharing some of the ambivalence of the typical frontiersman, Scott harbored no hatred for Indians in general, despite losing two sons under the scalping knives.

Aware of his own limitations, Scott never went beyond them; yet, when genuinely answering summonses to duty, he performed with energy and ability. A respected general of the Revolution, regarded as a "soldier's friend," he had stature in early Kentucky among the horde of army veterans—and, remarkably, entering the second phase of his life near age fifty on the frontier, continued to rise in esteem, accepting the highest honor from his fellow citizens at the end of his life. Scott, as much as anyone, represented and exemplified the character of the new American—the virtues and vices. If the era of the Revolution through to the War of 1812, the eve of America's national exuberance, was an epoch in securing American liberty, in Scott's career can be read America's coming into maturity.

ABBREVIATIONS

NOTES

BIBLIOGRAPHY OF
MANUSCRIPT SOURCES

INDEX

ABBREVIATIONS

AHR	*American Historical Review*
A-WP	W. W. Abbot, ed. *The Papers of George Washington. Colonial Series.* Vols. 1–4. Charlottesville, Va., 1983–84.
CJCLS	Church of Jesus Christ of Latter-day Saints Archives, Genealogical Department: microfilm collection of courthouse records, Salt Lake City
CS-UK	Charles Scott Papers, University of Kentucky Library
EJCC	H. R. McIlwaine et al., eds. *Executive Journals of the Council of Colonial Virginia.* 6 vols. Richmond, 1925–66.
FCHQ	*Filson Club Historical Quarterly*
FWW	John C. Fitzpatrick, ed. *The Writings of George Washington, 1745–99.* 39 vols. Washington, D.C., 1931–44.
HSP	Historical Society of Pennsylvania, Philadelphia
IHS	Indiana Historical Society, Indianapolis
JCC	Worthington C. Ford, ed. *Journals of the Continental Congress, 1774–89.* 34 vols. Washington, D.C., 1904–37.
JHB	John P. Kennedy and H. R. McIlwaine, eds. *Journals of the House of Burgesses, 1619–1776.* 13 vols. Richmond, 1905–15.
JP	Julian P. Boyd, ed. *The Papers of Thomas Jefferson.* 22 vols. to date. Princeton, N.J., 1950—.
KA	Kentucky Department for Libraries and Archives, Frankfort
KG	*Kentucky Gazette,* Lexington
LC	Library of Congress
MHS	Massachusetts Historical Society, Boston
NJHSP	*Proceedings of the New Jersey Historical Society*
NYHS	New-York Historical Society

Abbreviations

NYPL	New York Public Library
PCC	Papers of the Continental Congress, National Archives
PMHB	*Pennsylvania Magazine of History and Biography*
RKSHS	*Register of the Kentucky State Historical Society*
RV	William J. Van Schreeven, Robert L. Scribner, and Brent Tarter, eds. *Revolutionary Virginia: The Road to Independence.* 6 vols. Charlottesville, 1973–81.
SCHM	*South Carolina Historical and Genealogical Magazine*
VG	*Virginia Gazette* (Dixon and Nicolson), (Dixon and Hunter), (Pinckney), (Purdie), Williamsburg
VHS	Virginia Historical Society, Richmond
VMHB	*Virginia Magazine of History and Biography*
VSL	Virginia State Library
WMQ	*William and Mary Quarterly*
WP-LC	George Washington Papers, Library of Congress

NOTES

CHAPTER I

1. Goochland County Deed Book no. 1, 1728–34, June 1729, 97–98, 205, VSL; Scott Folder, Wyndham B. Blanton Papers, VHS; *The Edward Pleasants Valentine Papers*, 3 (Richmond, 1953): 1510–12, 1564–69; *WMQ* 1st ser., 23 (1915): 178n; "Bible Record of Josiah M. Jordan . . . ," ibid., 14 (1906): 32–33; C. G. Chamberlayne, ed., *The Vestry Book . . . St. Peter's Parish . . . , 1684–1786* (Richmond, 1937), passim; *EJCC*, May 4, 1717, 3:448, June 16, 1727, 4:142, April 29, 1730, 4:142, *JHB*, 1736–40, Nov. 2, 1738, 323; Malcolm H. Harris, *Old New Kent County*, 2 vols. (West Point, Va., 1977). One assertion, but not substantiated, is that Charles Scott's ancestors came from Newport, on the Isle of Wight, England (*WMQ*, 1st ser., 5 [1897]:282). The children of grandfather John Scott were: Samuel (Charles Scott's father, baptized Feb. 6, 1708/9), John, Jr., Edward, Joseph, Sarah, Martha, Judith, Jane (Jean), Jesse, and Mary. Edward, who served in the House of Burgesses, died in 1738. Like John, Jr., he also settled in Goochland County. He sold his Muddy Creek land to Gideon Patteson. A great-granddaughter of Charles Scott, Pattie (Martha Ann) Burnley, recalled that a Scott genealogy prepared for the family traced the ancestry back to the dukes of Buccleugh—of which no special credibility should be placed in view of her other faulty recollections. See *RKSHS* 1 (1903): 11.

2. Cumberland County Deed Book no. 1, Feb. 25, June 9, 1750, 276, 296, and no. 2, Sept. 22, 1753, 237–38, VSL; Cumberland County Order Book, 1752–58, March and April Court 1754, 152, VSL; *Valentine Papers*, 3:1514; "Council Journals of Virginia, 1726–53," *VMHB* 34 (1926): Oct. 11, 1728, 354, and 35 (1927): Sept. 24, 1753, 409.

3. Southam Parish, Powhatan County, Vestry Book, 1745–91, VSL; *Valentine Papers*, 3:1516; *VG* (Hunter), Feb. 6, 1752; *JHB*, 1752–58, 63, 108, 233; Cynthia Leonard, comp., *The General Assembly of Virginia* (Richmond, 1975), 83; William Meade, *Old Churches, Ministers, and Families of Virginia* (Philadelphia, 1861), 2:33–34; James H. Mosby, *Our Noble Heritage: The Moseby Family History* (Evansville, Ind., 1975), 117-18.

4. Cumberland County Will Book no. 1, June 21, 1755, Sept. 25, 1768, 95, 155, VSL; Cumberland County Order Book, 1752–58, June 23, 1755, July 28, 30, 1755, Feb. 25, 1756, 252, 277, 279, 281, 291–93, 300, 373. In 1746 and 1748 Samuel Scott was listed with six tithables (Jean A. Lurvey, *Goochland County, Virginia, Tithe Lists* [mimeographed, Springfield, Mo., 1979], 1:4, 2:7).

5. Cumberland County Order Book, 1752–58, June 28, 1756, March 28, 1757, 408, 459; J. P. Eggleston to Wyndham B. Blanton, Sr., May 6, 1942, Scott Folder, Blanton Papers, VHS; *VMHB* 22(1914): 427. Perhaps there was another sister, Sarah ("Bible Record . . . Jordan," *WMQ*, 1st ser., 14 [1906]: 32–33). Martha Scott married a Mr. Thomas and, secondly, Littlebury Mosby, Sr. (third marriage), no issue (G. Brown Goode, *Virginia Cousins: A Study of the Ancestry and Posterity of John Goode of Whitby* [Bridgewater, 1963], 221).

6. A Roll of Capt. David Bell's Company, July 13, 1756, WP-LC; Cumberland County Order Book, 1752–58, July 28, 1755, 292, and 1762–64, Aug. 24, Oct. 25, 1762, 41, 74.

7. Shane: William Mosby interview, Draper Collection, 11CC273, State Historical Society of Wisconsin, Madison.

8. A Roll of Capt. David Bell's Company, July 13, 1756, WP-LC; General Instructions . . . , Sept. 3, 1755, *A-WP*, 2:13.

9. Washington to Dinwiddie, Oct. 11, 1755, Evening Orders, Oct. 23, 1755, and Washington to Capt. David Bell, Oct. 28, 1755, *A-WP*, 2:105, 134, 144; Douglas S. Freeman, *George Washington*, 7 vols. (New York, 1949–57), 2:126.

10. Adam Stephen to Washington, Oct. 4, 1755, and Washington to Robert Hunter Morris, April 9, 1756, *A-WP*, 2:72, 345–46 and n; Freeman, *Washington*, 2:172.

11. Capt. Bell's Pay Roll and Receipt for May 1756 and pay receipt, June 30, 1756, WP-LC. Scott's pay was £1.9; privates received 15s. 4d. each; the ensign, £6.4.

12. A Muster of Capt. David Bell's Company at Maidstone, May 18, 1756, and A Weekly Return of Capt. Bell's Company, Aug. 1, 15, 22, 29, 1756, WP-LC; Washington to Bell, April 10, 25, 1756, Robert Stewart to Washington, July 3, 1756, Orders, July 12, 1756, Thomas Waggener to Washington, Aug. 10, 1756, and Washington to Bell, Sept. 6, 1756, *A-WP*, 2:347, 3:52, 235–36, 250–54, 340–42, 394–95; Louis K. Koontz, *The Virginia Frontier, 1754–63* (Baltimore, 1925), 316.

13. Council of War . . . , April 16, 1757, Dinwiddie to Washington, May 16, 1757, Washington to Capt. John Dagworthy, July 12, 1757, to Capt. Thomas Waggener, July 29, 1757, to Capt. Robert McKenzie, July 29, 1757, and to Dinwiddie, Aug. 3, 1757, *A-WP*, 4:136–37, 153–54, 300–301, 348–49, 352, 359–61, 361–62n.

14. Charles M. Stotz, "Defense in the Wilderness," *Western Pennsylvania Historical Magazine* 41 (1958): 90; Freeman, *Washington*, 2:309.

15. A Size Roll of Capt. Robert McKenzie's Company (ca. 1757–58), A Return . . . 1st Virginia Regiment . . . at Ft. Pleasant and . . . Artificers at Ft. Pearsall, June 28, 1758, A Weekly Return of the 2d Virginia Regiment . . . near Ft. Cumberland, July 10, 1758, and A Weekly Return of the Virginia Detachment Encamped at Raystown . . . , July 30, 1758, WP-LC.

16. A Return of the Six Companies of the 1st Virginia Regiment Encamped at Reastown, July 2, 1758, WP-LC; Washington to Bouquet, Aug. 19, 1758. James Burd to Forbes, [Aug. 31, 1758], to Bouquet, Sept. 1, 1758, S. K. Stevens et al., eds., *The Papers of Henry Bouquet*, 2 (Harrisburg, Pa., 1951): 389, 449, 459; Washington to Bouquet, Aug. 24, Sept. 2, 1758, *FWW*, 2:274, 286.

17. Return of his Majesty's Forces . . . , Nov. 4, 6, 1758, Return of the Invalids . . . , Nov. 18, 1758, and Return of the 1st Virginia Regiment . . . , Nov. 20, 1758, WP-LC; Alfred P. James, "Drums in the Forest: Decision at the Forks," *Western Pa. Hist. Mag.* 41 (1958): 52–53; Walter O'Meara, *Guns at the Forks* (Englewood Cliffs, N.J., 1965), 204. Washington's regiment at Loyalhanna totaled 765; Byrd's, 537; the total British, Pa., N.C., and Va. troops at Loyalhanna and vicinity, 4,600.

18. Dr. James Craik to Washington, Dec. 20, 1758, WP-LC; Forbes to Abercromby and Amherst, Nov. 26, 1758, Alfred P. James, ed., *Writings of General John Forbes* (Menasha, Wis., 1938), 263; Washington to Fauquier, Sept. 25, 1758, George Reese, ed., *The Official Papers of Francis Fauquier,* 3 vols. (Charlottesville, Va., 1980–83), 1:80.

19. Governor and Council [Minute, March 22, 1759], Marion Tinling, ed., *The Correspondence of the Three William Byrds . . . ,* 2 vols. (Charlottesville, Va., 1977), 2:671 and passim; Stephen to Stanwix, May 25, 1759, Major Tulleken to Bouquet, July 21, 1759, Bouquet to Col. Hugh Mercer, July 13, 1759, S. K. Stevens and Donald H. Kent, eds. *The Papers of Henry Bouquet* (mimeographed, Harrisburg, Pa., 1943), no. 21644, 153–55, 203, and no. 21655, 43.

20. *EJCC,* July 23, 1760, 6:168; William Crozier, ed., *Virginia Colonial Militia, 1651–1776* (New York, 1905), 30, 43; Tinling, *Correspondence of the Three Byrds,* passim; Reese, *Fauquier Papers,* vol. 2; the various returns in the Cornwallis Papers, War Office, Public Record Office, 34/47 (microfilm, VSL); Nellie Norkus, "Francis Fauquier . . ." (Ph.D. diss., University of Pittsburgh, 1954); David H. Corkran, *The Cherokee Frontier: Conflict and Survival, 1740–62* (Norman, Okla., 1962); N. B. and F. B. Kegley, *Early Adventures on the Western Waters* (Orange, Va., 1980), 64.

21. Cumberland County Order Book, 1758–62, Sept. 28, 1761, 418. For the French and Indian War service, Scott would be awarded in 1781 1,450 acres: 1,000 acres as a subaltern; 200 as a sergeant; 200 as a corporal; 50 as a "soldier" (Warrants nos. 611–14, March 8, 1781, French and Indian Warrants, Land Office, VSL).

22. Cumberland County Marriage Bonds, 1749–58, Feb. 22, 1762,

VSL. Pattie Burnley, great-granddaughter of Charles Scott, stated that Frances Sweeney's mother or grandmother was "Miss Howard, daughter of Frances Howard, of Gloucester county, Virginia. We have now some quaint old silver spoons, which belonged to that lady" (*RKSHS* 1 [1903]: 11).

23. See "Sweeney Family," *WMQ*, 1st ser., 16 (1908): 237–39; ibid., 24 (1916): 35–36; *Register of Ancestors: The National Society of the Colonial Dames* . . . (Richmond, 1979), 49, 81–82, 89; *Virginia Historical Register* 4 (1851): 135. Frances Sweeney may also, like the Scotts, have come from New Kent County, for there was a Sweeney branch there.

24. Cumberland County Order Book, 1758–62, April 26, 1762; Frances Scott's Will, July 11, 1804, Woodford County (Ky.) Will Book C. 79–83, CJCLS.

25. Cumberland County Tithables, List . . . , 1764 and 1768, VSL; A List of Tithables Sent the Lords of Trade—Cumberland, Feb. 23, 1756, Brock, *Dinwiddie Records*, 2:352–53. Tithables were defined as all white males eighteen years old and up and Negroes (male and female) over sixteen.

26. Cumberland County Order Book, 1758–62, Feb. 22, March 22, 1762, 445, 473, and 1762–64, Aug. 22, 1763 (signed/jury June 25, 1762), Nov. 29, 1763, 290–91, 371.

27. Ibid., 1762–64, May 24, Aug. 22, 1763, March 27, 1764, 212, 305, 411.

28. Robert D. Meade, *Patrick Henry: Practical Revolutionary*, 1 (Philadelphia, 1957): 106–7; Richard T. Couture, *Powhatan: A Bicentennial History* (Richmond, 1980), 75, 82; Cumberland County Records, July 28, 1766, *Valentine Papers*, 2:840.

29. *RKSHS* 1 (1903): 11.

30. *VG* (Purdie), July 7, 1775; H. R. McIlwaine, ed., *Proceedings of the Committee of Safety of Cumberland and Isle of Wight Counties, Virginia, 1775–76* (Richmond, 1919), Cumberland, May 3, 1775, 11–12.

31. McIlwaine, *Proceedings . . . Cumberland*, June 30, 1775, 16; Boynton Merrill, Jr., *Jefferson's Nephews: A Frontier Tragedy* (Princeton, N.J., 1976), 15; *VG* (Purdie), July 7, 17, 1775.

32. *VG* (Purdie), supplement, July 14, 1775.

33. George Gilmer to Jefferson, ca. July 26, 1775, R. A. Brock, ed., "Papers, Military and Political, of George Gilmer . . . Miscellaneous Papers," *Collections of the VHS*, n.s., 6 (1887): 101.

34. Officers . . . to Norfolk Borough Committee, July 19, 1775 *RV*, 3:322; [Officers to] John Blair, ca. July 22, 26, 1775 [notation by John Blair], Brock, "Gilmer Papers," *Colls. VHS*, n.s., 6:94–96, 99–100.

35. Address of the Officers . . . , July 26, 1775, Brock, "Gilmer Papers," *Colls. VHS*, n.s., 6: 98; Virginia Convention, July 28, 1775, *RV*, 3:361.

36. [Officers] to the President and Gentlemen of the Convention,

Aug. 2, 1775, Charles Scott Papers, Henry E. Huntington Library, San Marino, Calif.; George Gilmer to Charles Carter, July 15, 1775; Brock, "Gilmer Papers," *Colls. VHS,* n.s., 6:90–91; Virginia Convention, Aug. 3, 5, 1775, *RV,* 3:393, 401.

37. Vigrinia Convention, Aug. 5, 17, 1775, *RV,* 3:400–401, 457–59; An Ordinance . . . to settle the Accounts of the Militia . . . , William W. Hening, comp., *The Statutes at Large . . . Virginia,* vols. 6–13 (Richmond and Philadelphia, 1819–23), 9:71. The Virginia Committee of Safety, which carried on the routine business of the colony between sessions of the Convention, issued the commission at its meeting in Hanover Town on Sept. 19, 1775.

38. Brent Tarter, ed., "The Orderly Book of the Second Virginia Regiment, Sept. 27, 1775–April 15, 1776," *VMHB* 85 (1977): 162–63, 165n, 166–67.

39. W. B. Wallace to Michael Wallace, Nov. 12, 1775, Wallace Papers, University of Virginia Libary, Charlottesville; Thomas J. Wertenbaker, *Norfolk: Historic Southern Port* (Durham, N.C., 1931), 59.

40. *VG* (Purdie), supplement, Nov. 24, 1775; *RV,* 4:418n; Edmund Randolph, *History of Virginia,* ed. Arthur H. Shaffer (Charlottesville, 1970), 229; Ivor Noël Hume, *1775: Another Part of the Field* (New York, 1966), 367, 401–2.

41. Scott to Woodford, Nov. 26, 1775, Woodford to John Page, Nov. 26, 1775, *RV,* 4:476–77; Randolph, *History of Virginia,* 229; John R. Sellers, "The Virginia Continental Line, 1775–80" (Ph.D. diss., Tulane University, 1968), 86–89.

42. Tarter, "Orderly Book," *VMHB* 85 (1977): 180n; *RV,* 5:5; Sellers, "Virginia Continental Line," 89.

43. Extract, Scott to "His Friend in Williamsburg," 2 letters, Dec. 4, 1775, Peter Force, ed., *American Archives* (Washington, D.C., 1837–53), 4th ser., 4:171–72, 183–84.

44. Woodford to President of the Convention, Dec. 17, 1775, *RV,* 5:78.

45. Sellers, "Virginia Continental Line," 89–90; *RV,* 5:5.

46. Woodford to Pendleton, Dec. 9, 10, 1775, to the Virginia Convention, Dec. 10, 1775, D. R. Anderson, ed., "The Woodford, Howe, and Lee Letters," *Richmond College Historical Papers* 1 (1915): 115–17, 119–20; Woodford to President of the Convention, Dec. 11, 1775, *RV,* 5:109; Charles Stedman, *The History . . . of the American War* (London, 1794), 1:148; Howard H. Peckham, ed., *The Toll of Independence: Engagements and Battle Casualties of the American Revolution* (Chicago, 1974), 10; Benson J. Lossing, *Pictorial Field-Book of the Revolution* (New York, 1851, rept. 1969), 535–36; "The Battle of Great Bridge," *Virginia Historical Register and Literary Companion* 6, no. 1 (Jan. 1853): 1–5; Noël Hume, *1775,* 432–36.

47. A General Return . . . , Dec. 10, 1775, *RV,* 5:101; Scott to Capt.

Southall, Dec. 12, 1775, and A Morning Return . . . Colonel Howe, Force, *American Archives*, 4th ser., 4:245, 294; Tarter, "Orderly Book," *VMHB* 85 (1977): Dec. 16, 1775, 306–8 and n; Hugh F. Rankin, *The North Carolina Continentals* (Chapel Hill, 1971), 25; Extract, Scott to Capt. Southall, Dec. 17, 1775, Walter Clark, ed., *The State Records of North Carolina*, vols. 11–16 (Goldsboro, N.C., 1895–99), 11:353. The breakdown of Woodford's force: Va. 2d Rgt., 350; Minute Bn., 165; 1st Rgt., 172; N.C. 2d Rgt., 438; and N.C. Volunteers, 150.

48. Woodford and Howe to President of the Convention, Jan. 1, 1776, *RV*, 5:308–9; Tarter, "Orderly Book," *VMHB* 85 (1977): 314–15n; Wertenbaker, *Norfolk*, 67.

49. At a Council of War . . . , Jan. 9, 1776, Emmet Collection no. 6384, NYPL; Leven Powell to Mrs. Sarah Powell, Jan. 27, 1776, "Correspondence of Leven Powell," *John P. Branch Historical Papers of Randolph-Macon Colege* 1 (1901): 28–29; *RV*, 5:18, 371n; Tarter, "Orderly Book," *VMHB* 85 (1977): Jan. 24, 1776, 318n, 320, 322n.

50. Scott to Dunmore, Jan. 26, 1776, Chalmers Collection, NYPL; Scott to Capt. Southall, Dec. 12, 1775, Force, *American Archives*, 4th ser., 4:245; Ernest M. Eller, "Chesapeake Bay in the American Revolution," and Alf J. Mapp, Jr., "The 'Pirate' Peer: Lord Dunmore's Operations in the Chesapeake Bay," in Ernest M. Eller, ed. *Chesapeake Bay in the American Revolution* (Centreville, Md., 1981), 18–19, 90–91.

51. Pendleton to Howe, Feb. 18, 1776, Clark, *N.C. State Records*, 11:275.

52. *JCC*, Feb. 13, 1776, 4:131; Patricia G. Johnson, *General Andrew Lewis* . . . (Blacksburg, Va., 1980), 197; Proceedings, Virginia Committee of Safety, March 20, 25, 28, 1776, *RV*, 6:230, 249, 261; Tarter, "Orderly Book," *VMHB* 85 (1977): March 6, April 5, 1776, 327, 330–31 and n; Woodford to Charles Lee, May 2, 1776, VSL; R. A. Brock, ed., "Orderly Book of the Company of Captain George Stubblefield, 1776," *Misc. Papers, Colls. VHS*, n.s., May 9, 1776, 6:171; Mapp, "The 'Pirate' Peer," in Eller, *Chesapeake Bay*, 90.

53. Andrew Lewis to John Hancock, May 15, 1776, PCC; John Augustine Washington to Richard Henry Lee, May 18, 1776, Revolutionary Lee Papers, University of Virginia Lib.; Charles Campbell, ed., *The Orderly Book . . . of General Andrew Lewis . . .* (Richmond, 1860), June 19, 30, 1776, 52, 57; David Griffith to Col. Leven Powell, July 8, 1776, "Correspondence of Powell," *Branch Papers*, 1 (1901): 42; Lewis to Charles Lee, June 12, 1776, *Lee Papers*, 4 vols., NYHS, Collections, 4–7 (New York, 1872–75), 2:63; Sellers, "Virginia Continental Line," 129–30.

54. *JCC*, May 7, Aug. 13, 4:333–34, 5:649; Andrew Lewis to John Hancock, Aug. 22, 1776, PCC. Congress issued Scott a commission as colonel, dated June 19, 1776 (Etting Collection, HSP).

55. Rev. David Griffith to Leven Powell, June 16, 1776, Peter Force Collection, ser. 9, LC.

56. John F. Dorman, *Virginia Revolutionary Pension Applications,* 35 vols. (Washington, D.C., 1958–80), 25:30 (Philip Crowder); Lucy K. McGhee, comp., *Virginia Pension Abstracts of the Wars of the Revolution, 1812, and Indian Wars,* 35 vols. (Washington, D.C., 1950–66), 16:156 (John Davis).

57. Andrew Lewis to President of Congress, Sept. 10, 1776, PCC. Stephen was elected brigadier general, Sept. 4, 1776 (*JCC,* 5:733–34).

58. Board of War to Washington, Oct. 24, 1776, Paul H. Smith, ed., *Letters of Delegates to Congress,* 11 vols. (Washington, D.C., 1976–85), 5:375.

CHAPTER II

1. Stephen to Secretary Peters and to President of Congress, Nov. 16, 1776, William Livingston to John Hancock, Dec. 7, 1776, PCC; Stephen to Gov. William Livingston, Nov. 22, 1776, Gratz Collection, HSP; Washington to Greene, Nov. 8, 1776, Richard K. Showman, ed., *The Papers of General Nathanael Greene,* vols. 1–3 (Chapel Hill, N.C., 1980–83), 1:343, 344n; Gen. Mercer to the Board of War, Nov. 8, 1776, Stephen to the Board of War, Nov. 8, 1776, Force, *American Archives,* 5th ser., 3:600–601; *JCC,* Nov. 18, 1776, 6:957.

2. "Diary of Lt. James McMichael of the Pennsylvania Line, 1776–78," *PMHB* 16 (1982): Nov. 17, Dec. 9, 1776, 139; S. Sydney Bradford, ed., "A British Officer's Revolutionary War Journal, 1776–78," *Maryland Historical Magazine* 61 (1961): Nov. 29–Dec. 14, 1776, 165–66; Jared C. Lobdell, ed., "The Revolutionary War Journal of Sergeant Thomas McCarty," *NJHSP* 82 (1964): Nov. 23–Dec. 14, 1776, 37–39; Samuel Patterson to George Read, Nov. 30, 1776, William T. Read, ed., *Life and Correspondence of George Read* (Philadelphia, 1870), 216–17; Peckham, *Toll,* 26; Richard Hanser, *The Glorious Hour of Lt. Monroe* (New York, 1976), 101.

3. Return . . . , Dec. 22, 1776, Force, *American Archives,* 5th ser., 3:1401–2; Washington to President of Congress, Dec. 13, 1776, *FWW,* 6:364; James Wilkinson, *Memoirs of My Own Times* (Philadelphia, 1816), 1:119; Samuel S. Smith, *The Battle of Trenton* (Monmouth Beach, N.J., 1965), 10, 18.

4. Benjamin Rush to Richard Henry Lee, Dec. 21, 1776, Smith, *Letters of Delegates to Congress,* 5:640.

5. Freeman, *Washington,* 4:308n; Order of march to Trenton, Dec. 25, 1776, Knox Papers, MHS.

6. Weedon to John Page, Dec. 29, 1776, Weedon-Page Correspondence, Chicago Historical Society; Hanser, *Monroe,* 131, 135, 138, 143–44; William S. Stryker, *The Battles of Trenton and Princeton* (Boston, 1898), 18–27; Lyon G. Tyler, "The Old Virginia Line in the Middle States during the American Revolution," *Tyler's Quarterly Magazine* 12 (1931): 7; Max von Eelking, *The German Allied Troops in the North American War for Independence, 1776–83* (Albany, 1893), 64–71.

7. Richard Henry Lee to Patrick Henry, Jan. 9, 1777, William W. Henry, *Patrick Henry: Life, Correspondence, and Speeches,* 3 (New York, 1891): 37; G. Johnston to Lt. Col. Leven Powell, Jan. 14, 1777, "Old Virginia Line," *Tyler's Quarterly Mag.* 12 (1931): 109; Wilkinson, *Memoirs,* 1:136–38; Freeman, *Washington,* 4:327–30, 342–43; Stryker, *Trenton and Princeton,* 254–60; Varnum L. Collins, ed., *A Brief Narrative of the Ravages of the British and Hessians at Princeton in 1776–77* (New York, 1906, rept. 1968), 31; Samuel S. Smith, *The Battle of Princeton* (Monmouth Beach, N.J., 1967), 13–15.

8. Stryker, *Trenton and Princeton,* 261–64; Collins, *Brief Narrative,* 33.

9. "Anecdotes of Old Gen. Scott," newspaper clipping, Draper Coll., 26CC10.

10. George W. P. Custis, *Recollections and Private Memoirs of Washington* (New York, 1860), Jan. 2, 1777, 413.

11. Weedon to John Page, Jan. 6, 1777, Weedon-Page Corr., Chicago Hist. Soc.; Sellers, "Virginia Continental Line," 208; Stryker, *Trenton and Princeton,* 270, 285; Mark M. Boatner, *Encylopedia of the American Revolution* (New York, 1966), 891–93.

12. John Chilton Diary, Jan.–Feb. 1777, VHS; Christopher Ward, *The War of the Revolution* (New York, 1952), 1:319; William Duane, ed., *Extracts from the Diary of Christopher Marshall, 1774–81* (Albany, 1877), Jan. 10, 1777, 111; Lobdell, "Journal of McCarty," *NJHSP* 82 (1964): Jan. 13–29, 1777, 42–44; Ambrose E. Vanderpoel, *History of Chatham, New Jersey* (Chatham, 1959), 184.

13. William S. Powell, ed., "A Connecticut Soldier . . . Elisha Bostwick's Memoirs . . . ," *WMQ,* 3d ser., 6 (1946): 105–6; Washington to President of Congress, Feb. 5, 1777, *FWW,* 7:105; Harry M. Lydenberg, ed., *Archibald Robertson: His Diaries and Sketches in America, 1762–80* (New York, 1930), Feb. 1, 1777, 123–24; "Extract of a letter from an officer of distinction . . . ," Feb. 3, 1777, *Pennsylvania Gazette,* March 5, 1777, in William S. Stryker, ed., *Documents Relating to the Revolutionary History of . . . New Jersey . . . , New Jersey Archives,* 2d ser., 5 vols. (Trenton, 1901), 1:306; Lobdell, "Journal of McCarty," *NJHSP* 82 (1964): Jan.–Feb. 1777, 44–45; Jared C. Lobdell, "Two Forgotten Battles in the Revolutionary War," *New Jersey History* 85 (1967): 226–27; Peckham, *Toll,* 30. James Taylor's version of Scott's entreaty, recorded for Daniel Drake in the nineteenth century: "Shin them (shoot low) Shin the d——d rascals twill take two Well ones to carry off one crippled one, Shin them, G. D—them" (Draper Coll., 8CC166:5).

14. "Extract of a letter from a gentleman of distinction . . . ," Feb. 10, 1777, *VG* (Purdie), March 4, 1777; Stephen to Erskine and Erskine to Stephen, from the *Pennsylvania Evening Post,* May 10, 1777, in *Docs. Rev. Hist. N.J., N.J. Archives,* 2d ser., 1:364–67 (copy of Stephen's letter of Feb. 4, 1777, is in PCC).

15. Lobdell, "Two Forgotten Battles," *New Jersey History* 85 (1967): 229–30.

16. Washington to President of Congress, Feb. 5, 1777, *FWW*, 7:105; Robert Forsyth to Stephen, Feb. 15, 1777, "Extract of a letter . . . ," Feb. 10, 1777, *VG* (Purdie), March 7, 14, 1777.

17. *The Kemble Papers*, 2 vols., NYHS, Colls., 16–17 (1883–84), "Diary," 1:111; Leonard Lundin, *Cockpit of the Revolution: The War for Independence in New Jersey* (New York, 1940, rept. 1972), 224–25; Stephen to Maj. Angus McDonald, March 15, 1777, in Vanderpoel, *Chatham*, 187.

18. Col. William Harcourt to his father, Earl Harcourt, March 17, 1777, Edward W. Harcourt, ed., *The Harcourt Papers*, 11 (Oxford, Eng., n.d.): 208.

19. Ralph Falkner to Scott, March 16, 1777, CS-UK; General Orders, April 7, 1777, and Washington to Schuyler, April 23, 1777, *FWW*, 7:365, 453; *JCC*, April 1, 1777, 7:213; also PCC, reel 72, item 59, vol. 2, p. 10, n.d. The promotion was announced in *VG* (Dixon) and *VG* (Purdie), April 18, 1777.

20. Washington to Capt. Caleb Gibbs, May 3, 1777, and General Orders, May 11, 1777,. *FWW*, 8:11, 41; G. Johnston to Lt. Col. Jonah Parker, May 7, 1777, Washington to Woodford and to Scott, May 10, 1777, G. Johnston to Scott, May 19, 1777, WP-LC.

21. Henry Knox to Henry Jackson, June 19, 1777, Knox Papers, MHS; Col. Lewis Willis to Charles Yates, June 19, 1777, "Letters of Col. Lewis Willis," *VMHB* 2 (1895): 214; Lord Stirling to Sullivan, June 27, 1777, Otis G. Hammond, ed., *Letters and Papers of Major-General John Sullivan*, New Hampshire Historical Society, Collections, 13 (Concord, 1930), 1:402; Elias Boudinot to William Livingston, June 25, 1777, J. J. Boudinot, ed., *The Life . . . Letters of Elias Boudinot*, 1 (Boston, 1896): 49–50; Showman, *Greene Papers*, 2:107n; "At a Council . . . ," June 12, 1777, Worthington C. Ford, ed., "Defences of Philadelphia in 1777," *PMHB* 18 (1894): 2–3; Friedrich von Muenchhausen, *At General Howe's Side*, ed. Samuel S. Smith (Monmouth Beach, N.J., 1974), 58n; Theodore Thayer, *Nathanael Greene: Strategist of the American Revolution* (New York, 1960), 173–75; George F. Scheer and Hugh F. Rankin, *Rebels and Redcoats*, pbk. ed. (New York, 1957), 259.

22. John Chilton to his brother, June 29, 1777, Tyler, "Old Virginia Line," *Tyler's Quarterly Mag.* 12 (1931): 119; Scott to Sullivan, June 30, 1777, Gratz Coll, HSP; Hamilton to Scott, June 30, 1777, Harold C. Syrett, ed., *The Papers of Alexander Hamilton*, 1 (New York, 1961): 277–78; Washington to President of Congress, June 28, 29, July 1, 1777, to Putnam, June 30, 1777, *FWW*, 8:307–10, 324, 322; Muenchhausen, *At General Howe's Side*, 62; Emogene Van Sickle, *The Old York Road and Its Stage Coach Days* (Flemington, N.J., 1936), 83.

23. "Orderly Book . . . Muhlenberg," *PMHB* 34 (1910): Aug. 13–23, 1777, 182, 358, 443.

24. Scott to Col. Benjamin Harrison, Aug. 3, 1777, PCC; *JCC*, Aug. 8, 1777, 8:623.

25. See Harry M. Ward, *Duty, Honor, or Country: General George Weedon and the American Revolution* (Philadelphia, 1979), 53–54.

26. Ibid., 93–96; "Orderly Book . . . Muhlenberg," *PMHB* 34 (1910): Aug. 23, 1777, 443; Meeting of General Officers . . . , Aug. 7, 1777, Showman, *Greene Papers*, 2:134; "At a Council . . . ," Aug. 21, 1777, Ford, "Defences of Philadelphia," *PMHB* 18 (1894): 329–30.

27. John Chilton Diary, Sept. 1–7, 1777, VHS; Stephen to Richard Henry Lee, Sept. 5, 1777, Revolutionary Lee Papers, University of Virginia Lib.; Bradford, "A British Officer's . . . Journal," *Md. Hist. Mag.* 61 (1961): 168–69; Ward, *War of the Revolution*, 1:337–40; Dorman, *Va. Rev. Pension Applications*, 4:78 (Lewis Barlow); McGhee, *Va. Pension Abstracts*, 19:96 (Joseph Vance).

28. Weedon to [John Page], Sept. 11, 1777, Weedon-Page Corr., Chicago Hist. Soc.: ". . . Journal of Sergeant Thomas Sullivan . . . ," *PMHB* 31 (1907); Sept. 11, 1777, 412–17; ". . . Journal of Surgeon Ebenezer Elmer . . . ," ibid., 35 (1911): 104–5; John McKinly to Caesar Rodney, Sept. 9, 1777, George H. Ryden, ed., *Letters to and from Caesar Rodney, 1756–84* (Philadelphia, 1933), 221–22; Hammond, *Sullivan Papers*, Order of Battle, 1:448; Showman, *Greene Papers*, 2:158, 160–61; Samuel S. Smith, *The Battle of Brandywine* (Monmouth Beach, N.J., 1976), 16–23.

29. "Pickering Journal," Sept. 12–16, 1777, Octavius Pickering, *The Life of Timothy Pickering*, 1 (Boston, 1867): 158–61; Muenchhausen, *At General Howe's Side*, 32; John F. Reed, *Campaign to Valley Forge . . .* (Philadelphia, 1965), 148–56; Rankin, *N.C. Continentals*, 106–7; Scheer and Rankin, *Rebels and Redcoats*, 274.

30. Gen. McDougall's account . . . , Oct. 5, 1777, Bancroft Transcripts, vol. 1, NYPL; "Journal," Pickering, *Pickering*, 1:161; Council of War, Sept. 23, 1777, *FWW*, 9:261, 263n; Council of War, Sept. 28, 1777, Ford, "Defences of Philadelphia," *PMHB* 18 (1894): 341–42; Wayne K. Bodle and Jacqueline Thibaut, *Valley Forge Historical Research Report* 1 (1980): 17–21; Tyler, "Old Virginia Line," *Tyler's Quarterly Mag.* 12 (1931): 28–29; John W. Jackson, *With the British Army in Philadelphia, 1777–78* (San Rafael, Calif., 1979), 29–32, 43–44.

31. Weedon to John Page, Oct. 4, 1777, Weedon-Page Corr., Chicago Hist. Soc.; "Journal," Oct. 4, 1777, Pickering, *Pickering*, 1:169–71; von Eelking, *German Allies*, 115; Rankin, *N.C. Continentals*, 113–15; Thayer, *Greene*, 202–3; Freeman, *Washington*, 4:508–11; "The Diary of Robert Morton . . . ," *PMHB* 1 (1877): Oct. 5, 1777, 14.

32. [George Weedon], *Valley Forge Orderly Book . . .* (New York, 1971), Oct. 5, 1777, 68.

33. Scott to Frankey (Mrs. Scott), Nov. 15, 1777, Collection of John F. Reed, King of Prussia, Pa.

34. *FWW*, 10:103n, 133n; Gen. Scott's Opinion . . . , Nov. 25, Dec. 1, Dec. 4, 1777, WP-LC.

35. Weedon to John Page, Dec. 17, 1777, Weedon-Page Corr., Chicago Hist. Soc.; Lydenberg, *Robertson Diaries*, Dec. 4–8, 1777, 159–61; Ray Thompson, *Washington at Whitemarsh: Prelude to Valley Forge* (Fort Washington, Pa., 1974), 53–59.

36. John F. Reed, *Valley Forge: Crucible of Victory* (Monmouth Beach, N.J., 1969), 5–6, 70; Harry E. Wildes, *Valley Forge* (New York, 1938), 158; Edward Pinkowski, *Washington's Officers Slept Here* (Philadelphia, 1953), 143.

37. [Weedon], *Valley Forge Orderly Book*, Dec. 26–March 3, 1778; Reed, *Valley Forge*, 18.

38. Wildes, *Valley Forge*, 158.

29. Stephen to Washington, Oct. 9, 1777, WP-LC; After Orders, Oct. 25, 1777, *FWW*, 9:436; Rush's quote in Carl Binger, *Revolutionary Doctor: Benjamin Rush, 1746–1813* (New York, 1966), 129.

40. See ". . . Diary of Surgeon Albigence Waldo . . . ," *PMHB* 21 (1897): Dec. 28, 1777, 314–15.

Chapter III

1. Charles M. Lessler, *The Sinews of Independence: Monthly Strength Reports of the Continental Army* (Chicago, 1976), Jan. 1778, 58; Louis Gottschalk, *Lafayette Joins the American Army* (Chicago, 1937), 101–2; Committee of Conference Minutes [Feb. 17–18, 1778], Edmund C. Burnett, ed., *Letters of Members of the Continental Congress*, 8 vols. (Washington, D.C., 1921–36), 3:89; General Officers to Washington, March 4, 1778, Showman, *Greene Papers*, 2:297; General Orders, March 3, 1778, *FWW*, 11:19; *JCC*, March 19, 1778, 10:269; the brigadiers to President of Congress, Jan. 6, 1778, PCC.

2. General Scott's Observations . . . , Jan. 14, 1778, WP-LC. Dragoons originally were regarded as mounted infantrymen, as distinguished from cavalry, but eventually both were considered the same since both could dismount and fight. Dragoon units serving in the Continental army were "independent" groups, self-contained and unlike the light infantry drawn from the army itself.

3. Washington to Weedon, Feb. 10, 1778, *FWW*, 10:448; Henry Laurens to Gov. Johnson and to Gov. Caswell, March 14, 1778, to Col. William Aylett, March 19, 1778, PCC; Washington to Scott, May 22, 1778, WP-LC; Scott to Capt. McLane, May 23, 1778, McLane Papers, BV, sec. M, 1:48, NYSH; "Orderly Book . . . Col. Henry Bicker," *PMHB* 36 (1912): May 22, 1778, 337; Col. William Russell to Col. William Fleming, March 1, 1778, Reuben G. Thwaites and Louise P. Kellogg, *Frontier Defense on the Upper Ohio, 1777–78* (Madison, Wis., 1912), 211; J. Bennett Nolan, *Lafayette in America Day by Day* (Baltimore, 1934), 53; Rankin, *N.C. Continentals*, 151.

4. Scott's Opinion . . . , June 17, 18, 1778, WP-LC; Thomas Boyd, *Mad Anthony Wayne* (New York, 1929), 112.

5. Scott to Capt. McLane, June 19, 1778, McLane Papers, BV, sec. M. 1:51, NYHS; Washington to Scott, Henry Jackson to Washington, Jacob Morris to Washington, and Instructions, June 24, 1778, WP-LC; Washington to President of Congress, July 1, 1778, PCC; Washington to Philemon Dickinson and to Maxwell, June 24, 1778, *FWW*, 12:112–14, 115n; Lloyd A. Brown and Howard H. Peckham, eds., *Revolutionary War Journal of Henry Dearborn* (New York, 1939, rept. 1971), June 24, 1778, 124; Gottschalk, *Lafayette Joins American Army*, 207–9.

6. Hamilton to Washington and Steuben to Scott, June 25, 1778, WP-LC, Washington to Lafayette, June 25, 1778, Lafayette to Washington, June 26, 1778, Stanley J. Idzerda, ed., *Lafayette in the Age of the American Revolution: Selected Letters and Papers, 1776–90*, vols. 1–4 (Ithaca, N.Y., 1977–81), 2:87, 90; Brown and Peckham, *Dearborn Journal*, June 24–26, 1778, 124–25; Broadus Mitchell, "The Battle of Monmouth through Alexander Hamilton's Eyes," *NJHSP* 73 (1955): 248; Gottschalk, *Lafayette Joins American Army*, 210, 215–16; John M. Palmer, *General von Steuben* (New Haven, 1937), 181–82.

7. Washington to Charles Lee, June 26, *FWW*, 12:120; Showman, *Greene Papers*, 2:453n; Don Higginbotham, *Daniel Morgan: Revolutionary Rifleman* (Chapel Hill, N.C., 1961), 89; Gottschalk, *Lafayette Joins American Army*, 218–19; Boyd, *Wayne*, 116–17.

8. Court-martial proceedings, *Lee Papers*, vol. 3; Wayne to Scott, June 30, 1778, WP-LC; Showman, *Greene Papers*, 2:454n; Gottschalk, *Lafayette Joins American Army*, 219–23; Samuel Thomas, "William Croghan: A Pioneer Kentucky Gentleman," *FCHQ* 63 (1969): 38.

9. Charlemagne Tower, *The Marquis de La Fayette in the American Revolution*, 2 vols. (Philadelphia, 1901), 1:382–83; Samuel S. Smith, *The Battle of Monmouth* (Monmouth Beach, N.J., 1964), 18–19.

10. Theodore B. Lewis, "Was Washington Profane at Monmouth?" *New Jersey History* 89 (1971): 149–62.

11. Washington to President of Congress, July 1, 1778, *FWW*, 12:143–45; William S. Stryker, *The Battle of Monmouth* (Princeton, N.J., 1927), 193–97; Thayer, *Greene*, 246; Boatner, *Encyclopedia of Revolution*, 734–24.

12. "Journal of Ebenezer Wild," *Proceedings of the MHS*, 2d ser., 6 (1890): July 2–15, 1778, 110–12; Smith, *Monmouth*, 24; William B. Willcox, *Portrait of a General: Sir Henry Clinton . . .* (New York, 1964), 237; Rankin, *N.C. Continentals*, 160–61; Freeman, *Washington*, 50.

13. *Lee Papers*, Aug. 12, 1778, 3:208; John R. Alden, *General Charles Lee: Traitor or Patriot* (Baton Rouge, La., 1951), 234–39.

14. General Orders, July 22, 1778, *FWW*, 12:215–17; ibid., 12:388n; Christopher Ward, *The Delaware Continentals, 1776–83* (Wilmington, 1941), 282; Fred A. Berg, *Encyclopeedia of Continental Army Units . . .* (Harrisburg, Pa., 1972), 124, 127, 130; Proceedings of a Council of

General Officers, July 25, 1778, and Council of War, Sept. 1, 1778, WP-LC.

15. After Orders, Aug. 8, 1778, *FWW*, 12:300–301. Field officers for Scott's light infantry corps: colonels—Richard Parker (1st Va.), Mordecai Gist (3d Md.), Richard Butler (9th Pa.), David Henley (Additional Cont. Regiment), and Morris Graham (N.Y. militia regiment); lt. colonels—Josiah Harmar (6th Pa.), Charles Simms (6th Va.), and Isaac Sherman (8th Conn.); majors—John Stewart (2d Md.), Richard Taylor (13th Va.), and Benjamin Ledyard (4th N.Y.). Subsequently there were changes, for example, Josiah Harmar became "violently ill with pleursy" and had to leave Scott's corps (Josiah Harmar Papers, Nov. 11, 1778, Draper Coll., 1W1).

16. Washington to Scott, Aug. 14, 1778, WP-LC; [Orders], Aug. 14, 1778, Clark, *N.C. State Records,* 12:534.

17. Scott to Washington, Aug. 22, 28, 29, 30, 31, Sept. 2, 3, 10, 1778, Cols. Parker and Butler to Scott, Aug. 29, 1778, and Eli Leavenworth to Scott, Sept. 18, 1778, WP-LC; Morton Pennypacker, *General Washington's Spies on Long Island and in New York* (New York, 1939), 2; John Bakeless, *Turncoats, Traitors, and Heroes* (Philadelphia, 1959), 226.

18. Scott to Washington, Aug. 31, 1778, WP-LC; Joseph P. Tustin, ed., *Diary of the American War: A Hessian Journal, Captain Johann Ewald* . . . (New Haven, 1979), 144–45, 406n; Carson Ritchie, ed., "A New York Diary . . . ," *Narratives of the Revolution in New York* . . . (New York, 1975), Aug. 31, 1778, 254; John G. Simcoe, *Military Journal . . . Queen's Rangers* (New York, 1844), 74–86; Otto Hufeland, *Westchester County during the Amereican Revolution, 1775–83* (White Plains, N.Y., 1926), 259–60; Edward H. Hall, *Philipse Manor Hall at Yonkers, N.Y.* (New York, 1912), 168.

19. Edmund Pendleton to Woodford, Sept. 19, 1778, Mays, *Letters of Pendleton,* 1:270.

20. Scott to Washington, Sept. 14, 1778, Benjamin Tallmadge to Scott, Sept. 16 (letter no. 1), 1778, WP-LC; [Scott's] Instructions to Capt. McLane, Sept. 8, 1778, McLane Papers, BV, sec. M, 1:66, NYHS.

21. Washington to Scott, Sept. 15, 1778, WP-LC.

22. Scott to Washington, Sept. 12, 13, 15 (letters nos. 1, 2), 1778, Tallmadge to Scott, Sept. 16 (letter no. 2), 17, ibid.; Robert Bass, *The Green Dragoon: The Lives of Banastre Tarleton and Mary Robinson* (New York, 1957), 50; Hufeland, *Westchester County,* 262–63.

23. Scott to Washington, Sept. 17, 1778, WP-LC; Washington to the QM General, Sept. 15, 1778, to Greene, Sept. 22, 1778, *FWW*, 462, 480; Ward, *Delaware Continentals,* 283; Charles S. Hall, *Life and Letters of Samuel Holden Parsons* (Binghamton, N.Y., 1905), 193–94.

24. Scott to Washington, Sept. 20, 21, 1778, WP-LC.

25. Scott to Washington, Sept. 21, 29, Oct. 9, 13 (letter no. 1), Nov.

6, 1778, Washington to Scott, Sept. 30, 1778, ibid.; General Orders, Oct. 10, 1778, *FWW*, 13:60.

26. Tench Tilghman to Scott, Sept. 21, 1778, WP-LC.

27. Washington to Scott, Sept. 25, 1778, to Stirling, Sept. 24, 1778, Scott to Washington, Sept. 26 (letter no. 1), 1778, ibid.

28. Tustin, *Diary . . . Ewald*, Sept. 25–26, 1778, 149–50.

29. Scott to Washington, Sept. 27 (letter no. 2), 1778, WP-LC.

30. Washington to Scott, Sept. 29, 1778, to Greene and to Gates, Oct. 1, 1778, Tallmadge to Gates, Sept. 29, 1778, Scott to Washington, Sept. 29, 30 (letters nos. 1, 2), 1778, ibid.; David Griffith to Stirling, Oct. 20, 1778, VSL photostat; G. D. Scull, ed., *The Montresor Journals*, NYHS, Colls., 14 (1881), Sept. 28, 1778, 513; Ritchie, "New York Diary," *Narratives*, 243, 279; Thomas Jones, *History of New York during the Revolutionary War* (New York, 1879), 2:286; Stedman, *History . . . American War*, 2:41–42; Burt G. Loescher, *Washington's Eyes: The Continental Light Dragoons* (Ft. Collins, Colo., 1977), 69–76; David H. Murdoch, ed., *Rebellion in America . . .[Excerpts from the Annual Register]* (Santa Barbara, Calif., 1979), 1779, 666; Thomas H. Edsall, ed., "Journal of Lieutenant John Charles Philip von Kraft . . . ," NYHS, *Colls.* 15 (1882): Sept. 30, 1778, 62; *FWW*, 13:4n.

31. Scott to Washington, Sept. 21, Oct. 7, 10, 1778, to Gates, Oct. 8, 1778, Washington to Scott, Sept. 30, Oct. 8, 11, 1778, WP-LC; Tustin, *Diary . . . Ewald*, 152; Bernhard A. Uhlendorf, ed., *Revolution in America . . . Major Baurmeister of the Hessian Forces* (New Brunswick, N.J., 1957), 223; *FWW*, 13:47n. For a description of British patrols versus those of Scott, see Tustin, *Diary . . . Ewald*, 150–55, and Edsall, "Journal . . . Kraft," NYHS, *Colls.* 15 (1882): 63–72.

32. Washington to Scott, Oct. 11, 1778, WP-LC; Armand to Scott, Oct. 10, 12 and nn (ca. Nov. 1), 1778, "Letters of Col. Armand, 1777–91," NYHS, *Colls.* 11 (1878): 297–301; John H. Stutesman, Jr., "Colonel Armand and Washington's Cavalry," *NYHS Qurterly* 45 (1961): 18–23; George F. Scheer, *Private Yankee Doodle . . . Joseph Plumb Martin* (Boston, 1962), 57.

33. Washington to Scott, Sept. 25, 29, Oct. 18, 1778, Scott to Washington, Oct. 18 (letter no. 3), 1778, WP-LC; Greene to McDougall, Nov. 8, 1778, McDougall to Greene, Nov. 12, 1778, Showman, *Greene Papers*, 3:48, 64.

34. Tallmadge to Scott, Oct. 29, 1778, Scott to Washington, Nov. 7, 1778, WP-LC; Henry P. Johnston, "The Secret Service of the Revolution," *Mag. of Amer. Hist.* 8 (1882): 95–105; Corey Ford, *A Peculiar Service: A Narrative of Espionage . . . New York . . . American Revolution* (Boston, 1965), 142–54; Bakeless, *Turncoats*, 226–30; Charles S. Hall, *Benjamin Tallmadge, Revolutionary Soldier and American Statesman* (New York, 1942), 45–47.

35. Washington to Scott, Nov. 8, 1778, WP-LC.

36. Bakeless, *Turncoats,* 252–59.

37. Scott to Washington, Oct. 3, 4, 6, 9, 13 (letter no. 2), 15 (letter no. 1), 16, 17 (letters nos. 1, 2), 19, Nov. 2 (letter no. 2), 7, 10, 1778, Washington to Scott, Oct. 16, 31, 1778, to Brig. Gen. Clinton, Nov. 8, 1778, WP-LC; Washington to Scott, Oct. 11, 1778, *FWW,* 13:67.

38. Washington to Scott, Oct. 15, 1778, Scott to Washington, Oct. 18, 1778, WP-LC; Washington to Magistrates and Selectmen of Norwalk, Oct. 15, 1778, *FWW,* 13:81–82.

39. Washington to Scott, Oct. 18, 25, 1778, WP-LC.

40. Scott to Washington, Oct. 15 (letter no. 1), 1778, Washington to Scott, Oct. 17, 1778, ibid.; Washington to Col. Theodorick Bland, Oct. 17, 1778, *FWW,* 13:96.

41. Scott to Washington, Oct. 13, 21, 29, Nov. 4, 1778, Washington to Scott, Oct. 31, Nov. 5, 1778, WP-LC.

42. Scott to Washington, Nov. 6, 1778, Washington to Scott, Nov. 7, 1778, ibid.

43. Washington to Henley, Nov. 27, 1778, ibid.; Washington to Col. Nathaniel Gist, Feb. 22, 1779, *FWW,* 14:139–40; Ward, *Delaware Continentals,* 284.

44. Washington to Henley, Nov. 18, 1778, WP-LC; Scott to Greene, Dec. 8, 1778, Showman, *Greene Papers,* 3:109–10.

Chapter IV

1. Washington to Weedon, March 6, 1779, *FWW,* 15:205.

2. Washington to Scott, March 6, 1779, ibid., 203–4. For a description of activity at the tavern, April 1782, see marquis de Chastellux, *Travels in North America . . .* , ed. Howard Rice, Jr. (Chapel Hill, N.C., 1963), 2:416.

3. Lee A. Wallace, Jr., ed., *The Orderly Book of Captain Benjamin Taliaferro . . .* (Richmond, 1980), 6; Lessler, *Sinews,* 108; *JCC,* March 10, 1779, 15:1455; Proclamation, March 10, 1779, *FWW,* 15:222.

4. H. R. McIlwaine, ed., *Journals of the Council of State of Virginia,* 2 (Richmond, 1932): March 31, 1779, 252; Scott to Washington, March 22, 1779, Washington to Scott, April 10, 1779, WP-LC.

5. Scott to Washington, April 24, 1779, WP-LC.

6. Scott to Washington, April 28, 1779, Washington to Scott, May 12, 1779, ibid.; *VG* (Dixon and Nicolson), May 1, 1779.

7. Washington to John Augustine Washington, May 12, 1779, *FWW,* 15:60.

8. Washington to Richard Henry Lee, Henry Laurens, and Thomas Burke, May 5, 1779, to Col. Richard Parker, May 7, 1779, to Benjamin Harrison, May 5–7, 1779, to Meriwether Smith et al., May 25, 1779, ibid., 14:501, 15:11, 17, 148; Washington to Scott, May 5, 1779, WP-LC; Henry Laurens Statement (June 3, 1779), Burnett, *Letters,* 4:248.

Initially, the officers of the three regiments of Scott's new brigade were: 1st—Col. Richard Parker, Lt. Col. Samuel Hopkins, and Maj. Richard Clough Anderson; 2d—Col. William Heth, Lt. Col. Gustavus Brown Wallace, and Maj. James Lucas; and 3d—Col. Abraham Buford, Lt. Col. Ribert Ballard, and Maj. Thomas Ridley (William P. Palmer, ed., *Calendar of Virginia State Papers* . . . , 5 vols. [Richmond, 1875–85], May 12, 1779, 1:319; Bounty Land Warrants nos. 251–500, S 46372, Scott County: Abraham Buford, Aug. 16, 1828, VSL).

9. Washington to Gov. John Rutledge, May 7, 1779, *FWW*, 5:19.

10. George Collier, *A Detail of Some Particular Services . . . Journal aboard the Ship Rainbow* . . . (New York, 1835), 76–80; Patrick Henry to John Jay, May 12, 1779, Scott to Washington, May 12, 1779, WP-LC; Weedon to Walter Stewart, May 18, 1779, Stewart Papers, NYHS; Sellers, "Virginia Continental Line," 351–52; Robert Fallaw and Marion W. Stoer, "The Old Dominion under Fire: The Chesapeake Invasions, 1779–81," in Eller, *Chesapeake Bay*, 443–49; Marshall Butt, *Portsmouth under Four Flags, 1752–1970* (Portsmouth, Va., 1971), 14–15; Lossing, *Field-Book*, 2:538.

11. H. R. McIlwaine, ed., *Official Letters of the Governors . . . Virginia* (Richmond, 1926–29), Journal House of Delegates, May 10, 15, 1779, 1:366, 370.

12. Gov. Henry to President of Congress, May 21, 1779, ibid., 374; Scott to Washington, May 18, 1779, WP-LC; Sellers, "Virginia Continental Line," 352.

13. Washington to Scott, May 25, 1779, WP-LC; McIlwaine, *Official Letters*, Journal House of Delegates, May 20, 1779, 1:373.

14. Scott to Washington, May 27 (letters nos. 1, 2), 1779, WP-LC; extract of a letter from Col. Marshall to Brig. Gen. Nelson, May 26, 1779, *VG* (Dixon and Nicolson), May 29, 1779.

15. *VG* (Dixon and Nicolson), June 5, 1779; McIlwaine, *Official Letters*, Journal House of Delegates, May 29, 1779, 1:378; Jefferson to Scott, June 21, 1779, *JP*, 3:8–9.

16. Scott to Washington, May 27, June 10, 1779, WP-LC; G. B. Wallace to Col. John Cropper, May 12, 1779, Palmer, *Calendar State Papers*, 1:319.

17. Scott to Washington, June 28, July 20, 1779, Washington to Scott, July 8, 26, 27, 1779, WP-LC; Wallace, *Taliaferro Orderly Book*, 10; Morris Saffron, *Surgeon to Washington: Dr. John Cochran* (New York, 1977), 215; Jefferson to Scott, June 21, 1779, to John Rutledge, Nov. 11, 1779, *JP*, 3:7–8, 180; John D. McBride, "The Virginia War Effort, 1775–83; Manpower Policies and Practices" (Ph.D. diss., University of Virginia, 1977), 103–5.

18. Scott to Washington, July 20, 1779, WP-LC; Col. Abraham Buford to Scott, June 2, 1779, Misc. MSS, Buford, NYHS.

19. Benjamin Lincoln to John Jay, Sept. 1, 1779, John Jay to Scott, July 29, 1779, PCC; *JCC*, July 27, 1779, 14:893.

20. Franklin B. Hough, ed., *The Siege of Charleston* . . . (Spartanburg, S.C., 1867, rept. 1975), from Rivington's *Gazette*, March 18, 1780; Wallace, *Taliaferro Orderly Book*, 12; R. L. T. Beale, ed., "Revolutionary Service . . . Robert Beale," *Southern Magazine* 17 (1875): 606–7. Buford marched from Petersburg Aug. 27, 1780 (Muhlenberg to Gates, Aug. 27, 1780, Gates Papers, NYHS). Enlistment of Scott's levies was eighteen months.

21. Washington to Scott, Oct. 19, Dec. 14, 1779, WP-LC; Samuel Huntington to Lincoln, Nov. 11, 1779, PCC; *JCC*, Nov. 11, 1779, 15:1256.

22. Wallace, *Taliaferro Orderly Book*, 18–19, 22–23; William T. Bulger, ed., "Sir Henry Clinton's Journal . . . ," *SCHM* 66 (1965): 147; *VG* (Dixon and Nicolson), March 11, 1780; Robert Simons, ed., "Regimental Book of Captain James Bentham, 1778–1800," *SCHM* 44 (1953): 154; Thomas Pinckney to Mrs. Harriott Pinckney, May 30, 1780, in Jack L. Cross, ed., "Letters of Thomas Pinckney, 1775–80," ibid., 58 (1957): 236–37; Alexander R. Stoesen, "The British Occupation of Charleston, 1780–82," ibid., 63 (1962): 71; Edward J. Lowell, *The Hessians and Other German Auxiliaries* . . . (Williamsport, Mass., 1884, rept. 1970), 244–45.

23. "Notes on Threatened British Invasion," Dec. 1779, Jefferson to Theodorick Bland, Jan. 18, 1779, to Washington, Feb. 17, 1780, *JP*, 3:252–53, 263, 296–97.

24. Lincoln to President of Congress, March 4, 1780, PCC; Lincoln to Washington, July 17, 1780, Benjamin Lincoln Papers, MHS; "Revolutionary Army Orders, 1778–79," *VMHB* 22 (1914): 12–13; Joseph I. Waring, ed., "Lieutenant John Wilson's Journal . . . ," *SCHM* 66 (1965): April 1, 1780, 178; Samuel Baldwin, "Diary of Events in Charleston, S.C. . . . ," *NJHSP* 2 (1846–47): March 31, 1780, 80; *VG* (Dixon and Nicolson), March 11, 1780; William Croghan to Michael Gratz, April 8, 1780, Robert W. Gibbes, ed., *Documentary History of the American Revolution* . . . *South Carolina*, 3 vols. (New York, 1853–57), 2:129–30; Wallace, *Taliaferro Orderly Book*, April 2, 1780, 120 and n; Thomas, "William Croghan," *FCHQ* 43 (1969): 41. Scott's brigade, April 16, 1780, had 1,208 rank and file, with 676 fit for duty (Draper Coll., Sumter MSS, 1VV37); on May 9, it had 1,171, with 615 fit for duty (U.S. Cont. Army Return, Charleston, May 9, 1780, Sir Henry Clinton Papers, William L. Clements Library, Ann Arbor,Mich.).

25. Lincoln to Gen. Clinton and Admiral Arbuthnot, April 10, 1780, PCC; Edward McCrady, *The History of South Carolina in the Revolution, 1775–80* (New York, 1901, rept. 1969), 507; John C. Cavanaugh, "American Military Leadership in the Southern Campaign: Benjamin Lincoln," in W. Robert Higgins, ed., *The Revolutionary War in the South* . . . (Durham, N.C., 1979), 125; Thomas, "William Crogan," *FCHQ* 43 (1969): 41; Frances Williams, *A Founding Family: The Pinckneys of South Carolina* (New York, 1978), 153; William G. Simms, *South-Carolina in the Revolutionary War* (Charleston, 1853), McIntosh letter, 121.

26. Wallace, *Taliaferro Orderly Book*, 28; *The Annual Register* (London), 1780, 783; McGrady, *South Carolina in the Revolution*, 471–72; William B. Willcox, ed., *The American Rebellion: Sir Henry Clinton's Narrative* . . . (New Haven, 1954, rept. 1971), 164, 166; William Croghan's Journal, April 18 and 22, 1780, Draper Coll., 3N107; Baldwin, "Diary of Events," *NJHSP* 2 (1846–47): 85; Williams, *Founding Family*, 154; Boatner, *Encyclopedia of Revolution*, 210; Waring, "Wilson's Journal," *SCHM* 46 (1965): 180.

27. Lincoln to Gen. Clinton, April 21, 1780, PCC; Council of War, April 20, 21, 1780, no. 7713, Emmet Coll., NYPL; McCrady, *South Carolina in the Revolution*, 478–81; William Croghan's Journal, April 24, 1780, Draper Coll., 3N120; Simms, *South-Carolina in the Revolutionary War*, 134 (De Brahm); Orderly Book, April 24, 1780, in Gibbes, *Doc. History*, 2:132; Wallace, *Taliaferro Orderly Book*, 30, 32, 143–44.

28. Council of General and Field Officers, May 8, 1780, PCC; McCrady, *South Carolina in the Revolution*, 495–501; Lydenberg, *Robertson Diaries*, May 9, 1780; Williams, *Founding Family*, 157.

29. Lydenberg, *Robertson Diaries*, May 11, 1780, 228–29.

30. Return . . . Troops from Virginia . . . Scott's Brigade taken prisoner at Chas. Town, May 12th, 1780, Return of the Officers of Genl Scott's Brigade, and Return of Regiments in Genl Scott's Brigade, May 17, 1780, Sumter MSS, Draper Coll., 1VV54–55, 61; Tustin, *Diary* . . . *Ewald*, 238; Banastre Tarleton, *A History of the Campaigns of 1780 and 1781* (Spartanburg, S.C., 1787, rept. 1967), 22–23; Mabel L. Webber, ed., "Josiah Smith's Diary, 1780–81," *SCHM* 33 (1932): 2–3; Stoessen, "British Occupation of Charleston," ibid., 63 (1962): 72; Bernhard A. Uhlendorf, ed., *The Siege of Charleston* . . . *Diaries and Letters of Hessian Officers* . . . (Ann Arbor, Mich., 1938), Jungkenn letters, May 13, 1780, 411 and n. 7; Rivington's *Gazette*, June 7, 1780, Clinton and Arbuthnot to Lincoln, May 11, 1780, in Hough, *Siege of Charleston*, 78–80, 114; McCrady, *South Carolina in the Revolution*, 507, 511; Wallace, *Taliaferro Orderly Book*, 56n; Dorman, *Va. Rev. Pension Applications*, 16:78; George C. Rogers, *Charleston in the Age of the Pinckneys* (Norman, Okla., 1969), 47.

31. Moultrie, *Memoirs*, 2:116, ca. May 18, 1780; Marvin R. Zahnizer, *Charles Cotesworth Pinckney: Founding Father* (Chapel Hill, N.C., 1967), 64, 66.

32. Moultrie to Capt. Turner, May 28, 1780, to Patterson [Paterson], June 15, 16, 1780, Moultrie, *Memoirs*, 2:112–13, 118.

33. Duportail to La Luzerne, July 7, 1780, Elizabeth S. Kite, ed., *Brigadier-General* . . . *Duportail* (Baltimore, 1933), 178.

34. Job Colcock to Scott, Aug. 28, 1780, CS-UK.

35. Scott to Jefferson, Dec. 1780, *JP*, 4:278; Account Book with Virginia officers, Jan. 12, March 3, 1781, Presbyterian Historical Society, Philadelphia; Scott to Lt. Col. Jonathan Clark, Jan. 25, Jan. 29, 1781,

Nathaniel Gist to Clark, Jan. 26, 1781, Clark Papers, Draper Coll., 2L9, 12, 10; Fraser to Scott, Jan. 30, 1781, Cornwallis Papers, War Office, PRO, 30/11/92, 17.

36. Scott to Jefferson, Feb. 2, 1781, Emmet Coll., no. 7668, NYPL; Scott to Jefferson, Jan. 30, 1781, Jefferson to William Phillips, March 31, 1781, *JP*, 4:481, 5:307; "Recd of Gen. Charles Scott . . . ," signed Job Colcock, n.d., PCC; Scott to Col. Balfour, Jan. 30, 1781, Palmer, *Calendar State Papers*, 1:474.

37. David Jameson to James Madison, March 10, 1781, Willaim T. Hutchinson and William M. E. Rachal, eds., *The Papers of James Madison*, 3 (Chicago, 1963): 15, 16n; Scott to Clark, Jan. 25, 1781, Emmet Coll., no. 9120, NYPL; Jefferson to David Ross, March 13, 1781, Scott to Jefferson, March 1, 1781, *JP*, 5:141, 38–39; Lafayette to Cornwallis, June 20, 1781, PCC; Cornwallis to Lafayette, June 28, 1781, Cornwallis Papers, War Office, PRO 30/11/92.

38. Wilmer L. Hall, ed., *Journals of the Council of State of Virginia*, 3 (Richmond, 1952): Dec. 12, 1781, 11–12; Col. Davies to the Governor, Jan. 23, 1782, Palmer, *Calendar State Papers*, 3:43.

39. Report of Board of Treasury, Dec. 3, 1783, Report on certificate of Dr. Oliphant, Sept. 25, 1786, Old Accounts, Oct. 1–31, 1786 (concerning Board of Treasury Report, Sept. 22, 1786), Genl. Scott's Memorial recd Sept. 19, 1786, Referred to the Board of Treasury Acted on Oct. 3, 1786, Expenditures . . . Contingencies for Jan. 1 to 31, 1786, Report of Board of Treasury, Aug. 29, 1786, the U.S. to Charles Scott for Sundry Hospital Stores, Sept. 25, 1786, Board of Treasury Report, Feb. 5, 1787, PCC; Edward Carrington to Scott, Aug. 18, 1789, Scott Papers, Huntington Lib.; Scott to Maj. William Croghan, March 27, 1789, Meyers Coll., no. 1269, NYPL; *JCC*, 31:689, 758; Louis C. Duncan, *Medical Men in the American Revolution* (Carlisle Barracks, Pa., 1931), 317.

40. Germain to Cornwallis, Nov. 9, 1780, Charles Ross, ed., *Correspondence of . . . Cornwallis*, 1 (London, 1859): 80; Moultrie to Greene, Moultrie, *Memoirs*, Feb. 28, 1781, 2:162; David Ramsay, *The History of the Revolution of South-Carolina . . .* (Trenton, 1785), 2:295.

41. Scott to Cornwallis, Jan. 30, 1781, Cornwallis Papers, War Office, PRO, 30/11/93.

42. Gen. Scott's Memorial, recd. Sept. 19, 1786, PCC; Greene to Scott, April 14, 1781, Janin Family Collection, Huntington Lib.; William Pierce (ADC to Greene) to Scott, April 21, 1781, Nathanael Greene Papers, Clements Lib.

43. Gen. James Taylor, written for Daniel Drake, Dec. 1838, Draper Coll., 8CC166; also another version: Shane interview with William McClelland, n.d., ibid., 11CC184.

44. Woodford County Will Book C, Will of Frances Scott, July 11, 1804, 79–83; Job Colcock to Scott, Feb. 21, 1782, Janin Coll., Huntingɡ-

ton Lib.; Blanton Folder, VHS; Emma J. Walker and Virginia Wilson, comps., *Kentucky Bible Records*, 3 (Lexington, 1963): 23.

45. Cornwallis to Lafayette, July 18, 1781, and Lafayette to the British Officer having charge of the American Prisoners, July 25, 1781, Cornwallis Papers, War Office, PRO, 30/11/92–93, 26–27, 34; John Mathews to Greene, April 30, 1781, Edmund Randolph to Madison, July 23, 1781, Hutchinson and Rachal, *Madison Papers*, 3:66, 193, 195n; Roll of the Continental Officers . . . for Exchange, Aug. 4, 1781, *Original Papers Relating to the Siege of Charleston . . . Emmet Collection NYPL* (Charleston, S.C., 1898), 79; Dorman, *Va. Pension Applications*, 16:38 (Joseph Carter), 17:53 (Robert Chambers); Zahniser, *Pinckney*, 66.

46. Washington to President of Congress, Feb. 18, 1782, *FWW*, 24:4; Boatner, *Encyclopedia*, 289.

47. Washington to Rochambeau, Feb. 21, 1782, ibid., 17–18; Moultrie to John Hanson, Feb. 21, 1782, Cornwallis to Joshua Loring, July 3, 1782, Loring to the Secretary at War (Benjamin Lincoln), Sept. 3, 1782, PCC; Scott to Washington, July 24, 1782, WP-LC.

48. Greene to Scott, Oct. 31, 1782, Janin Coll., Huntington Lib.; Gov. Harrison to Recruiting Officer in Chesterfield County, Nov. 1, 1782, McIlwaine, *Official Letters*, 3:361; Hall, *Journals of Council of State*, Nov. 1, 1782, 3:165.

49. Scott to Washington, Oct. 27, 1782, WP-LC; Dorman, *Va. Pension Applications*, 8:47, 31:38, 15:85, 14:23.

50. Scott to Gov. of Va., Dec. 20, 1782, Arthur G. Mitten Collection, IHS (also Dreer Coll., HSP); Harrison to Scott, Dec. 16, 18, 1782, McIlwaine, *Official Letters*, 3:403, 405–6; Greene to Gov. Harrison, Feb. 3, 21, 1783, Col. Edward Carrington to Harrison, Feb. 21, 1783, Palmer, *Calendar State Papers*, 3:428, 438–39; Greene to Lincoln, Feb. 5, 1783, and John Banks's Certificate, Jan. 3, 1783, Syrett, *Hamilton Papers*, 10:432–55; Henry Banks, *The Vindication of John Banks . . .* (Frankfort, Ky., 1826), 5–7, 11, 46, 70–71; Thayer, *Greene*, 414–19.

51. Greene to Scott, Feb. 18, 1783, Scott Papers, Huntington Lib.; Harrison to Greene, Dec. 24, 1782, McIlwaine, *Official Letters*, 3:412–13.

52. Greene to Scott, May 20, 1783, Janin Coll., Huntington Lib.; Non Commissioned Officers of Bailor's [Baylor's] Regiment to Gov. Nelson [actually Gov. Harrison]—read June 10th referred to Supt. of Finance & Secy at War, PCC; Hall, *Journals of Council of State*, May 29, 30, 1783; 3:261, 263; Greene to Gov. Harrison, May 21, 1783, Palmer, *Calendar State Papers*, 3:486; Higginbotham, *Morgan*, 175–76.

53. *Journal of the House of Delegates* (Richmond, 1828), May session 1783, May 20, 1783, 13; "Virginia's Soldiers . . . ," *VMHB* 20 (1912): 184.

54. Scott to McIntosh, May 3, 1783, Gratz Coll., HSP.

55. According to congressional resolution, Sept. 30, 1783, *JCC*, 25:633.

CHAPTER V

1. Hening, *Statutes at Large,* Oct. 1780 session, 10:374–75; Patricia Watlington, *The Partisan Spirit: Kentucky Politics, 1779–92* (New York, 1970), 14–15.

2. William T. Hutchinson, *The Bounty Lands of the American Revolution in Ohio* (New York, 1979), 249–51.

3. R. C. Clough Papers, Virginia Continental Army Lands, Feb. 15, 1822, Box 14, VSL; Location for Genl Scott's Military claim, July 26, 1784, Account Book with Virginia Officers, Presbyterian Hist. Soc.; Weedon to Steuben, April 7, 1782, Steuben Papers, NYHS; Scott to McIntosh, May 3, 1783, Gratz Coll., HSP; *Journal of the House of Delegates,* May session 1783, 22, 171; Willard R. Jillson, *Old Kentucky Entries and Deeds . . .* (Louisville, 1926), warrants nos. 815 and 2012, 144, 359; Mosby, *Noble Heritage,* 123.

4. *Heads of Families at the First Census . . . 1790, Virginia, 1782–85* (Baltimore, 1952), 59; Scott to James McDowell, Oct. 11, 1783, Etting Coll., HSP. Tradition has it that the original name of the Powhatan county seat, Scottville (est. 1777), honored Scott. Nancy's date of birth is based on mention in Frances Scott's will that she would come of age for her inheritance after Aug. 1, 1804. Scott referred to her as a twin in his letter of Dec. 14, 1797, to his daughter-in-law.

5. Willard R. Jillson, ed., "A Description of Kentucky . . . 1792" by Harry Toulmin, in *A Transylvania Trilogy* (Frankfort, Ky., 1932), 139; Mann Butler, *Valley of the Ohio,* ed. G. Glenn Clift and Hambleton Tapp (Frankfort, Ky., 1971), 198.

6. [Wilkinson?] to Scott, June 16, 1785, CS-UK; Wilkinson to Scott, May 1785, quoted in Thomas R. Hay and M. R. Werner, *The Admirable Trumpeter* (New York, 1941), 62; Wilkinson to Scott, May 11, 1785, Thomas R. Hay, ed., "Letters of Mrs. Ann Biddle Wilkinson from Kentucky, 1788–89," *PMHB* 56 (1932): 41n; *Woodford Sun,* Jan. 1944.

7. William Christian to Mrs. Elizabeth Christian, Aug. 17, Nov. 4, 1785, Hugh Grigsby Papers, VHS; Hay, "Mrs. Ann B. Wilkinson Letters," *PMHB* 56 (1932); 41n; Richard K. McMurtry, *John McMurtry and the American Indian* (Berkeley, Calif., 1980), 46. For Scott's accounts with Short, see Peyton Short Account Books, LC. Short loaned cash to Scott's son Daniel in Oct. 1785—the first mention of Daniel. Traffic on the Ohio River grew rapidly; in 1785 some 1,000 boats with several families each descended the river; during the first forty days of 1786, 2,000 boats.

8. Anecdotes . . . Scott and interview with Jesse Graddy, Draper Coll., 26CC10 and 13CC132.

9. Powhatan Order Book 2, Sept. 15, 1785, and Powhatan Deed Book 1, Sept. 14, 1785, VSL; Edward Carrington to Joseph Carrington, Feb. 12, 1786 and A State of debts for which Joseph Carrington and Edward Carrington are engaged in behalf of Genl. Scott, Edward Carrington

Letters, VHS; Edward Carrington to Scott, Feb. 26, Aug. 18, 1786, Joseph Carrington to Scott, Aug. 7, 1786 (including Scott's account with Joseph Carrington, Aug. 7), Scott Papers, Huntington Lib.

10. See above, chap. 4; Scott's Narrative, sworn before James Duane, Mayor, Aug. 29, 1786: the U.S. to Charles Scott, PCC.

11. [Wilkinson?] to Scott, June 16, 1785, CS-UK; Josiah Harmar Papers, Jan. 19, 1787, Draper Coll., 1W274; Lee Shepard, ed., *Journal of Thomas Taylor Underwood*, March 26, 1792, to March 18, 1800 (Cincinnati, 1945), 12; George Imlay, *A Topographical Description of the Western Territory of North America* (London, 1793), 106–7, 162; Archer B. Hulbert, *Waterways of Westward Expansion: The Ohio River . . .* , vol. 9 of *Historic Highways* (Cleveland, 1903), 113, 118–19, 165; Charles Ambler, *A History of Transportation in the Ohio Valley* (Glendale, Calif., 1932), 41–42; Lowell H. Harrison, *John Breckinridge: Jeffersonian Republican* (Louisville, Ky., 1969), 39. For details of the entire route, see Thomas Speed, *The Wilderness Road: A Description of the Routes of Travel . . . Kentucky* (Louisville, 1886), 57–59.

12. Hening, *Statutes at Large*, Oct. 1787 session, 12:580; *Woodford Sun*, Jan. 1944.

13. *Woodford Sun*, Jan. 1944; *Scott County [Ind.] Journal and Chronicle*, April 29, 1969; letter of Moss Vance, ed., *Woodford Sun*, to the author, July 9, 1982; U.S. Geodetical Survey Map (1979).

14. Shane interview, William Mosby, Draper Coll., 11CC270–74.

15. Ibid.: Gen. James Taylor, narrative written for Daniel Drake, and interview, William McClelland, ibid., 8CC166:2, 11CC184.

16. Extract of a letter from Col. Levi Todd to the Gov. of Va., [May/ June] 1787, PCC; Timothy Flint, *Indian Wars of the West* (Cincinnati, 1833), April 11, 1787, 104.

17. John (Jack) Jouett, Jr., to Gov. Randolph, 1787, Edward S. Jouett, "Jack Jouett's Ride," *FCHQ* 24 (1950): 154; Shane interview, William Mosby, Draper Coll., 11CC270–74; Shane interview, William Tillery, in Willard R. Jillson, "Early Kentucky History in Manuscript—A Brief Account of the Draper and Shane Collections," *RKSHS* 33 (1935): 140; Mrs. William H. Coffman, "Big Crossing Station . . . ," *FCHQ* 5 (1931): 9; William E. Railey, "Woodford County," *RKSHS* 19 (1921): 58.

18. Hening, *Statutes at Large*, 12:580–82; George H. Reese, ed., *Journals of the Council of State of Virginia*, 5 (Richmond, 1967): Oct. 2, 21, 1788, 286, 297; James R. Robertson, ed., *Petitions . . . Kentucky to the General Assembly of Virginia*, Filson Club Publication no. 27 (Louisville, 1914), Sept. 12, 1787, 105; *KG*, Dec. 6, 1788; Draper Coll., n.d., 11CC251; Levi Todd et al., eds., *Some Pre-1800 Kentucky Tax Lists . . .* (Anchorage, Ky., 1965), Fayette County, 9.

19. *KG*, Dec. 5, 22, 1787.

20. Ibid., Jan. 25, 30, Feb. 14, 21, 28, March 14, 21, 1789; Mrs. Wilkinson to John Biddle, April 18, 1789, Hay, "Ann B. Wilkinson Letters,"

PMHB 56 (1932): 43 and n. John Jordan established a shipyard at Scott's Landing around 1788, making chiefly flatboats and later sailing vessels (Charles Scott Private Account, Jan. 17, 1789, Presbyterian Hist. Soc.; *KG*, March 12, May 28, 1805, Feb. 18, 1806).

21. A List of purchasers of Lotts in Petersburg . . . , Nov. 1, 1788, Charles Scott Private Account, Presbyterian Hist. Soc.

22. Samuel M. Wilson, "Matthew Harris Jouett: A Review," *FCHQ* 13 (1939): 95.

23. Shane interview, Herman Bowman, Draper Coll., 13CC172.

24. From "Excursion in the U.S. and Canada, 1822–23," by William N. Bane (1824), ibid., 8CC164; Lewis Collins, *Historical Sketches of Kentucky* (Cincinnati, 1847), 516.

25. *KG*, Dec. 1, 15, 22, 1787, Feb. 13, 1790.

26. Lord Dorchester to Lord Sydney, Aug. 27, 1789, R. C. B. Thruston, "Filson's History and Map of Kentucky," *FCHQ* 8 (1934): 33; E. A. Benians, ed., *A Journal by Thomas Hughes . . . 1778–79* (Cambridge, Eng., 1947), March 18, 1788, 164; A. C. Quisenberry, *The Life and Times of Hon. Humphrey Marshall* (Winchester, Ky., 1892), 47; John M. Brown, *Political Beginnings of Kentucky*, Filson Club Pub. no. 6 (Louisville, 1889), 209; Butler, *Valley of Ohio*, 264. For the court versus the country party at this time in Kentucky, see Watlington, *The Partisan Spirit*.

27. Harry Innes to Washington, Dec. 18, 1788, Harry Innes Papers, LC; John Connolly to Scott, April 6, 1789, CS-UK.

28. John F. Dorman, "Woodford County Militia Officers before 1792," *Kentucky Genealogist* 16 (1974): Dec. 6, 1788, 85.

29. Leonard, *General Assembly of Virginia Register*, 175.

30. *Journal of the House of Delegates*, Oct. 1789 session; To the President . . . The Memorial . . . delegates from the district of Kentucky, Nov. 28, 1789, WP-LC.

31. Patrick Henry to Scott, July 20, 1790, Etting Coll., HSP; Donald Jackson and Dorothy Twohig, eds., *The Diaries of George Washington*, 6 (Charlottesville, 1979): April 9, 1790, 108; Wilkinson to Harmar, March 17, 1790, Harmar Papers, Draper Coll., 2W184.

32. Charles E. Slocum, *The Ohio Country between the Years 1783 and 1815* (New York, 1910), 49–51; Wilkinson to Harmar, April 7, 1790, Harrison Papers, Draper Coll., 2W193.

33. Knox to Harmar, June 7, 1790, Draper Coll., 2W268–69; Kenton Papers, April 1790, ibid., 8BB85–86; Harry Innes to William Fleming, May 13, 1790, William Fleming Papers, Washington and Lee University Library, Lexington, Va.; *KG*, April 26, May 3, 1790; Edna Kenton, *Simon Kenton . . .* (New York, 1930), 200; Allan W. Eckert, *The Frontiersmen: A Narrative* (Boston, 1967), 336–37; Jackson and Twohig, *Washington Diaries*, July 9, 1790, 6:91; Harmar to Knox, June 9, 1790, in John B. Dillon, *The History of Indiana . . .[to] 1816*, 1 (Indianapolis, 1843): 260.

34. Knox to Harmar, June 7, 1790, Harmar to Robert Elliot, Aug. 15, 1790, to Maj. John Hardin, Aug. 18, 1790, Draper Coll., 2W68–69, 90, 291; Jack J. Gifford, "The Northwest Indian War, 1784–95" (Ph.D. diss., UCLA, 1964), 102; Court of Inquiry, Dec. 24, 1791, *American State Papers . . .* , Class V, *Military Affairs*, 1 (Washington, D.C., 1832): 24.

35. Scott to Muter, Sept. 11, 1790, Gunther Coll., Chicago Hist. Soc.

36. Shane interview, Hugh Garrett, Draper Coll., 11CC246; William A. Pusey, *The Wilderness Road to Kentucky: Its Location and Features* (New York, 1921), 26–27, 51–52, 62, 65.

37. *Journal of the House of Delegates*, Oct. 1790 session, Oct. 25, 29, Dec. 8, 1790, 4, 14, 26, 123; Leonard, *General Assembly of Virginia Register*, 179; Mary F. Caldwell, *General Jackson's Lady* (Nashville, 1936), 122, 154–55; Edgar E. Hume, ed., *Papers of the Society of the Cincinnati . . . Virginia, 1783–1824* (Richmond, 1938), Minutes, Oct. 26–27, 1790, 38–39.

38. Woodford Order Book A, April 6, 1790, 88; John Armstrong Papers, Notebook, 1790, Sept. 30, 1790, IHS; Harmar to Knox, Nov. 23, 1790, Draper Coll., 14U166; Shane interview, William Mosby, ibid., 11CC272; Harmar to Sec. of War, Nov. 4, 1790, *American State Papers*, Class II, *Indian Affairs*, 4 (actually vol. 1): 104; Randolph C. Downes, *Frontier Ohio, 1788–1803*, Ohio Historical Colls., 3 (Columbus, 1935): 24; Samuel Metcalf, *A Collection . . . Narratives of Indian Warfare in the West . . .* (Lexington, Ky., 1821), 106–7; William E. Connelley and E. M. Coulter, *History of Kentucky*, 5 vols. (New York, 1922), 1:382; Eckert, *Frontiersmen*, 342.

39. Harmar to Hamtramck, Nov. 29, 1790, Harmar to Knox, Nov. 23, 1790, Draper Coll., 2W352, 14U166; Basil Meek, "General Harmar's Expedition," *Ohio Archaeological and Historical Publications* 20 (1911): 86–87; John A. M'Clung, *Sketches of Western Adventure . . . 1755 to 1794* (Dayton, Ohio, 1836, rev. ed., 1852), 245.

40. Wilkinson to Hugh M'Ilwain, March 17, 1791, quoted in Mary Verhoeff, *The Kentucky River Navigation*, Filson Club Pub. no. 28 (Louisville, 1917), 227; Hamtramck to Harmar, Feb. 18, 1791, Gayle Thornbrough, ed., *Outpost on the Wabash, 1787–91 . . .* , IHS, Publications, 19 (Indianapolis, 1957), 279 and n; Frederick J. Turner, "The Origins of Genet's Projected Attack on Louisiana and the Floridas," *AHR* 3 (1898): 652–53; John C. Parish, "The Intrigues of Doctor James O'Fallon," *Miss. Valley Hist. Review* 17 (1930): 237–57, 245n; Jackson and Twohig, *Washington Diaries*, 6:70n; Peter C. Magrath, *Yazoo . . . Fletcher v. Peck* (Providence, 1966), 4–5; Arthur Campbell to Scott, March 23, 1791, CS-UK.

CHAPTER VI

1. Samuel M. Wilson, "George Washington's Contacts with Kentucky," *FCHQ* 6 (1932): 241; Federal Writers Project, WPA, *Military His-*

tory of Kentucky (Frankfort, 1939), 55; James R. Albach, *Annals of the West* . . . (Pittsburgh, 1857), 559; Richard H. Kohn, *Eagle and Sword: The Federalists and the Creation of the Military Establishment in America, 1783–1802* (New York, 1975), 108–9; Beverley Randolph to Scott, Dec. 30, 1790, Exec. Letter Book no. 9, 184–85, VSL; *KG*, Feb. 5, 12, 1791; Slocum, *Ohio Country*, 623. The commission is in the Kentucky Historical Society.

2. A Copy of the Orders for the Rangers, Feb. 23, 1791, CS-UK; A List of the Posts . . . garrisoned by the militia of Kentucky . . . commanded by General Scott, March 21, 1791, Draper Coll., 2W408; WPA, *Military History of Kentucky*, 56; Kenton, *Kenton*, 201; *KG*, Feb. 5, 12, 1791; Paul W. Beasley, "The Life and Times of Isaac Shelby, 1750–1826" (Ph.D. diss., University of Kentucky, 1968), 102.

3. Caleb Wallace to William Fleming, April 28, 1791, Grigsby Papers, VHS; David Williams to Scott, April 25, 1791, Henry Lee to Scott, April 23, 1791, CS-UK; Scott to Henry Lee, April 30, 1791, Scott Papers, Huntington Lib.; *KG*, Feb. 5, April 23, 1791; Downes, *Frontier Ohio*, 26.

4. John Belli to Scott, Feb. 17, 1791, CS-UK; *The Public Statutes at Large of the U.S.A.*, ed. Richard Peters, 1 (Boston, 1845): sess. III 1791, March 3, 1791, 222–23; [Sec. of War's] Instructions to Scott, March 9, 1791, *American State Papers*, Class II, *Indian Affairs*, 4:130; Downes, *Frontier Ohio*, 26–27; Calvin Young, *Little Turtle* . . . (Greenville, Ohio, 1917), 49–50.

5. Extracts from the Minutes of the Board, May 2, 1791, CS-UK.

6. E.g., see *KG*, May 7, 1791.

7. Harry Innes to Sec. of War, May 20, 1791 (copy), Harry Innes Papers, LC; William Leger, "The Public Life of John Adair" (Ph.D. diss., University of Kentucky, 1953), 41; St. Clair to Sec. of War, May 26, 1791, William Smith, ed., *The St. Clair Papers . . .* , 2 (Cincinnati, 1882, rept. 1971), 212–13; Gifford, "The Northwest Indian War" 145; Young, *Little Turtle*, 48.

8. Oscar J. Craig, "Ouiatanon," IHS, *Pubs.* 2 (1893): 338–39; David R. Edmunds, "Wea Participation in the Northwest Indian Wars, 1790–95," *FCHQ* 46 (1972): 247–48; John D. Barnhart and Dorothy L. Riker, *Indiana to 1816: The Colonial Period* (Indianapolis, 1971), 287; J. C. A. Stagg, *Mr. Madison's War: Politics, Diplomacy, and Warfare in the Early American Republic, 1783–1830* (Princeton, N.J., 1983), 185.

9. William Clark, A Journal of Genl. Charles Scott's Proceedings from the 23d of May to the 16th of June 1791, transcript, E. G. Voorhis Memorial Coll., Missouri Historical Society, St. Louis; WPA, *Military History of Kentucky*, 57. Except where noted, the description of the attack on the Indian towns is taken from Scott to St. Clair, June 20, 1791, CS-UK, and Scott to Sec. of War, June 28, 1791, *American State Papers*, Class II, *Indian Affairs*, 4:131–32; the report in *KG*, June 1, 1791, is essentially the same as Scott's report to St. Clair. For Scott's route, see also J. W.

Whickcar, "General Charles Scott and His March to Ouiatenon," *Indiana Magazine of History*, 21 (1925): 95–96.

10. Shane interview, John Craig, Draper Coll., 12CC146.

11. A Journal . . . Scott's Proceeding . . . , Voorhis Coll., Mo. Hist. Soc.; Wilkinson to Scott, June 3, 1791, *American State Papers*, Class II, *Indian Affairs*, 4:132; A. M. Gibson, *The Kickapoos: Lords of the Middle Border* (Norman, Okla., 1963), 45.

12. Jonathan Williams to Knox, July 5, 1791, Knox Papers, MHS.

13. [Scott's Proclamation], June 4, 1791, *American State Papers*, Class II. *Indian Affairs*, 4:132–33.

14. [Anon.] to Col. A. McKee, June 26, 1791, "Colonial Office Records . . . ," *Michigan Pioneer Historical Society Colls.* 24 (1895): 273; John Cleves Symmes to Jonathan Dayton, Aug. 15, 1791, Beverley W. Bond, ed., *The Correspondence of John Cleves Symmes* (New York, 1926), 150; Eugene F. Bliss, ed., *Diary of David Zeisberger . . .* , 2 vols. (Cincinnati, 1885), July 8, 1791, 2:199; Edmunds, "Wea Participation," *FCHQ* 46 (1972): 248.

15. Scott to Daniel Scott, June 3, 1791, Emmet Coll., no. 5958, NYPL; List of Indian Prisoners . . . , *American State Papers*, Class II, *Indian Affairs*, 4:133; A Journal . . . Scott's Proceeding . . . , Voorhis Coll., Mo. Hist. Soc.; *KG*, June 25, 1791.

16. St. Clair to the Committee of Kentucky, June 24, 1791, Smith, *St. Clair Papers*, 2:222–23; St. Clair Journal, June 25, 1791, Northwest Territory Coll., IHS.

17. Harry Innes to Scott, June 30, 1791, Gratz Coll., HSP; Scott to St. Clair, July 18, 1791, Palmer, *Calendar State Papers*, 5:359; St. Clair to Scott, July 19, 1791, Smith, *St. Clair Papers*, 2:226–27; Charles G. Talbert, *Benjamin Logan: Kentucky Frontiersman* (Lexington, 1962), 254–55; Scott to Gov. of Virginia, Aug. 2, 1791, misc. item, HSP; Charles Scott, Harry Innes, John Brown to commanding officer of Mercer County, July 5, 1791, Harry Innes Papers, LC; *KG*, July 19, 1791.

18. St. Clair Journal, May 25, 1791, Northwest Terr. Coll., IHS; John Cleves Symmes to Jonathan Dayton, Aug. 15, 1791, Bond, ed., *Symmes Correspondence*, 149; Lucien Beckner, ed., "A Sketch . . . William Sudduth . . . ," *FCHQ* 2 (1928): 57–58; WPA, *Military History of Kentucky*, 60.

19. St. Clair to Wilkinson, July 31, 1791, Wilkinson to St. Clair, Aug. 24, 1791, Smith, *St. Clair Papers*, 2:227, 233–39; John Brown to William Irvine, Aug. 22, 1791, Syrett, *Hamilton Papers*, 9:210; Leger, "John Adair," 42–43; William H. Guthman, *March to Massacre: A History of the First Seven Years of the U.S. Army, 1784–91* (New York, 1975), 204–5; Gibson, *Kickapoos*, 47; Erminie Wheeler-Voegelin et al., *Miami, Wea, and Eel-River Indians of Southern Indiana: An Anthropological Report . . .* (New York, 1974), 128.

20. Scott to Gov. of Virginia, Aug. 23, 1791, Draper Coll., Frontier

Wars, 4U187; Scott to the County Lieutenants, Sept. 23, 1791, to Col. Barnett, Feb. 1, 1792, CS-UK; Beverley Randolph to Scott, Aug. 4, Oct. 28, 1791, Executive Letter Book, no. 9, 233, 247–48, VSL.

21. Scott to the Gov. of Virginia, Sept. 26, 1791, Palmer, *Calendar State Papers*, 5:370.

22. St. Clair to Knox, Nov. 1, 1791, Smith, *St. Clair Papers*, 2:250–51; "Winthrop Sargent's Diary . . . ," *Ohio Arch. and Hist. Pubs.* 33 (1924): Oct. 10, 1791, 243; Frazer Wilson, ed., *Journal of Captain Daniel Bradley* (Greenville, Ohio, 1935), Oct. 4–Nov. 4, 1791, 17–29; William H. Denny, ed., "Military Journal [Ebenezer Denny]," *Memoirs of HSP* 7 (1860): Oct. 2–4, 1791, 358–59; Harry M. Ward, *Department of War, 1781–95* (Pittsburgh, 1962), 136–37.

23. Circular letter . . . Scott to the different county lieutenants, Nov. 11, 1791, in *KG*, Nov. 12, 1791; Scott to Henry Lee, Nov. 11, 1791, Draper Coll., Kenton Papers, 3BB47.

24. "Winthrop Sargent Diary," *Ohio Arch. and Hist. Soc. Pubs.* 33 (1924): Nov. 24, 26, 269–70; St. Clair to Knox, Nov. 24, 1791, Smith, *St. Clair Papers*, 2:271; Gifford, "The Northwest Indian War," 232.

25. St. Clair to Scott, Dec. 2, 1791, Draper Coll., 3BB49; *KG*, Feb. 18, 1792; Glenn Tucker, *Tecumseh's Vision of Glory* (Indianapolis, 1956), 61; Robert R. Jones, *Fort Washington at Cincinnati* (Cincinnati, 1902), 42.

26. John A. Caruso, *The Great Lakes Frontier* (Indianapolis, 1961), 170–71.

27. Ward, *Department of War*, 138, 143; Francis P. Prucha, *The Sword of the Republic* (Toronto, 1969), 27–28; Kohn, *Eagle and Sword*, 122, 127.

28. Opinion of the General Officers, n.d., Washington to Gov. Henry Lee, June 30, 1792, *FWW*, 31:509–15, 32:77–78; "Washington's Opinion of His General Officers," *Mag. of Amer. Hist.* 3 (1879): 81; Harry E. Wildes, *Anthony Wayne: Trouble Shooter of the American Revolution* (New York, 1941), 346–48; Prucha, *Sword of the Republic*, 29; Freeman, *Washington*, 6:341–42.

29. G. Glenn Clift, comp., *The "Corn Stalk" Militia of Kentucky, 1792–1814* (Frankfort, 1957), 15; Ward, *Department of War*, 143; Joseph A. Thacker, Jr., "The Kentucky Militia from 1792 to 1812" (M.A. thesis, University of Kentucky, 1954), 10–11.

30. Woodford County Order Book B, 1791–94, Sept. 7, 1791, March 5, Oct. 1, 1793, 36, 273, 322, and Order Book C, 1794–1812, April 3, 1797, 188, CJCCS; Hening, *Statutes at Large*, Oct. 1791 session, 13:272; Verhoeff, *Kentucky River Navigation*, 74; David Ross to George Raily [Revily?], May 8, 1792, Scott Papers, Huntington Lib.

31. *KG*, March 21, 1795; Woodford County Order Book B, July 3, 1792, 195–96, and Order Book C, May 1795, 70.

32. David Ross to Scott, Dec. 17, 1791, CS-UK; *KG*, March 3, 1792; Thomas D. Clark, "Salt, a Factor in the Settlement of Kentucky," *FCHQ* 12 (1938): 43.

33. Richard C. Wade, *The Urban Frontier: The Rise of Western Cities, 1790–1815* (Cambridge, Mass., 1959), 29–30, 34.

34. Petition . . . , Aug. 1792, CS-UK; Beasley, "Isaac Shelby," 120–21; Wilson, "Matthew Harris Jouett," *FCHQ* 13 (1939): 95; Verhoeff, *Kentucky River Navigation*, 76–77n; Willard R. Jillson, *Early Frankfort and Franklin County* (Louisville, Ky., 1936), 32–33, 77–78. For inducements offered by Frankfort, see Henry E. Everman, *Governor James Garrard* (n.p., 1981), 30.

35. Edmund Thomas to Daniel Scott, n.d. [1791], and Oct. 30, 1791, J. Holcome to Daniel Scott, April 2, 1792, Scott Papers, Huntington Lib.; Carrington to—, Nov. 10, 1791, Edward Carrington Letters, VHS.

36. Powhatan Marriage Bonds, 1777–94, 676; Charles Scott to Daniel Scott, Jan. 17, 1792, Scott Papers, Huntington Lib.

37. Charles Scott, Jr., to Daniel Scott, Feb. 24, 1792, Scott, Sr., to Daniel Scott, Feb. 25, 1792, Scott Papers, Huntington Lib.

38. Charles Scott, Jr., to Daniel Scott, July 10, 1792, ibid.; Talbert, *Logan*, 262.

39. Scott, Sr., to Daniel Scott, Oct. 4, 1792, Scott Papers, Huntington Lib.

40. Isaac Shelby Memorandum Book, 1792–94, April 19, 1793, Shelby Family Papers, LC; A Muster Roll . . . , March 29, 1792, and A Pay Abstract . . . , Aug. 26, 1792, CS-UK; Isaac Shelby to Scott, June 19, 1793, Durrett Coll., University of Chicago Lib.; Scott to Gov. of Kentucky, June 19, 1792, Lloyd W. Smith Collection, Morristown National Historical Park; Wayne to Knox, Aug. 1792, A. G. Mitten Coll., IHS; Thacker, "Kentucky Militia," 54–56; Arthur Campbell to ———, Feb. 17, 1792, Arthur Campbell Papers, Filson Club.

CHAPTER VII

1. E.g., see *KG*, April 6, 13, May 25, June 8, 15, 1793.

2. Lewis Collins (revised by Richard H. Collins), *History of Kentucky*, 2 vols. (Frankfort, 1874, rept. 1966), 1:23; A. Graham, "The Military Posts . . . State of Ohio," *Ohio Arch. and Hist. Soc. Pubs.* 3 (1890–91): 304; Young, *Little Turtle*, 65–67; Thacker, "Kentucky Militia," 53–54; "Narrative of John Heckewelder's Journey to the Wabash in 1792," *PMHB* 12 (1888): July 2, 1792, 39.

3. Scott to Wayne, May 23, 1793, Wayne to Scott, June 14, 1793, Wayne Papers, HSP; Wayne to Knox, June 20, 1793, Richard C. Knopf, ed., *Anthony Wayne, a Name in Arms: The Wayne-Knox-Pickering-McHenry Correspondence* (Pitsburgh, 1960), 245; extract of letter of Shelby to Wayne, May 27, 1793, CS-UK.

4. Report of General Officers, June 24, 1793, Wayne Papers, HSP.

5. Scott to Wayne, June 27, 1793, ibid.; Wayne to Knox, July 2, 1793,

Knopf, *A Name in Arms*, 252; Scott to Isaac Shelby, July 5, 1793, Draper Coll., King's Mountain: Isaac Shelby Papers, 11D51; *KG*, July 6, 1793.

6. Scott to Wayne, July 10, 17, Aug. 10, 1793, Wayne to Scott, Aug. 13, 1793, Wayne Papers, HSP; Knox to Wayne, Sept. 3, 1793, Knopf, *A Name in Arms*, 271; Wildes, *Wayne*, 395.

7. Wayne to Knox, June 20, 1793, Knopf, *A Name in Arms*, 244–45; Wildes, *Wayne*, 395–96; Scott to Wayne, July 17, 1793, Wayne Papers, HSP.

8. Scott to Wayne, Aug. 1, 1793, Wayne Papers, HSP; Scott to Brig. Gen. Posey, Aug. 15, 1793, Thomas Posey Coll., IHS.

9. Scott to Wayne, Aug. 1, 7, 15, 1793, Wayne to Scott, Aug. 5, 22, 1793, Wayne Papers, HSP.

10. Wayne to Scott, Sept. 12, 1793, Scott to Wayne, Sept. 16, 1793, ibid.; Scott to Brig. Gen. Todd, Sept. 14, 1793, William H. English Coll., University of Chicago Lib.; Wayne to Knox, Sept. 17, 1793, Knopf, *A Name in Arms*, 273; Orderly Books Wayne, Jan. 17, 1793–July 10,, 1794, Filson Club (microfilm); Scott to Shelby, Sept. 14, 1793, Draper Coll., Frontier Wars, 5U25.

11. E.g., see *KG*, Sept. 28, 1793, extract of letter of Wayne to Scott, Sept. 18, 1793.

12. General Orders, Sept. 24, 1793, copy, Journal of Gen. Charles Scott's Campaign in the year 1793, Filson Club; Scott to Wayne, Sept. 18, 1793, Wayne Papers, HSP; Circular [Isaac Shelby] to sundry Gent. on the Southside of Kentucky, Sept. 24, 1793, Durrett Coll., University of Chicago Lib.; Shelby to Scott, Sept. 18, 1793, Northwest Terr. Coll., Clements Lib.; Scott to Wayne, Sept. 22, 1793, Wayne Papers, ibid., Humphrey Marshall, *The History of Kentucky*, 2 vols. (Frankfort, 1824), 2:83–84.

13. Wayne to Scott, Sept. 26, 1793, Wayne Papers, HSP (also in James Love Papers, Filson Club); *KG*, Oct. 5, 1793.

14. Scott to Todd, Sept. 29, 1793, Todd to Wayne, Oct. 3, 1793, Robert Todd Orderly Book and Diary, IHS; General Return of the Division of Mounted Volunteers, Oct. 26, 1793, CS-UK; Scott to Wayne, Sept. 30, Oct. 3, 11, 1793, Wayne to Scott, Oct. 14, 1793, Wayne Papers, HSP; Barbee to Scott, Oct. 1, 1793, CS-UK; Richard C. Knopf, ed., "Two Journals of the Kentucky Volunteers, 1793 and 1794," *FCHQ* 27 (1953): 250–51; Shepard, *Underwood Journal*, Oct. 11, 1793, 6.

15. Wayne to Scott, Oct. 14, 1793, Wayne Papers, HSP; John M. Scott to John Armstrong, Oct. 22, 1793, John Armstrong Papers, IHS; Knopf, "Two Journals," 1793, *FCHQ* 27 (1953): Oct. 13–20, 1793, 252; Young, *Little Turtle*, 69–70.

16. Wayne to Scott,Oct. 23, 24, 1793, Scott to Wayne, Oct. 24, 1793, Wayne Papers, HSP; Knopf, "Two Journals," 1793, *FCHQ* 27 (1953): Oct. 19–23, 1793, 253; *KG*, Nov. 2, 1793.

17. Scott to Wayne, Nov. 1, 1793, Wayne to Scott, Nov. 2, 1793,

Wayne Papers, HSP; Answer to Genl. Wayne's Queries, Nov. 1, 1793, CS-UK.

18. Wilkinson to Wayne, Sept. 14, 1793, photostat, University of Kentucky Lib.; Bliss, *Zeisberger Diary*, Nov. 28, 1793, 2:331; Wayne to Knox, Oct. 28, 1793, Knopf, *A Name in Arms*, 278.

19. Wayne to Scott, Nov. 2, 1793, Wayne's Campaigns of 1793–94, Kentucky Volunteers, 1, Draper Coll., 16U16–22.

20. Wayne to St. Clair, Nov. 7, 1793, A. G. Mitten Coll., IHS; Wayne to Knox, Nov. 15, 1793, Knopf, *A Name in Arms*, 282–83; Knopf, "Two Journals," 1793, *FCHQ* 27 (1953): Nov. 3–10, 1793, 255–57.

21. Scott to Wayne, Nov. 9, 10, 13, 22, 1793, Wayne Papers, HSP.

22. Joan W. Coward, *Kentucky in the New Republic: The Process of Constitution Making* (Lexington, 1979), 97–99; Gifford, "Northwest Indian War," 392; Kohn, *Eagle and Sword*, 148; Beasley, "Isaac Shelby," 138–39.

23. Scott to Wayne, Dec. 17, 1793, Jan. 13, 1794, Wayne Papers, HSP.

24. Wayne to Knox, Jan. 8, 1794, Knopf, *A Name in Arms*, 297; Scott to Wayne, Jan. 25, 1794, Wayne Papers, HSP; Freeman Cleaves, *Old Tippecanoe: William Henry Harrison and His Time* (New York, 1939), 16; Wildes, *Wayne*, 408–9.

25. Scott to Wayne, Jan. 25, 1794, Wayne Papers, HSP.

26. Wayne to Scott, Jan. 4, 1794, Scott to Wayne, March 6, 1794, ibid.; Knox to Wayne, Nov. 25, 1793, March 31, 1794, Wayne to Knox, May 7, 1794, Knopf, *A Name in Arms*, 286–87, 314, 322–23.

27. Scott to Wayne, April 20, 1794, Wayne Papers, HSP; Knox to Bodley, May 16, 1794, Thomas Bodley Papers, photostat, University of Kentucky Lib.; William Meihen [Meiten?] to Scott, April 27, 1794, CS-UK; Jackson and Twohig, *Washington Diaries*, 4:330n.

28. Scott to Knox, April 30, 1794, CS-UK.

29. Knox to Wayne, May 16, 1794, Knopf, *A Name in Arms*, 328; Richard H. Kohn, "General Wilkinson's Vendetta with General Wayne . . . ," *FCHQ* 45 (1971): 362–64; Wildes, *Wayne*, 404–5.

30. Knox's Instructions to Scott, May 17, 1794, Wayne Papers, HSP; [Appointments to the Kentucky Board], May 17, 1794, signed by Knox, William H. English Coll., University of Chicago Lib.

31. Scott to Wayne, June 5, 6, 1794, Wayne Papers, HSP; Knox to Bodley, May 16, 1794, Thomas Bodley Papers, photostat, University of Kentucky Lib.; Campbell Smith to Richard C. Anderson, R. C. Anderson Papers, VSL; Knox to Wayne, May 16, 1794, Knopf, *A Name in Arms*, 329–30; Postmaster General [Timothy Pickering] to Maj. Isaac Craig, May 24, 1794, Clarence E. Carter, ed., *The Territorial Papers of the United States* (Washington, D.C., 1934), 1:482.

32. Wayne to Scott, June 10, 29, 1794, Scott to Wayne, June 21, 1794, Wayne Papers, HSP; Wayne to Capt. Thomas Lewis, May 26, 1794, Northwest Terr. Coll., IHS.

33. Extract of letter of Wayne to Wilkinson, June 8, 1794, Northwest Terr. Coll., IHS; Knox to Wilkinson, July 12, 1794, Knox Papers, MHS.

34. Sec. of War to President, June 25, 1794, Carter, *Territorial Papers,* 2:486–87; James O'Hara (QMG) to Isaac Craig, June 26, 1794, Mary C. Darlington, ed., *Fort Pitt and Letters from the Frontier* (Pittsburgh, 1892), 265; Extract of a letter from a gentleman of distinction . . . , July 13, 1794, in *KG,* July 26, 1794; Wayne to Knox, July 7, 1794, Knopf, *A Name in Arms,* 345–48; Young, *Little Turtle,* 75–77; Tucker, *Tecumseh,* 68; Caruso, *Great Lakes Frontier,* 17.

35. Paper . . . by Col. John Johnson . . . , Dec. 11, 1857, Charles R. Staples, *The History of Pioneer Lexington, 1779–1806* (Lexington, 1939), 101; Scott to Wayne, July 12, 16, 1794, Wayne to Scott, July 16, 1794, Wayne Papers, HSP; Scott to Todd, July 11, 1794, Todd to Major Price, July 11, 1794, Draper Coll., Wayne's Campaigns, 1793–94, Kentucky Volunteers, 1, 16U27–30; Knopf, "Two Journals," 1794, *FCHQ* 27 (1953): July 16, 1794, 260.

36. Winthrop Sargent to Knox, July 23, 1794, extract of letter of Scott to Knox, July 21, 1794, Knox Papers, MHS; "Extracts . . . Sargent's Journal, 1793–95," *Ohio Arch. and Hist. Soc. Pubs.* 33 (1924): July 22, 1794, 278.

37. Peyton Short, Business Papers . . . , 1794, Papers of Short-Harrison-Symmes Families, LC; Todd . . . Diary, July 22–25, 1794, IHS; Knopf, "Two Journals," 1794, *FCHQ* 27 (1953): July 25, 27, 1794, 260; Boyd, *Wayne,* 260; Wildes, *Wayne,* 372–73; Harrison Bird, *War for the West, 1790–1813* (New York, 1971), 55.

38. For the ensuing account, see Randolph [pseud.], "A Precise Journal of General Wayne's Last Campaign," ed. Richard C. Knopf, *Procs. of the American Antiquarian Society,* n.s., 64 (1954): 273–302; Lt. John Boyer, "Daily Journal of Wayne's Campaign . . . ," ed. Richard C. Knopf, *American Pioneer* 1 (1844): July 28–Nov. 2, 1794, 315–22, 351–57; Wilson, *Journal of Capt. Daniel Bradley,* 69–74; M. M. Quaife, ed., "General James Wilkinson's Narrative of the Fallen Timbers Campaign," *Miss. Valley Hist. Review* 16 (1930): 81–90; Shepard, *Underwood Journal,* 16–21; "William Clark's Journal . . . ," *Miss. Valley Review* 1 (1914–15): 418–44; Dwight L. Smith, ed., "From Greene Ville to Fallen Timbers . . . ," *IHS Pubs.* 16, no. 3 (1952): 237–333; Orderly Book, William Buckner, Draper Coll., 16U2; Todd Orderly Book and Diary, 1794, IHS; Knopf, "Two Journals," 1794, *FCHQ* 27 (1953): 258–67; Wayne to Knox, Aug. 28, 1794, *American State Papers,* Class II, *Indian Affairs,* 4:491.

39. Smith, "From Greene Ville to Fallen Timbers," *IHS Pubs.* 16, no. 3 (1952): Aug. 15–16, 1794, 279–81; Wildes, *Wayne,* 419–20.

40. Quote in Robert M. McElroy, *Kentucky in the Nation's History* (New York, 1909), 180.

41. "William Clark's Journal," *Miss. Valley Hist. Review* 1 (1914–15):

Aug. 30, 1794, 434; Orderly Book, William Buckner, Aug. 12, 28, Oct. 2, 1794, Draper Coll., Kentucky Volunteers, 16U49, 70, 119; Knopf, "Two Journals," *FCHQ* 27 (1953): Sept. 21, 28, 1794, 272–73; Wilkinson to John Brown, Aug. 28, 1794, in Quaife, ed., "Wilkinson's Narrative," *Miss. Valley Hist. Review* 16 (1930): 89–90.

42. Knopf, "Two Journals," *FCHQ* 27 (1953): Oct. 2, 1794, 273–74; Boyer, "Daily Journal," *American Pioneer* 1 (1844): 354–55; Wayne to Scott, Oct. 13, 1794, Wayne Papers, HSP.

43. Wayne to Capt. Edward Butler, Oct. 16, 1794, ibid.; Sec. of War to Scott, n.d. (copy), James Love Papers, Filson Club; Todd Orderly Book and Diary, Oct. 21, 1794, IHS; Wayne to Knox, Oct. 17, 1794, Knopf, *A Name in Arms*, 360.

44. Sec. of War to Scott, n.d. (copy), Love Papers, Filson Club; Wayne to Knox, Jan. 24, 1795, Knopf, *A Name in Arms*, 379.

45. Proclamation, March 24, 1794, *FWW*, 33:304–5; Knox to Pickering, Oct. 25, 1794, Pickering Papers, MHS; Thacker, "Kentucky Militia," 63–64; Talbert, *Logan*, 277–79.

46. *KG*, March 14, 1795, Proclamation, Feb. 22, 1795; Leitch J. Wright, Jr., *Britain and the American Frontier, 1783–1815* (Athens, Ga., 1975), 98–99.

47. Scott to Wayne, Sept. 28, 1795, Wayne Papers, Clements Lib.

48. Scott to Wayne, April 15, 1795, Wayne Papers, HSP.

49. Scott to Wayne, Aug. 5, Sept. 14, 1795, Wayne to Scott, Sept. 9, 1795, Wayne Papers, HSP; Scott to Wayne, Sept. 28, 1795, Wayne Papers, Clements Lib.

CHAPTER VIII

1. Charles Royster, "Founding a Nation in Blood: Military Conflict and American Nationality," in Ronald Hoffman et al., eds., *Arms and Independence: The Military Character of the American Revolution* (Charlottesville, Va., 1984), 26.

2. Woodford County Order Book C, Nov. 1, 1796, April 3, 1797, Feb. 4, Oct. 7, 1799, April 1, Sept. 1, 1800, Feb. 6, 1804, 164, 188, 277, 303, 321, 341, 477.

3. Scott to Mrs. Daniel Scott, Dec. 14, 1797, Scott Papers, Huntington Lib.; Woodford County Order Book C, April 1, Sept. 1, 1800, Nov. 7, 1803, 322, 341, 472; Mrs. Anne W. Bell, *Records of Marriages in Woodford County, Kentucky, 1788 to 1851* (mimeographed, Frankfort, n.d.), 2:29. Daniel's widow, Martha Mosby Scott married Robert Nicholas, July 17, 1801 (Catherine L. Knorr, *Marriage Bonds and Ministers' Returns of Powhatan County . . . 1777–1830* (Pine Bluff, Ark., 1957), 47).

4. *KG*, July 28, 1801, Sept. 18, 1894; *Stewart's Kentucky Herald*, May 30, 1797, July 28, 1801; *Palladium*, Dec. 19, 1799; Clift, *"Corn Stalk" Militia*, 55.

5. *Palladium,* Nov. 11, 25, 1800; *KG,* Nov. 24, Dec. 8, 1800.

6. *KG,* Nov. 22, 1803; James W. Hammack, Jr., "Kentucky and Anglo-American Relations, 1803–1815" (Ph.D. diss., University of Kentucky, 1974), 14–15.

7. Scott to Sec. of War, May 9, 1803 (copy), CS-UK; Autobiography of James Taylor, 1792–1817, transcript microfilm, 44–46, Filson Club; deed for the site of "Newport Barracks," Campbell County Deed Book B, July 28, 1803, 345, in Allen W. Smith, comp., *Beginning at "The Point": A Documented History of Northern Kentucky* . . . (Park Hills, 1977), 25; Scott to Dearborn, Aug. 26, 1803, Misc. Coll., LC.

8. Autobiography of James Taylor, 46, Filson Club; Anecdotes, Draper Coll., 8CC166:3; Smith, *Beginning at "The Point,"* 29.

9. Scott to Dearborn, July 1804, CS-UK.

10. Robert Sobel and John Raimo, *Biog. Directory of the Governors of the United States, 1789–1978* (Westport, Conn., 1978), 509; *KG,* May 8, 22, 1804; *Palladium,* Nov. 24, 1804. Scott was unopposed in Woodford County (*KG,* Oct. 16, 1804).

11. *KG,* Oct. 9, 1804.

12. Woodford County Will Book C, July 11, 1804, court Nov. 4–5, 1804, 79–84; Mosby, *Our Noble Heritage,* 110, 127. Betsy (Eliza) married Bartholomew Truehart; she died in 1821.

13. Walker and Wilson, *Kentucky Bible Records,* 3:20, 23–24, and 100; Connelley and Coulter, *History of Kentucky,* 2:1088; Alice E. Trabue, *A Corner in Celebrities* (Louisville, Ky., 1923), 33–34; John S. Goff, "The Last Leaf: George Mortimer Bibb," *RKSHS* 59 (1961): 333–34; Mrs. Frank Stewart, *Bibb Family of America,* 1 (Centre, Ala., 1979); Thomas M. Green, *Historic Families of Kentucky* (Baltimore, 1889, rept. 1964), 90. The children of George and Martha Scott Bibb were: Charles Scott (d. 1832), Edward Booker (d. 1827), George Allison (d. 1827), Henry Power Broadnay (d. 1823), Richard Augusta (d. 1806), Lucien Iramba (d. 1831), Frances Ann (d. 1891, wife of A. T. Burnley), Richard (d. 1833), Titus Pomponius Atticus (d. 1872), Lucy Mary Pocahantas (d. 1844), and John Jorden Critten (d. 1853). Martha Ann Burnley, great-granddaugther of Scott, was born July 2, 1831, died Nov. 16, 1919, age eighty-eight.

14. *KG,* Oct. 16, Nov. 6, 13, 27, Dec. 4, 11, 18, 25, 1804, Jan. 1, 8, 15, 22, 29, Feb. 5, 12, 19, 1805; Woodford County Deed Book C, May 29, 1802, 351–53, and Deed Book D, Sept. 22, 1806, 1–2.

15. *KG,* June 11, July 5, 9, 1805; Staples, *Pioneer Lexington,* 36.

16. E.g., Woodford County celebration, *KG,* July 12, 1806.

17. Robert P. Hay, "A Jubilee for Freeman: The Fourth of July in Frontier Kentucky, 1788–1816," *RKSHS* 64 (1966): 179; *KG,* Aug. 25, 1806.

18. Dale M. Royalty, "Banking, Politics, and the Commonwealth, Kentucky, 1800–25" (Ph.D. diss., University of Kentucky, 1971), 11–

38; Basil W. Duke, *History of the Bank of Kentucky, 1792–1895* (Louisville, 1895), 7–14; Hammack, "Kentucky and Anglo-American Relations," 49.

19. *KG*, July 8, Aug. 25, Sept. 1, 1806; Reuben G. Thwaites, "The Ohio Valley Press before the War of 1812–15," *Procs. of the Amer. Antiquarian Soc.*, n.s., 19 (1909): 331–33; William B. Allen, *A History of Kentucky . . .* (Louisville, 1872), 70–73; Leger, "John Adair," 100–102.

20. *Palladium*, June 26, Oct. 23, Nov. 6, 1806, April 16, 1807; *KG*, Nov. 13, 1804, July 1, 29, 1806.

21. Hammack, "Kentucky and Anglo-American Relations," chaps. 3, 4.

22. *Palladium*, April 23, Aug. 20, 1807; Christopher Greenup to Scott, Aug. 1, 1807, CS-UK; James W. Hammack, Jr., *Kentucky and the Second American Revolution: The War of 1812* (Lexington, 1976), 3–4.

23. Autobiography of James Taylor, 21, Filson Club; Samuel C. Williams, "Nathaniel Gist, Father of Sequoyah," *East Tennessee Hist. Soc. Pub.*, no. 5 (1933): 39–54; Elbert B. Smith, *Francis Preston Blair* (New York, 1980), 6–7. For Mrs. Judith Scott's background, see Robert K. Brock, *Archibald Cary . . .* (Richmond, 1937), 18, 145–49; Wilson Gee, *The Gist Family of South Carolina and Its Maryland Antecedents* (Charlottesville, Va., 1934), 8–9; Getha G. Bell, *The Bells in the U.S.A. . . .* (n.p., 1977), 180; and Jean M. and Maxwell J. Dorsey, *Christopher Gist of Maryland . . . Descendants . . .* (Chicago, 1958), 25–35, 38–39, 41–49. Over the next five years Scott was listed as having patented 8,300 acres at Tigerts Creek, Greenup County; 250 acres at Stoner Creek, Clark County; and 5,500 acres at Big Sandy, Floyd County; and having 16 slaves above age sixteen (Clark County Taxbooks, 1793–1809, Aug. 15, 1805, and 1810–24, passim).

24. Rebecca Gratz to Maria Gratz, Aug. 27, 1837, David Philipson, ed., *Letters of Rebecca Gratz* (Philadelphia, 1929), 243; Smith, *Blair*, 8–9; James Flanagan, "Canewood: The Seat of the Gist Family and Home of Governor Chas. Scott," *FCHQ* 20 (1946): 41–42. Canewood was originally a 6,000-acre military grant. Gist sold the southern half in 1793 to Thomas Lewis of Fayette County. Benjamin Gratz, through his wife, Maria, inherited the 177½ acres on which the residence stood. Gratz used Canewood as a summer residence, 1834 to 1853, when he sold it to Matthew Hume. The original house, built in 1793, burned in the mid-nineteenth century, and a later one has also disappeared.

25. Hammack, "Kentucky and Anglo-American Relations," 63.

26. *KG*, Feb. 16, 1808.

27. Cassius M. Clay, *The Life of Cassius Marcellus Clay: Memoirs, Writings, and Speeches*, 1 (Cincinnati, 1886): 29, 38.

28. E.g., see *KG*, March 1, 1808, signed "an Old Soldier."

29. James F. Hopkins, ed., *The Papers of Henry Clay*, 1 (Lexington, Ky., 1959): 72; Walter W. Jenings, *Transylvania: Pioneer University of the West*

(New York, 1955), 22, 114, 240, 258; Col. Orlando Brown, "The Governors of Kentucky," *RKSHS* 49 (1951): 110n; *Biog. Directory of the American Congress,* Senate Doc., 92d Congress, 1st session, 1971, 84, 603. In addition to serving as Kentucky secretary of state under Scott, Bledsoe was a state representative in 1813, U.S. senator, March 4, 1813–Dec. 24, 1814, when he resigned, and a state senator, 1817–20; he headed the law department at Transylvania University until 1826, when it was discontinued. Bledsoe became a Disciple of Christ minister. In 1833 he moved to Mississippi and in 1835 to Texas; he died May 1836, near Nacogdoches. In 1819 Bledsoe married Scott's stepdaughter Sarah Howard Gist.

30. *KG*, June 28, 1808; Robert G. Bodenger, "Soldiers' Bonuses: A History of Veterans' Benefits in the United States, 1776–1967" (Ph.D. diss., Pa. State University, 1971), 21; Thomas Hall to Scott, March 24, 1808, CS-UK.

31. *KG*, Jan. 10, 1808.

32. *Reporter,* June 4, July 23, 1808.

33. *KG*, June 14, 1808.

34. "Regulus" to the People, ca. May 31 and July 9, 1808, and "Regulus" in Reply to "A Farmer," ca. June 21, 1808, Hopkins, *Clay Papers,* 1:333, 361–67, 349–53.

35. Dr. Anthony Hunn's Reply to "Regulus," ca. June 7, 1808, from the *Western World,* June 30, 1808, reprint from *The Lamp,* and letter from Anthony Hunn, from *Reporter,* July 2, 1808, ibid., 335–36, 359–60.

36. *Reporter,* June 18, July 16, 1808; *KG*, July 5, 1808.

37. *KG*, June 21, 1808.

38. E.g., *Reporter,* July 23, 1808.

39. David L. Smiley, *Lion of White Hall: the Life of Cassius M. Clay* (Madison, Wis., 1962), 7.

40. *Reporter,* June 18, 1808.

41. E.g., from a Woodford County man, one of the first, in *KG*, June 28, 1808.

42. Ibid., June 28, July 2, 1808.

43. Ibid., July 5, 12, 1808.

44. E.g., see *Reporter,* July 16, 1808.

45. Ibid.; *KG*, July 19, 1808 (letter dated July 9).

46. Anecdote, Draper Coll., 26CC10.

47. Flanagan, "Canewood," *FCHQ* 20 (1948): 45.

48. *Reporter,* July 16, 1808.

49. Connelley and Coulter, *History of Kentucky,* 1: 477–79; *KG*, Aug. 2, 6, 16, 23, 1808; *Reporter,* Aug. 25, 1808.

50. *KG*, Aug. 30, 1808.

51. Ibid., Sept. 6, 1808.

52. Ibid., Sept. 13, 1808.

53. Draper Coll., 26CC10.

54. Papers of the Governors of Kentucky—Scott, Executive Journal no. 1, Sept. 22, 29, Oct. 9, 14, 1808, KA; *KG*, Nov. 29, Dec. 13, 1908.

55. *KG*, Nov. 22, 1808; *Reporter*, Nov. 21, 1808; Hammack, "Kentucky and Anglo-American Relations," 134–38.

56. Papers of the Governors—Scott, Exec. Journal no. 2, Dec. 13, 1808, KA; *Journal of the House of Representatives* (Ky.), 1808–9, 13–18; Hammack, "Kentucky and Anglo-American Relations," 138–39.

57. Papers of the Governors—Scott, Exec. Journal no. 2, Dec. 4, 1809, KA; Brown, "Governors of Kentucky," *RKSHS* 49 (1951): 111.

CHAPTER IX

1. Fortesque Cuming, "Sketches of a Tour to the Western Country . . . ," in Reuben G. Thwaites, ed., *Early Western Travels*, 4 (Cleveland, 1904), 189–93; e.g., "Memoranda Made by Thomas R. Joynes on a Journey . . . Ohio and Kentucky, 1810," *WMQ*, 1st ser., 10 (1902): 156–57.

2. Papers of the Governors—Scott, Exec. Journal no. 2, Jan. 31, Dec. 4, 8, 1809, Feb. 20, 1810, KA; *KG*, April 10, 1810.

3. Papers of the Governors—Scott, Exec. Journal no. 2, Jan. 25, 1809, KA.

4. Ibid., no. 1, Jan. 17, Aug. 7, 16, Sept. 28, 1809, Feb. 17, 1812; *Reporter*, Jan. 21, Feb. 22, 1812.

5. Papers of the Governors, Exec. Journal nos. 1, 2, Jan. 3, 1811, April 15, June 25, July 9, 1812, KA.

6. Ibid., no. 2, Dec. 4, 1811; Paul W. Gates, "Tenants of the Log Cabin," *Miss. Valley Hist. Review* 49 (1962): 4–14; Royalty, "Banking . . . Kentucky," 73.

7. Papers of the Governors—Scott, Exec. Journal no. 2, Feb. 4, 1809, KA; *Journal of the Senate*, 1808–9, 182–83.

8. Papers of the Governors—Scott, Exec. Journal no. 2, Jan. 26, 1809, KA; *Journal of the Senate*, *1808–9*, *147–53*, *156;* Connelley and Coulter, *History of Kentucky*, 1:482 and n. The Senate overrode the veto, 17–10.

9. *Journal of House of Representatives*, 1809–10, Dec. 7, 1809, 34–35, and 1810–11, March 3, 1810; Papers of the Governors—Scott, Exec. Journal no. 2, Jan. 3, Dec. 7, 1809, KA.

10. *KG*, Aug. 29, 1809, Connelley and Coulter, *History of Kentucky*, 458.

11. *KG*, May 30, July 11, 1809.

12. Papers of the Governors—Scott, Exec. Journal no. 2, Dec. 4, 1809, KA; Hammack, "Kentucky and Anglo-American Relations," 162–63; *Palladium*, extra issue, Dec. 23, 1809.

13. Thomas A. Bailey, *A Diplomatic History of the American People* (New York, 1950), 125–27; Connelley and Coulter, *History of Kentucky*, 1:547.

See Thomas D. Clark, "Kentucky in the Northwest Campaign," in Philip P. Mason, ed., *After Tippecanoe: Some Aspects of the War of 1812* (East Lansing, Mich., 1963), 80, for the Kentucky perspective.

14. Reginald Horsman, *The Frontier in the Formative Years, 1783–1815* (Albuquerque, N.M., 1975), 169–70; Harry Coles, *The War of 1812* (Chicago, 1965), 26–37; Roger H. Brown, *The Republic in Peril: 1812* (New York, 1971), 76, 81.

15. Clay's Speech . . . , ca. Feb. 22, 1819, Hopkins, *Clay Papers*, 1:449–50, 452n.

16. Harrison to Scott, March 10, April, 1810, Logan Esarey, ed., *Messages and Letters of William Henry Harrison*, IHS, Colls., 8 (Indianapolis, 1922), 1:400–417; Tucker, *Tecumseh*, 134.

17. Papers of the Governors—Scott, Exec. Journal no. 2, Dec. 4, 1810, KA; *Journal of House of Representatives*, 1810–11, Dec. 4, 1810, 9–14.

18. *KG*, July 9, 1811.

19. E.g., see *Palladium*, July 13, 20, 1811.

20. *KG*, Sept. 13, 1811; *American Republic*, Sept. 6, 1811; Cleaves,*Old Tippecanoe*, 86–87; Glen Tucker, *Poltroons and Patriots: A Popular Account of the War of 1812*, 1 (Indianapolis, 1954): 114; Alec R. Gilpin, *The War of 1812 in the Old Northwest* (East Lansing, Mich., 1958), 10.

21. Bledsoe to Scott, Oct. 16, 1811, William Henry Harrison Coll., IHS.

22. *American Republic*, Nov. 15, 1811; W. A. Wentworth, "Tippecanoe and Kentucky Too," *RKSHS* 40 (1962): 39; Scott to Harrison, Nov. 27, 1811, Esarey, *Harrison Messages*, 1:643.

23. John Johnston to Sec. of War, Nov. 28, 1811, William Henry Harrison Papers, LC.

24. Quoted in *KG*, Nov. 19, 1811.

25. Harrison to Scott, Dec. 13, 1811, Esarey, *Harrison Messages*, 1:666–72.

26. Hammack, "Kentucky and Anglo-American Relations," 201–2, quoting from *Reporter*, Nov. 23, 1811, May 23, 1812.

27. Ibid., 202–3.

28. Papers of the Governors—Scott, Exec. Journal no. 2, Dec. 3, 1811, KA.

29. Gabriel Slaughter to Scott, in Senate, Dec. 18, 1811, Slaughter Misc. MSS, NYHS (also in *KG*, Jan. 7, 1812); Hammack, "Kentucky and Anglo-American Relations," 216.

30. G. Glenn Clift, *Remember the Raisin! Kentucky and Kentuckians . . . at Frenchtown . . . War of 1812* (Frankfort, 1961), 10.

31. *Reporter*, March 31, 1812; Marshall, *History of Kentucky*, 2:552.

32. *Palladium*, Feb. 6, May 6, 1812; *KG*, April 28, 1812; *Reporter*, April 25, 1812; *American Republic*, April 24, 1812.

33. *Reporter*, May 9, 1812; Clift, *Remember the Raisin!*, 13; *KG*, May 12,

1812, quoted in Clark, "Kentucky in the Northwest Campaign," in Mason, *After Tippecanoe*, 84.

34. Clift, *Remember the Raisin!*, 11, 17, quoting from *Niles' Weekly Register.*

35. *Palladium*, July 8, 1812; *Reporter*, July 1, 4, 1812; Hammack, *Second American Revolution*, 31–32.

36. Cleaves, *Old Tippecanoe*, 114; Clift, *Remember the Raisin!*, 16; *Reporter*, Aug. 8, 1812; Harrison to Sec. of War, Aug. 6, 12, 1812, William Henry Harrison Papers, LC; Harrison to Acting Gov. John Gibson [Indiana Territory], Aug. 17, 1812, Carter, *Territorial Papers*, 8:201–2; Richard C. Knopf, ed., *Document Transcriptions of the War of 1812 in the Northwest*, 10 vols. (Columbus, Ohio, 1957–62), "National Intelligencer Reports the War," Aug. 22, 1812, 5, pt. 1:127.

37. Scott to Isaac Shelby, Aug. 10, 1812; Papers of the Governors— Scott, Exec. Journal no. 1, July 27–28, 1812, KA; *Reporter*, Aug. 1, 1812.

38. Gov. Ninian Edwards to Scott, Feb. 4, 1812 (copy), *KG*; Ninian Edwards to Scott, Aug. 4, 1812, *Journal of the Ill. State Hist. Soc.* 24 (1931–32): 186; Knopf, *Doc. Transcriptions*, "Nat. Intelligencer . . . ," [June 9, 1812], 5, pt. 1:93; George W. Ranck, *History of Lexington, Kentucky . . .* (Cincinnati, 1872), 251; Martin D. Hardin to Henry Clay, July 6, 1813, Hopkins, *Clay Papers*, 1:807–8; Harrison to Sec. of War, Aug. 18, 1812, William Henry Harrison Papers, LC; Harrison to Gibson, Aug. 17, 1812, Carter, *Territorial Papers*, 8:201. Two thousand Kentucky volunteers went up the Wabash, with only one week's provisions, and finding the Indians had scorched the prairie, returned home.

39. *Reporter*, Aug. 15, 1812; Orders, Frankfort, Aug. 6, 1812, Knopf, *Doc. Transcriptions*, "Nat. Intelligencer . . . ," Aug. 22, 1812, 5, pt. 1:129; Brown, "Governors of Kentucky," *RKSHS* 49 (1951): 111.

40. *KG*, Aug. 18, 1812; Elias Darnell, *Journal . . . Kentucky Volunteers and Regulars Commanded by General Winchester, 1812–13* (Philadelphia, 1854), 6–7; Speech to Troops at Georgetown, Aug. 16, 1812, Hopkins, *Clay Papers*, 1:715; Ranck, *Lexington*, 250–51; Clift, *Remember the Raisin!*, 20, 21; Pierre Berton, *The Invasion of Canada*, 1 (Boston, 1980): 267.

41. Scott to Madison, July 30, 1812, quoted in Stagg, *Mr. Madison's War*, 212.

42. Scott to [Sec. of War], Aug. 25, 1812, with enclosure [the "caucus" to Thomas Buford], Daniel Parker Papers, HSP; Henry Clay to James Monroe, Aug. 25, 1812, Hopkins, *Clay Papers*, 1:719–20; Harrison to Sec. of War, Aug. 28, 1812, Esarey, *Harrison Messages*, 2:98.

43. Scott to [Sec. of War], Aug. 25, 1812, Daniel Parker Papers, HSP.

44. Scott to Harrison, Aug. 25, 1812, ibid.; General Orders . . . , Aug. 25, 1812, in *Reporter*, Aug. 29, 1812; *KG*, Sept. 1, 1812.

45. B. Logan to Mrs. Jane Allen, Sept. 19, 1812, Allen-Butler Family Papers, University of Kentucky Lib.; Harrison to Sec. of War, Aug. 28, 1812, William Henry Harrison Papers, LC; *Niles' Weekly Register*, Sept.

12, 1812, 3:25; Berton, *Invasion of Canada,* 269; Cleaves, *Old Tippecanoe,* 116.

46. Sylvia Wrobel and George Grider, *Isaac Shelby* . . . (Danville, Ky., 1974), 110–13; Reginald Horsman, *The War of 1812* (New York, 1969), 84–85; Caruso, *Great Lakes Frontier,* 274–75; Berton, *Invasion of Canada,* 288–302; Clark, "Kentucky in the Northwest Campaign," in Mason, ed., *After Tippecanoe,* 94, 98; John K. Mahon, *The American Militia: Decade of Decision, 1789–1800,* University of Florida Monographs, no. 6 (Gainesville, 1960), 130–31.

47. Mrs. Benjamin Gratz to [Mrs. Charles Scott], 1830, William V. Byars, ed., *B. and M. Gratz, Merchants in Philadelphia, 1754–98: Papers of Interest* (Jefferson City, Mo., 1916), 288.

48. William E. Smith, *The Francis Preston Blair Family* . . . (New York, 1933), 21–22; E. B. Smith, *Blair,* 7–9; Philipson, *Letters of Rebecca Gratz,* 43n.

49. F. P. Blair to Maria Gratz, Feb. 5, 1831, Byars, *Gratz,* 292–93.

50. *KG,* Oct. 26, 1813.

51. *Reporter,* Nov. 6, 1813; *Niles' Weekly Register,* Feb. 25, 1815, supplement vol. 7:20.

52. Charles E. Slocum, *The Ohio Country between the Years 1783 and 1815* (New York, 1910), title page.

53. Hammack, "Kentucky and Anglo-American Relations," 378, 383.

54. Obituary Addresses . . . Nov. 8, 1854 (Frankfort, 1855). Mrs. Scott died in 1833 during the cholera epidemic in Lexington (*KG,* June 22, 1833).

BIBLIOGRAPHY OF
MANUSCRIPT SOURCES

Many of the manuscripts are available on microfilm and other photo-duplication and through interlibrary loan and individual order. For the most part, this listing cites the actual depositories of the manuscripts.

Chicago Historical Society
    Gunther Collection
    Collections: Charles Scott, Ninian Edwards, William Croghan, Thomas Posey
    George Weedon–John Page Correspondence
Church of Jesus Christ of Latter-day Saints Archives, Genealogical Department, Salt Lake City
    Clark County, Kentucky, Taxbook, 1793–1809 and 1810–24
    Woodford County, Kentucky, Order Books: A (1789–91); B (1791–94); C (1794–1812); D (1812–21)
    Woodford County, Kentucky, Will Books: A, B, and C, 1789–1815
    Woodford County, Kentucky, Deed Book C
William L. Clements Library, Ann Arbor, Mich.
    Nathanael Greene Papers
    Anthony Wayne Papers
    Northwest Territory Collection
    Sir Henry Clinton Papers
    U.S. Continental Army Returns
Detroit Public Library
    Francis Navarre Papers
Filson Club, Louisville, Ky.
    Arthur Campbell Papers
    James Love Papers

Orderly Books of Major General Wayne, Jan. 17, 1793, to July 10, 1794 (Lt. Samuel Tinsley et al.)
Isaac Shelby Papers
Autobiography of James Taylor—typescript
Journal of General Charles Scott's Campaign . . . 1793
Journal of a Campaign . . . 1794 . . . Scott
Harvard University, Cambridge, Mass.
Sparks MSS
Historical Society of Pennsylvania, Philadelphia
Anthony Wayne Papers
Simon Gratz Collection
Etting Collection: Revolutionary War Papers
Dreer Collection: Letters of the Generals of the American Revolution
Society Collections: Revolutionary War Generals
John Randolph of Roanoke Papers
Daniel Parker Papers
Henry E. Huntington Library, San Marino, Calif.
Janin Family Collection
Charles Scott Papers (chiefly relating to Daniel Scott)
Charles Scott et al. petition, Aug. 2, 1775
Indiana Historical Society, Indianapolis
John Armstrong Papers
Northwest Territory Collection
Arthur G. Mitten Collection
William Henry Harrison Miscellaneous Collection
Orderly Book and Diary of Robert Todd
Kentucky State Historical Society, Frankfort
James Wilkinson Papers
George M. Bibb Letters
Sale of Slaves / Judith Gist
Scott Miscellaneous Folder
Kentucky Department for Libraries and Archives, Frankfort
Papers of the Governors—Charles Scott
Papers of the Governors: Executive Journals, 1808–12 (nos. 1 and 2); Enrolled Bills, 1808–11
Library of Congress, Washington, D.C.
George Washington Papers
William Henry Harrison Papers
Robert Honeyman Diary
Harry Innes Papers

Miscellaneous Collections—Charles Scott
Shelby Family Papers
Peyton Short Account Book (Papers of Short-Harrison-Symmes Families)
Peter Force Collection
Massachusetts Historical Society, Boston
Henry Knox Papers
Benjamin Lincoln Papers
Missouri Historical Society, St. Louis
William Clark, Journal of General Scott's Expedition, 1791, E. G. Voorhis Memorial Collection—transcript
Morristown National Historical Park, Morristown, N.J.
Lloyd W. Smith Collection
National Archives, Washington, D.C.
Papers of the Continental Congress
Charles Scott Service Record
New-York Historical Society, New York City
Allen McLane Papers
Horatio Gates Papers
Steuben Papers
Walter Stewart Papers
Miscellaneous MSS: Abraham Buford; Gabriel Slaughter
New York Public Library
Bancroft Transcripts: Revolutionary Papers
Chalmers Collection
Emmet Collection
Meyers Collection
Miscellaneous Collection
Presbyterian Historical Society, Philadelphia
Charles Scott Account Books: the State of Virginia in Account with Officers of the Revolution; Private Accounts
Public Record Office: War Office, Great Britain, Virginia Records Project, Virginia State Library
Cornwallis Papers
Reed, John F. (private collection, King of Prussia, Pa.)
Charles Scott to Frankey [Frances Scott], Nov. 15, 1777
State Historical Society of Wisconsin, Madison
Draper Collection:
Jonathan Clarke Papers, 1728–94
William Croghan Papers, 1779–1814

L
N

Frontier Wars   U
Harmar Papers   W
King's Mountain (Shelby) Papers   DD
Kentucky Manuscripts   CC
Shepherd Papers   SS
Sumter Manuscripts   VV
South Carolina Papers   TT
Tecumseh Manuscripts   YY
Virginia Papers   ZZ
University of Chicago
  Durrett Collection
  William H. English Collection
University of Kentucky, Lexington
  Allen-Butler Family Papers
  Charles Scott Papers
  Charles Scott: land warrant, correspondence relating to
  E. Williams to Gen. Williams, Aug. 24, 1788
  James Wilkinson to Anthony Wayne, Sept. 14, 1792
  Thomas Bodley Papers (photostats)
  Letters to Joseph Lawrence
University of Virginia, Charlottesville
  Revolutionary Lee Papers
  Wallace Papers
Virginia Historical Society, Richmond
  Hugh Grigsby Papers
  Louise Este Bruce Papers
  Letters of Edward Carrington
  John Chilton Diary
  Blanton Family Papers
  Wyndham B. Blanton Papers
Virginia State Library, Richmond
  Richard Clough Anderson Papers
  Patteson Family Papers
  Executive Letter Books
  Christian Febiger Orderly Book, 1778 and Letter Book, 1780–82 (microfilm)
  Virginia Land Office—French and Indian War Warrants
  Miscellaneous Legislative Petitions
  Arrangement of the Virginia Line, 1781
  Southam Parish, Powhatan County, Vestry Book, 1745–91

William Woodford to Charles Lee, May 2, 1776
David Griffith to Lord Stirling, Oct. 20, 1776
Bounty Land Warrants
Cumberland County Order Books, 9 volumes, 1749–78
Cumberland County Will Book 1
Cumberland County Marriage Bonds, 1749–78
Goochland County Deed Book no. 1
Goochland County Marriage Bonds, 1777–94
Powhatan County Marriage Bonds, 1777–94
Powhatan County Order Book no. 1
Cumberland County Deed Books nos. 1 and 2
Cumberland County Tithables
Washington and Lee University, Lexington, Va.
William Fleming Papers

INDEX